Heidegger

Heidegger

An Introduction

J. Jeremy Wisnewski

ROWMAN & LITTLEFIELD PUBLISHERS, INC.
Lanham • Boulder • New York • Toronto • Plymouth, UK

Published by Rowman & Littlefield Publishers, Inc.
A wholly owned subsidiary of The Rowman & Littlefield Publishing Group, Inc.
4501 Forbes Boulevard, Suite 200, Lanham, Maryland 20706
www.rowman.com

10 Thornbury Road, Plymouth PL6 7PP, United Kingdom

British Library Cataloguing in Publication Information Available

Library of Congress Cataloging-in-Publication Data
Wisnewski, Jeremy.
Heidegger : an introduction / J. Jeremy Wisnewski.
p. cm.
Includes bibliographical references and index.
ISBN 978-1-4422-1925-0 (cloth : alk. paper)—ISBN 978-1-4422-1926-7 (pbk. : alk. paper)—ISBN 978-1-4422-1927-4 (electronic)
1. Heidegger, Martin, 1889-1976. I. Title.
B3279.H49W53 2012
193—dc23
2012029577

The paper used in this publication meets the minimum requirements of American National Standard for Information Sciences Permanence of Paper for Printed Library Materials, ANSI/NISO Z39.48-1992.

Printed in the United States of America

Contents

List of Figures

List of Tables

Preface

How to Use This Book

Heidegger is one of the most controversial philosophers of the twentieth century. He may be *the* most controversial. He is often dismissed as obscure—even deliberately so—or as writing just plain nonsense. Many who've heard of Heidegger know only that he was a member of the Nazi Party. Despite the notorious difficulty of Heidegger's texts, and despite Heidegger's political activities, he has exerted a tremendous influence on the intellectual culture of the twentieth and twenty-first centuries.[1] Those directly influenced by Heidegger offer us a roll call of significant philosophical schools and approaches: Hannah Arendt, Maurice Merleau-Ponty, Jean-Paul Sartre, Emmanuel Levinas, Hans-Georg Gadamer, Jacques Derrida, Paul Riceour, Charles Taylor, and Richard Rorty are but some of the most famous contemporary thinkers who have labored under Heidegger's influence. That influence is felt today as strongly as ever. There is little doubt that Heidegger has entered the philosophical pantheon and that he will remain there: he is among the philosophical gods, whether we like it or not.

This means that we must reckon with Heidegger, no matter how we judge his character or his works. The primary aim of this introduction is to help you grapple with this philosophical giant. A second, though equally important, goal is to convince you that the struggle is *worth* the effort.

While my aim is to introduce Heidegger, the diversity of possible interpretations makes it necessary to take a stand on issues throughout the book. Because of length constraints, I've also had to leave out a good deal of detail that emerges in Heidegger's thinking. To ease my sense of guilt, I have placed a list of recommendations for further reading at the book's end. These recommendations are organized according to relevant topics.

Chapters

Like most introductions, this one proceeds in a cumulative fashion. For those already familiar with Heidegger, skipping around while reading shouldn't cause any problems. For those unfamiliar with Heidegger, I recommend reading the chapters in the order presented.

The first chapter of the book focuses on Heidegger's life while also introducing some basic concepts. I explore Heidegger's early intellectual development, his rise to philosophical fame, and his subsequent involvement with National Socialism. I've devoted a fair amount of space to Heidegger's involvement with the Nazis, partly because of the attention Heidegger's politics has generated, and partly because the issues involved are complicated ones. As with other issues, you will find further sources to consult in the section on further reading.

Chapters 2 through 7 take up particular topics found in *Being and Time*. As I am convinced that Heidegger's path of thinking is a continuous one, there is much that is relevant to Heidegger's later philosophy in these chapters as well. There are Heidegger scholars who maintain that Heidegger's thinking after "the turn" (*die Kehre*) of the early 1930s is radically different from the thinking of *Being and Time*. I am not among them. For more on this issue, see the section in chapter 1 called "The 'Turn.'"

Chapter 8 takes up a range of concepts that permeate Heidegger's later thought: dwelling, thinking, poetry, art, and technology. It is notoriously difficult to summarize Heidegger's later work (indeed, Heidegger refers to his later writing as "ways, not works"). There are actually good philosophical reasons for this, and hence also for avoiding the *desire* to summarize. But one must begin somewhere, and this *is* an introduction to Heidegger after all. My compromise is to look at some of the themes in Heidegger's later work and to use these as a window for Heidegger's thinking after *Being and Time*. In the final chapter I offer some comments on Heidegger's continuing influence.

Jargon

Heidegger's work is full of gerund and infinitive constructions, nouns made into verbs, neologisms, and other linguistically annoying devices. Part of the explanation for this style of writing lies in Heidegger's thinking about language. The language we use structures our thinking and the way we experience the world around us. Language shapes and displays the world for the speaker. To use the standard vocabulary for addressing what Heidegger sees as a forgotten question, then, would amount to being unable to even *express* the question, let alone answer it. New questions require new ways of seeing and thinking, and the only way to accomplish this is to disrupt the normal understanding of things—an understanding that has become sedimented in the language we speak.

To help you through the jargon, I have provided definitions of a handful of basic concepts in "A Quick Terminology Guide for Getting Started." These definitions should be regarded as pedagogical tools, not definitive statements concerning the essence of whatever it is that's being defined. I have offered a gloss of those terms Heidegger uses from the first pages of *Being and Time*, as these terms often create unnecessary difficulties for readers new to Heidegger. Understanding the definitions, I want to reiterate, is only a place to begin thinking about Heidegger's work. It is no substitute for the work itself. (The same can be said of any introduction to Heidegger.) Terms not in the terminology guide, of course, can be found by consulting the index.

I have also provided quick translations of Greek and Latin terms that Heidegger employs in *Being and Time* (particularly in the introduction) and which he doesn't translate.

Too Many Translations?

Readers of Heidegger are fortunate to have two very good translations of Heidegger's major work, *Being and Time* (*Sein und Zeit*). The first translation, and the one I use throughout this book, is by John Macquarrie and Edward Robinson. A second translation, which has become available more recently, is by Joan Stambaugh. Both of these translations have their strengths and weaknesses. For the sake of consistency, I have utilized the first translation throughout this introduction, though I occasionally alter wording to clarify certain concepts. When I think other translations of key terms are simply better, I provide these alternatives, as well as an account of why I think they're better.

Reading This Book in Conjunction with Heidegger's Writings

This introductory text, as the title makes clear, is meant to guide the reader. In a Heideggerian mood, we might ask what it *means* to guide one somewhere—to lead them down a path and into a way of thinking about the world. We might ask what the meaning of the Being of "guiding" is. If this sounds peculiar, this is indeed the book for you.

There are two ways to be guided by this book. A reader might read it straight through, hoping for an overview of Heidegger's thought. Alternatively, one can read this book in conjunction with Heidegger's major works, a section at a time. In the event that one follows this latter course, I offer the following guidance.

Chapter 1 Biographical background; can be read with "My Way to Phenomenology"
Consult also *Plato's Sophist*

Chapter 2 *Being and Time*, introductions 1 and 2 (pp. 17–64)
Consult also *History of the Concept of Time*

Chapter 3 *Being and Time*, Division I, chapters 1–3 (pp. 67–148)

Chapter 4 *Being and Time*, Division I, chapters 4–5 (pp. 149–224)

Chapter 5 *Being and Time*, Division I, chapter 6 (pp. 225–73)
           On the concept of truth, consult also *Logic; Parmenides*

Chapter 6 *Being and Time*, Division II, chapters 1–3 (pp. 274–382)

Chapter 7 *Being and Time*, Division II, chapters 4–6 (pp. 383–488)
           Consult also *Basic Problems of Phenomenology*

Chapter 8 "The Question Concerning Technology"
           "Modern Science, Metaphysics, and Mathematics"
           "The End of Philosophy and the Task of Thinking"
           "Building Dwelling Thinking"
           "The Origin of the Work of Art"
           "Letter on Humanism"

Chapter 9 Consult selected readings from the end of the book

The Unseen Country

No book of this size can cover all the rich terrain of Heidegger's thought. The most we can do is try to get a rough lay of the land, passing over much that would be worth our time. I have tried to rectify this by supplying suggestions for additional readings in the form of both primary and secondary sources.

NOTE

1. Ludwig Wittgenstein is perhaps the only twentieth-century philosopher who could claim to rival Heidegger's influence.

Acknowledgments

I have been thinking about Heidegger since I was an undergraduate at the College of William and Mary. A number of philosophers have guided me along the way: Dwight Furrow, Bernd Magnus, Pierre Keller, and Larry Wright have each helped me grapple with Heidegger's thought— sometimes in unexpected ways. I have further enjoyed conversations with a number of philosophers working in the phenomenological tradition, each of whom helped me, sometimes unwittingly, to grapple with Heidegger. I would like to thank Janet Donohoe, in particular, for her ear and her intellectual generosity.

Several people read portions of this book and offered valuable feedback. I would like to thank Joe Jones, Meg Lonergan, Jordan Liz, Dan Morse, Josh Simmonds, Bob Stolorow, Dorothy Wisnewski, and Tim Christie for their time and their feedback.

As always, my family makes possible all things. I want to thank my wife, Dorothy, for more support than anyone could ever expect. She even read this book and commented on it, reminding me of my audience at several crucial points. I also want to thank my children, Audrey and Lucian, for keeping me mindful of what's important.

Abbreviations

BT	*Being and Time*
BDT	"Building Dwelling Thinking"
BP	*Basic Problems of Phenomenology*
LH	"Letter on Humanism"
MWP	"My Way to Phenomenology"
OWA	"The Origin of the Work of Art"
QCT	"The Question Concerning Technology"
WCT	"What Is Called Thinking?"

ONE

The Philosopher from Meβkirch

This chapter offers an overview of Heidegger's life, focusing on his intellectual development. In doing so, we'll have occasion to see several of the philosophical themes that permeate his work. Finally, we'll consider Heidegger's relationship to the Nazis.

THE EARLY YEARS

Martin Heidegger was born in the small town of Meβkirch, Germany, in 1889. His family belonged to the Roman Catholic Church in a period when calls for reform were being heard in Heidegger's hometown.[1] Heidegger's father played an active role in church life, serving as a sexton. As children, Martin and his younger brother, Fritz, helped with church services. "They were servers, they picked flowers to decorate the church, they ran errands for the priest, and they rang the bells" (Safranski, 7). The church permeated their daily lives. From the very beginning of young Martin's life, organized religion in general—and Catholicism in particular—played an important part in Heidegger's development.

The part played by the church is nowhere as apparent as in the young Heidegger's education. The local priest encouraged the Heideggers to send their eldest son, Martin, to Catholic seminary to further his studies, seeing in him tremendous intellectual potential. This same priest gave the young Heidegger lessons in Latin, enabling him to enroll in the seminary gymnasium to pursue his studies (Safranski, 9). Although by no means destitute, the Heideggers were of modest means. When Martin showed substantial promise, members of the church arranged for the young Heidegger to obtain a grant and enter the Catholic seminary. In a significant sense, then, Heidegger owed his education to the church and its membership. It was perhaps due to a sense of obligation to the church that Hei-

1

degger was reluctant to give up his studies in theology despite an intense and growing interest in the traditional questions of philosophy.

But give up his theological studies he did. In the winter semester of 1911–1912, Heidegger enrolled in the University of Freiburg in a course of study that set theology aside. The young Heidegger began his study of mathematics, physics, philosophy, and chemistry (Safranski, 42). He was initially interested in philosophical issues arising in mathematics and the mathematical sciences. Eventually, when Heidegger's funding required that he pursue topics in the Medieval Catholic tradition, he devoted himself to problems of medieval logic. (His dissertation was on a text then thought to be by the medieval philosopher Duns Scotus.)

While studying at Freiburg, Heidegger met his future wife, Elfride Petri, who was attending the university to study economics. Despite the fact that Heidegger was to have at least two extramarital affairs with students during his marriage to Elfride[2] (one with Hannah Arendt, who would go on to become a famous philosopher in her own right, and one with the lesser-known Elisabeth Blochman), he seems to have loved his wife deeply throughout their marriage. Heidegger's letters to Elfride are often in a devotional key, and his love for her is apparent. Indeed, Heidegger wrote and published poems to his wife early in their relationship, seemingly recognizing even then a point that would come to dominate his later thinking: some things in the world cannot be adequately expressed in expository writing; it is only through poetics that certain things can be brought to light. No matter how much we learn about the physiology of love, for example, a treatise on love will never do it justice if it does not reach *beyond* the physiology to the experiences that constitute this emotion.

The issue of the relationship of our experiences to our descriptions of these experiences is a central concern for Heidegger, even in these early years. The inability of Catholic dogmatism to capture certain experiences at least arguably contributed to Heidegger's estrangement from the Catholic Church (Heidegger remarked later, however, that "Ich bin niemals aus der Kirche getretten"—that he'd "never left the church") (Sheehan, 72).

Edmund Husserl, the father figure of phenomenology, sparked Heidegger's interest from the start. He was embarking on an exciting research project that set Heidegger's imagination on fire. However, the elder philosopher was somewhat standoffish to Heidegger when they first met, largely due to the perception that Heidegger was a "Catholic philosopher." This perception was one that Heidegger did not initially try to combat. Indeed, in his early years of philosophical study, Heidegger was being groomed for the Chair of Catholic Philosophy at Freiburg University by his mentors, Arthur Schneider and Heinrich Finke.

THE ENCOUNTER WITH PHENOMENOLOGY

Heidegger had been reading the work of Husserl, a pioneer in the phenomenological movement, since his first semester in seminary. He borrowed both volumes of Husserl's *Logical Investigations* from the university library, and they became constant companions in Heidegger's early efforts to penetrate the questions of philosophy (MWP, 74–75). Even after Husserl published his *Ideas*, the *Logical Investigations* didn't lose its power over Heidegger. He was "still captivated by [their] never-ceasing spell" (MWP, 78).

Part of the spell cast by Husserl was, Heidegger confessed, an inability to fully grasp what Husserl was up to—what this thing "phenomenology" was supposed to be about. Heidegger remarked that his "perplexity decreased slowly, my confusion dissolved laboriously, only after I met Husserl personally in his workshop" (MWP, 78).

Heidegger became Husserl's assistant in Freiburg in 1918. He remained there until 1923, lecturing to students and studying with the master. While Husserl maintained that philosophy needed to concentrate on "the things themselves," and hence could dispense with the academic study of the "great philosophers," Heidegger remained dedicated to the study of Greek thought even during the five years he was assisting Husserl. Heidegger's "involvement with the Greeks was of fundamental importance to him; it distinguished him from all other phenomenologists early on" (Gadamer, "The Greeks," 142).

Husserl eventually saw in Heidegger a potential successor—an incredibly gifted young philosopher who would take Husserlian phenomenology to its next stages. Heidegger saw in Husserl a great teacher as well as an exciting new approach to philosophy that had the potential to open up the interpretation of classical philosophical texts.

> The clearer it became to me that the increasing familiarity with phenomenological seeing was fruitful for the interpretation of Aristotle's writing, the less I could separate myself from Aristotle and the other Greek thinkers. Of course I could not immediately see what decisive consequences my renewed occupation with Aristotle was to have. (MWP, 78)

And, indeed, the consequences were significant. Heidegger's phenomenological confrontation with Aristotle resulted in a manuscript, the strength of which led the faculty of Marburg to offer Heidegger a permanent position. As Gadamer recalls, reading a copy of this manuscript "was like being hit by a charge of electricity" ("Martin Heidegger—85 Years," 114).

It was Heidegger's lectures on Aristotle, in fact, that drew the young Hans-Georg Gadamer first to Freiburg and then on to Marburg shortly thereafter (though of course Husserl was much more famous at the time).

Apparently, attending a Heidegger lecture was an experience that many were drawn to.

> The great monologues from texts lost their precedence with Heidegger. What he offered was much more: It was the complete supply of all his power—and what ingenious power—of a revolutionary thinker who would literally startle himself with his own ever more radical questions and who was so filled with the passion of thought that it was carried over into the auditorium, unable to be stopped by anything. (Gadamer, "Martin Heidegger—85 Years," 114)

Heidegger's lectures were not the only thing that set him apart from those around him. Rather than donning the standard suit and tie of other academics, Heidegger wore clothing that resembled farmer's attire. His students called it his "existential suit" (Gadamer, "Martin Heidegger—85 Years," 115). Heidegger's very appearance suggested that philosophy would be carried out in a new way—that the old set of expectations should be set aside, as they no longer applied.

> No matter what he lectured on—whether Descartes or Aristotle, Plato or Kant formed the starting point—his analysis always penetrated behind the concealments of traditional concepts to the most primordial experience of Dasein [human beings]. . . . The remarkable phenomenological power of intuition Heidegger brought to his interpretation liberated the original Aristiotelian text so profoundly and strikingly from the sedimentation of the scholastic tradition and from the lamentably distorted image of Aristotle contained in the criticism of the time . . . that it began to speak in an unexpected way. (Gadamer, "Heidegger and Marburg Theology," 201–2)

The movement to Marburg marked Heidegger's professional coming-of-age. He had completed his academic training, both writing a dissertation and completing his habilitation (a kind of second dissertation required in much of Europe prior to university professorship) and then serving under Husserl as his primary research assistant (following Edith Stein), meanwhile teaching as a *Privatdozent* (a person without a permanent position at a university) at his alma mater. Based on the strength of his teaching and research (his unpublished manuscript on Aristotle), Heidegger found himself with a permanent appointment to a chair of philosophy in Marburg. He had come into his own.

HEIDEGGER AS A REVOLUTIONARY

Heidegger remained at Marburg from 1923 until 1928. He lectured widely, but the bulk of his attention remained on a radical reinterpretation of Aristotle in light of phenomenology.

From 1918 (when he became Husserl's research assistant) until 1927, Heidegger published absolutely nothing. In 1927, however, a job opened up, and Heidegger learned he was being considered for it. The job in question was a dream one: it was to succeed Husserl as the Chair of Non-Catholic Philosophy at the University of Freiburg. To win the position, though, he needed to publish. As Heidegger recalls in "My Way to Phenomenology," the dean of the philosophical faculty at Marburg asked him if he had anything he could publish. He did indeed have a manuscript, albeit one that was far from finished. Heidegger decided to publish it. In 1927 he thus published what we now know as *Being and Time*. It constitutes two parts of a projected six-part work. Heidegger's fame, already widespread, grew tremendously and nearly instantaneously.

Comically, when Heidegger published the first pages of *Being and Time* in the *Jahrbuch für Philosophie und phänomenologische Forschung*, the committee at Freiburg wrote back that the work was "insufficient" to warrant granting Heidegger the position. When subsequent parts went to press, of course, the committee reversed its decision and granted Heidegger the position. One of Husserl's favorite comments—"Phenomenology—that's me and Heidegger"—proved correct in the eyes of the Freiburg community, as well as in the eyes of the philosophical community at large. The "rumor of the hidden king" that circulated around Heidegger (as Hannah Arendt once characterized Heidegger's reputation) proved to be true. In one magnificent moment, Heidegger had changed the face of phenomenology. *Being and Time* has proven to be one of the most important works in twentieth-century philosophy. It may even by the *most* important. Its influence began even before it was published—in the ideas that Heidegger was exploring in his classroom lectures and seminar discussions—and it continues to this day.

Upon its publication, *Being and Time* sent shock waves through the European intellectual scene. Jürgen Habermas called this work "the most significant philosophical event since Hegel's *Phenomenology*" (Habermas, 156). He made this claim in an article devoted to criticizing Heidegger's shameful political behavior in the years following the publication of his magnum opus. Although Heidegger was famous before he published any of the works for which he is widely known, *Being and Time* marked him as epoch-making.

Heidegger remained at Freiburg until 1946, when he was banned from teaching for five years as a response to his involvement with the National Socialist movement and his promotion of the university policies of Adolf Hitler.

BEING AND TIME: A WORK OF GENIUS

What is so unique about *Being and Time*? Why is it so important? How could a work have enough force to direct philosophical questioning across an entire continent—indeed, several continents!—for decades to come?[3]

Being and Time sets out to examine the meaning of Being. The pathway chosen to investigate this issue is one that passes through what Heidegger calls "Dasein"—a German term that is frequently translated, in other contexts, as "existence." For Heidegger, *Dasein* is a term that picks out those beings who interpret themselves, who care about their existence, and who have an understanding of the world. Thus, in investigating the meaning of Being, Heidegger is investigating *the very beings we are.*

And what sort of beings are we? We are beings who find ourselves existing in a world we must grapple with—who find ourselves with commitments and obligations we did not ask to have, condemned to death. We thus find ourselves in a world, obligated to act in *some way*, despite the fact that we never asked to be born. We find ourselves in a world with a life to which we must give some meaning—either by accepting what others say as meaningful or by inventing some meaning ourselves. And yet, no matter how much work we put into constructing a meaningful life, no matter how much we sweat and stress about what we will do with our lives—none of us will escape death.

By examining the structures of such an existence, Heidegger thinks, we can restore an understanding of the world that we have forgotten—we can become cognizant once again of *what it means to be.* This, of course, requires reexamining some of our philosophical dogma—that the person is independent of his world, that the world is composed of distinct objects with properties, that persons have an "inner world" of mental life, that to know the world requires getting "outside" of our inner world, and so on. As Heidegger argues, our condition involves misunderstanding ourselves systematically and pervasively. To understand our condition, and to recognize how we deceive ourselves, we must set aside the usual views of common sense along with the usual modes of thinking. This task is only accomplished by a confrontation with our condition directly—by the anxiety brought on by a recognition of our fundamental finitude and our inescapable mortality. Once we understand ourselves for what we are, we can likewise understand the world for what it is—a place imbued with significance, where things are disclosed and hidden from each of us, and within which history runs its course.

Obviously, there is no way to do justice to *Being and Time* in a few paragraphs. Indeed, there is no way to do justice to it even in the span of an introductory book. The previous remarks, however, should be sufficient to set the stage for the much more thorough exploration of the themes of *Being and Time* in chapters 2–7.

THE "TURN"

It was in the early years following the publication of *Being and Time* that Heidegger underwent what he called *"die Kehre,"* or "the turn." Both the significance of the turn and its content are the subject of some dispute. There are those who claim that the turning marks a fundamental change in Heidegger's basic orientation—a time when Heidegger gave up the systematic philosophizing of the Western tradition—one dominated by reason and explication, and turned toward meditative, nonrepresentational thinking instead. Others claim that the turn is not a turn *toward* meditative thinking so much as a turn *away from* the anthropocentrism of Heidegger's early analyses. On this view, *Being and Time* centered too much on human existence (under the term *Dasein*) and too little on Being as such. Still others claim that the turning isn't really a change at all; it is, rather, a shift of focus. Heidegger moves away from an investigation of Dasein to an investigation of disclosure; he moves from the question of the meaning of Being to the *truth* of Being.

I think those who see continuity in Heidegger's work are closer to the mark than those who do not. Nevertheless, I'll leave such matters to the readers for the most part. Chapter 8 will cover writings after Heidegger's "turn."

HEIDEGGER'S INVOLVEMENT WITH THE NAZI PARTY

Is There an Issue?

One of the first things people tend to learn about Heidegger is that he was a Nazi. Before inquiring into the extent of Heidegger's involvement with the Nazis, we should ask whether or not this involvement is *relevant* to assessing Heidegger's philosophical thought.

There is a difference, after all, between a person's private life, on the one hand, and the philosophical views he defends, on the other. In assessing the philosophical work of Gottlob Frege, for example, I have never heard anyone claim that Frege's advances in symbolic logic or the view he defends concerning how terms refer to the world are somehow infiltrated by his deep anti-Semitism. Likewise, few people claim that Aristotle's entire corpus, or the work of Bertrand Russell, or of Jean-Paul Sartre, is infected by their varying degrees of misogyny. Most people have moral blindspots, and philosophers are no exception. Like everyone else, even the greatest philosophers get things wrong—and sometimes in the worst ways. One would be hard-pressed to find even a few single philosophers who had never had a questionable ethical view and had committed no ethically questionable actions.

Criticizing a view or an argument based on the way someone behaves, in fact, is traditionally considered a fallacy. The standard name for this kind of error in reasoning is *ad hominem* (Latin for "to the man"). Whenever one criticizes what someone says by referring to what that person does, an ad hominem fallacy has been committed. The smoker who criticizes smoking is indeed a hypocrite, and probably a fool, but the fact that he smokes does not make his criticisms of smoking *incorrect*. Likewise, a deeply immoral person who criticizes immorality may be a nasty person, but this doesn't make his views false or his arguments implausible.

Is it simply an error, then, to ask questions about Heidegger's affiliation with Nazism in a book about Heidegger's philosophy? Let us assume that Heidegger was a total moral monster. This may entitle us to judge his character, but why would it entitle us to dismiss his philosophy?

Of course, the Nazis' crimes outstrip average moral failures by several orders of magnitude. Perhaps this is reason enough to rethink any philosopher's connection with this political party. Likewise, the charge has sometimes been made that there is something inherently Nazi-like in Heidegger's thinking—that, if one embraces Heidegger's thinking, one is more likely to be led to fascistic forms of philosophical reflection. If this is true, the ad hominem charge is irrelevant, for there would be a tight connection between Heidegger's thinking and his political stance— namely, embracing Heidegger's thinking would involve embracing Heidegger's politics.

To claim that Heidegger's thinking somehow leads *directly* to Nazism faces serious objections. One of the primary objections is the number of philosophers both influenced by Heidegger *and* hostile to the Nazi movement. If Heidegger's thinking leads directly to Nazism, then we would be forced to say that his most famous students have misunderstood that thinking, despite having worked directly with Heidegger in many cases and in some cases maintaining lifelong relationships with him. (If they understood it, after all, they would be fascists. This is what it means to say that the two things are *directly* connected.) This same objection can be raised against the view that Heidegger's work is somehow anti-Semitic, or conducive to anti-Semitism. Among those who have been influenced by Heidegger, appropriating his work to ends radically opposed to Nazism, are Hannah Arendt, Herbert Marcuse, Hans Jonas, and Emmanuel Levinas (all of whom were Jewish).

Of course, it's possible that all of these thinkers have misunderstood Heidegger, and that his work really does lead to Nazism. I know of no compelling argument for this view over the alternate appropriations of Heidegger by thinkers like Arendt and Jonas. Certainly, it is possible to be a Nazi and a Heideggerian (a proposition that Heidegger himself proved in 1933–1934), but this is a far cry from claiming that any Heideggerian is *automatically* committed to the Nazi cause or something similar enough.

Of course, Heidegger *himself* viewed National Socialism as connected to his philosophy. This is a primary piece of evidence used by those who defend the view that Heidegger's philosophy is intrinsically related to Nazism (or anti-Semitism). If Heidegger saw his own philosophy manifested in the fascism of his day, who are we to deny this? Certainly Heidegger understands his own philosophy better than others, so shouldn't we take him at his word?

The answer, in short, is no. Like much else in Heidegger's thinking, his remarks about the relationship between his philosophy and National Socialism can't be taken at face value. Karl Jaspers saw precisely this. In his recommendation to the denazification committee, Jaspers remarked that "the National Socialism which [Heidegger] embraced had little in common with existing National Socialism" (Jaspers, 149). If Heidegger contended that National Socialism arose from his philosophy, but did not think of National Socialism as others did, it just isn't clear *what* Heidegger saw as stemming from his philosophy.[4] In Heidegger's "Introduction to Metaphysics" lectures, he claims that the "greatness" of National Socialism could be found in its confrontation with the industrialized technological machine of the modern world—that it provided an alternative to the dominant way of thinking about history, human existence, and technology. One can easily see how the need for such an alternative would stem from Heidegger's philosophy; it's less clear what this has to do with the understanding of National Socialism that most people have.

An Unapologetic Nazi

However personalized Heidegger's Nazism was, his political involvement with the Nazis is a black eye on the history of philosophy. To understand this involvement, we should neither exaggerate nor diminish Heidegger's actions and attitudes. The claim that Heidegger was a Nazi is one that, in perfect Heideggerian fashion, both conceals and reveals something about Heidegger. It is true that Heidegger was a Nazi—but this can be taken in at least two ways.

The term *Nazi* suggests, at least to some, an evil group of people bent on world domination and genocide. Certainly there were Nazis who fit that description with horrifying accuracy. It is nevertheless a mistake to think that *most* Nazis fit this description. After all, a Nazi, in the strictest sense, was just someone who had joined the National Socialist Party in Germany. There is no doubt whatsoever that Heidegger was a Nazi in this sense. He joined the Party in 1933 and paid dues until 1945. This does not automatically mean, however, that Heidegger was evil, or that he was racist. What can we infer from Heidegger joining the Nazis?

While the fascist elements of the party were spelled out in detail, not every action or ambition of the party was equally clear. In the early 1930s, for example, the way in which the Nazis would pursue anti-Semitism was by no means clear to all of its members. Many thought, in fact, that the rabid anti-Semitism they saw in the party was simply a fringe phenomenon that would disappear as the Nazis ascended to power.

Of course, anti-Semitism was hardly uncommon in Germany at the time, regardless of one's political affiliations. The Nazis implemented their prejudices in concrete policies early on in their acquisition of political power. They made employment of Jews in the university system illegal, for example, and stripped those of Jewish descent of civil and political rights at every turn. Given these facts, one cannot tell the story of the Nazis without telling the story of anti-Semitism, no matter how much the average German did or did not know about those Nazi solutions to the so-called Jewish problem.

Heidegger joined the Nazi Party in 1933 as part of his acceptance of the rectorship of Freiburg University (only members of the party could hold such high-level administrative positions). Heidegger supported Nazi policies while in this office, though how strictly and unquestioningly is a subject of some debate. (Heidegger asserts that he frequently refused to implement Nazi policies; the evidence is not so clear). In 1934, ten months after taking the rectorship position, Heidegger stepped down. In the years that followed, his classes were monitored by representatives of the Nazi regime. Publication of (and reference to) his works was strictly limited by the Nazis.

Heidegger's relationship with the Nazis was not a straightforward one. To say that Heidegger supported Nazi policies is accurate, but the extent to which he did this, and the *reason* he did it, are nowhere near so clear. Heidegger's own account of his membership in the political party presents a man stuck in a particular historical moment—one in which he has to carry out certain orders (like terminating Jewish professors and suspending academic freedom). Heidegger's personal account of his actions can be found in a letter to the rector of Freiberg University of 1945, as well as in his posthumously published interview with *Der Spiegel*, a prominent news magazine in Germany.

Heidegger claims he was "absolutely convinced that an autonomous alliance of intellectuals [*der Geistigen*] could deepen and transform a number of essential elements of the 'National Socialist movement' and thereby contribute in its own way to overcoming Europe's disarray and the crisis of Western spirit" (Heidegger, "Letter to the Rector," 61–62). But if Heidegger's account is to be believed, it was not only the view that the party could be reformed from within that led to Heidegger's acceptance of the position of rector. In fact, according to Heidegger, he was *implored* to take the position by Rector von Möllendorf and Vice Rector Sauer. They urged Heidegger to take the position so that a "party functionary" would not be named rector (*Der Spiegel*, 93). Even with such urging, Heidegger was reluctant. He agreed to take the position only "in the interest of the University, but only if [he] could be certain of a unanimous agreement of the Plenum" (*Der Spiegel*, 93).

Heidegger's condition was met. He was "unanimously elected Rector (with two abstentions) in a plenary session of the university" (Heidegger, "Letter to the Rector," 61). As Heidegger insists in his letter of 1945, he was not "appointed by the National Socialist minister," nor did he desire to occupy any administrative office. Heidegger maintained, both in 1945 and in his 1966 interview with *Der Spiegel*, that he had no interest in politics, and hence that politics had not been a motivation for becoming the rector of Freiburg. "I never belonged to a political party nor maintained a relation, either personal or substantive, with the NSDAP [the Nazi Party] or with governmental authorities. I accepted the rectorship reluctantly and in the interest of the university alone" (*Der Spiegel*, 61).

Despite Heidegger's version of the story, it is widely thought that he joined the Nazi Party either as a matter of political expediency or as a matter of true commitment to certain Nazi ideals. There is evidence for both of these views—enough evidence, at any rate, to make Heidegger's version of events seem unlikely.

Heidegger's account of his relationship to the Nazi Party is, at any rate, far too selective. He viewed his participation in the party as having world-historical significance; he thought of himself as the "philosopher of the Reich"; he even envisioned himself as eventually being the philosopher to whom the Führer would turn to clarify the philosophical destiny of the German people. The hubris and arrogance behind these thoughts is undeniable.

Heidegger's speeches and brief political writings of this period (1933–1934) suggest a stronger commitment to Nazification than do his retrospective accounts of his motivations for joining the Nazi Party and taking up the Nazi cause in the university. In 1933, for example, Heidegger wrote that "the National Socialist revolution is bringing about the total transformation of our German existence [*Dasein*]" (Heidegger, "Political Texts," 46). He goes on to say that "the Führer alone *is* the present and future German reality and its law" (Heidegger, "Political Texts," 47). A week later Heidegger gave an address in Leipzig (one of many) declaring his allegiance to Adolf Hitler and the National Socialist state. He concluded the address in what became his customary way during his time as rector: "Sieg Heil!"

Despite Heidegger's failure to admit the extent of his involvement in and support for Nazi politics, this involvement or support should also not be exaggerated. To be sure, Heidegger's membership in the Nazi party was a devoted one, and one for which he never adequately made amends. It was also short lived—though perhaps not as short lived as Heidegger implied. Heidegger's account of his relationship to the party after 1934 may well play down the length of his political activities. But his account also shows how quickly he became disillusioned with politics in general—and how quickly the Nazi party had become suspicious of Heidegger himself.

When Heidegger saw that change from within the Nazi Party was not possible—when he confronted the same kind of dogmatism that had led him away from Catholic doctrine—he resigned his rectorship and returned to the classroom. This, at any rate, is the explanation Heidegger gives of the growing tension between himself and the party he had joined only ten months earlier. "National Socialist ideology became increasingly inflexible and increasingly less disposed to a purely philosophical interpretation" (Heidegger, "Letter to the Rector," 64). As Heidegger recounts events, his teaching after his resignation took up the issue of language, and Heidegger "sought to show that language was not the biological-racial essence of man, but conversely, that the essence of man was based in language as a basic reality of spirit" (Heidegger, "Letter to the Rector," 64). Moreover, as he explicitly says in a letter to Herbert Marcuse in 1948, "in 1934 I recognized my political error and resigned my rectorship in protest against the state and party" (Marcuse and Heidegger, 162).

It is certainly understandable to criticize Heidegger for not speaking out against the Nazis more explicitly and more loudly. It is a mistake, however, to criticize Heidegger for a naïve view of blood and race that one found in standard Nazi ideology, as some have.[5] Heidegger did *not* advocate such racist views. When read in context, the claims Heidegger makes about race stand directly opposed to the eugenics of National Socialism.

Aside from the transcripts of Heidegger's lectures in this period, the Nazi reaction to Heidegger's scholarship reveals that officials within the party viewed Heidegger as increasingly hostile to it. Heidegger was excluded from attending the International Philosophy Conference as part of the German delegation. He was likewise told he could not be part of the German delegation to a Descartes Conference taking place in Paris in 1937, despite the fact that the organizers of the conference had specifically requested that Heidegger attend.

But these actions were the least of the Nazi distrust of Heidegger after 1934. Heidegger's second book, *Kant and the Problem of Metaphysics*, was banned. Moreover, Heidegger notes that "from 1938 on, one could no longer cite my name nor evaluate my works as a result of secret instructions given to general editors" (Heidegger, "Letter to the Rector," 65). Publication of essays by Heidegger—in particular his essay "Plato and the Concept of Truth," as well as some work on Hölderlin—was forbidden by the Nazis. Heidegger also claimed that the Gestapo regularly kept tabs on his lectures. Toward the end of the war, finally, the Nazis, short on man-power, began sending "nonessential" personnel to the front to contribute to the war effort. This included even university professors who weren't regarded as "essential" to the functioning of intellectual life in Germany. Despite Heidegger's incredible international fame, he was among the first of those sent.

Heidegger claimed that he began protesting the Nazi Party "by not participating in its gatherings, by not wearing its regalia, and, as of 1934, by refusing to begin my courses and lectures with the so-called German greeting [Heil Hitler!]" (Heidegger, "Letter to the Rector," 65). In the eyes of many, including some of Heidegger's former students, this form of "protest" was insufficient, to say the least. What most wanted was an *acknowledgment*, offered publicly, for the political mistakes Heidegger had made. Heidegger's silence, some suggested, was an implicit endorsement of National Socialist policy and practice—even at its bloodiest. Heidegger's speeches and addresses endorsed Nazi policies; to fail to acknowledge one's mistakes in this regard was to imply that one had not *made* any mistakes. Herbert Marcuse expressed precisely these concerns in a private letter to Heidegger.

> You have never publicly retracted [your writings and speeches in support of Nazism]—not even after 1945. You have never publicly explained that you have arrived at judgments other than those which you expressed in 1933–34 and articulated in your writings. You remained in Germany after 1934, though you could have found a position abroad practically anywhere. You never publicly denounced any of the actions or ideologies of the regime. Because of these circumstances you are still today identified with the Nazi regime. (Marcuse and Heidegger, 160–61)

Heidegger's response to Marcuse's letter was anything but satisfactory. "You are entirely correct that I failed to provide a public, readily comprehensible counter-declaration; it would have been the end of both me and my family. On this point, Jaspers said: that we remain alive is our guilt" (Marcuse and Heidegger, 163). It's not clear why Heidegger thought publicly acknowledging his mistakes and distancing himself from earlier positions would "be the end" of him and his family.

CONCLUSION

Ultimately, Heidegger's silence was probably more damaging than any admission of guilt would have been. He was banned from teaching for five years, upon the recommendation of onetime friend Karl Jaspers, and was allowed to keep his pension. He returned to teaching at Freiburg for one year after his exile from the university, and then retired. Although Heidegger continued to offer seminars for the rest of his life, he spent most of his days in his small cabin at Todtnauberg, in the Black Forest region of southern Germany. He died in 1976. His writings continue to exert an immense influence on all of the inhabited continents.

NOTES

1. Meβkirch was thus embroiled in what is known as the "Kulturkampf" (cultural struggle).

2. Out of fairness, it should probably be noted that Elfride also had an extramarital affair.

3. *An autobiographical note—to be ignored if you're not interested in a personal anecdote! Being and Time* changed my life. I try not to write in clichés, but this one deserves to be written. I was twenty years old when I first read *Being and Time* in a seminar at William and Mary, where I was an undergraduate. Not only did it prove decisive in my decision to go to graduate school in philosophy, it has also been decisive in my thinking through just about everything since then. This is not to say that I simply accept everything Heidegger says, as though it were manna from heaven or the word of God. Certainly Heidegger is not right about everything—and he may well be flat-out wrong about a number of things. But Heidegger has influenced the way I think about questions, objections, and even the role of thinking. Reading *Being and Time*, in particular, has managed to do what great literature often does: it changed the way I perceive the world and the place of humanity within it. One can hardly ask for more from a work of philosophy.

4. There are several nuanced treatments of this issue. See, for example, Julian Young, *Heidegger, Philosophy, Nazism*.

5. See Víctor Farías, *Heidegger and Nazism*.

TWO

The Forgotten Question

Heidegger begins *Being and Time* by claiming that we've forgotten the question of the meaning of Being. In this chapter, we'll explore this question, as well as how Heidegger hopes to answer it. We'll also introduce and explore some of Heidegger's central terminological distinctions.

IS THERE A *REAL* QUESTION ABOUT THE MEANING OF BEING?

Is there really a question about the meaning of Being? Certainly Heidegger thought so. Several critics of Heidegger, old and new, seem ready to dismiss the question out of hand. Bertrand Russell sums up a common criticism of Heidegger as follows:

> Highly eccentric in its terminology, his philosophy is extremely obscure. One cannot help suspecting that language is here running riot. An interesting point in his speculations is the insistence that nothingness is something positive. As with much else in Existentialism, this is a psychological observation made to pass for logic. (Russell, 303)

The underlying view here—one also found in A. J. Ayer and Rudolf Carnap—is that Heidegger doesn't actually say anything. He uses words in peculiar ways that make it seem like there's a real issue at stake. In reality, however, there's no issue. This is one way that a question might fail to be a question—it might fail to have what analytic philosophers call "propositional content." If I ask whether a witch has blue blood or red blood, or whether or not dreams weigh more than fairy dust, it *looks like* I'm asking a question. After all, my sentences are in interrogative form. Moreover, I'm using words that you've seen before. Am I asking a real question? For many traditional analytic philosophers (like Ayer and Russell), the answer must be no. I'm not asking an actual question because

I'm not talking about anything *real*. There's no such thing as fairy dust, and there aren't any witches (excepting Wiccans, of course). One might think Heidegger is embroiled in a similar mistake: there's no such thing as "Being." Given that "Being" doesn't pick out anything in the world, we can't ask questions about it.

In one respect, Heidegger agrees. There isn't anything called "Being" that exists independently of beings. But there *are* beings (lower case *b*). The distinction here (between "Being" and "beings") actually represents two different words in the original German: *Sein* (Being) and *Seiende* (beings). Individual entities are beings. Each individual being, however has a *kind* of Being. We will use capitalization when translating and discussing the noun *Sein* (Being). We will not capitalize when translating the noun *seiende* (beings). We should be careful, however, not to interpret this as having any special significance. All nouns are capitalized in German. As we'll see, Being can only be investigated through *beings*, so we should fight the temptation to view the use of capitalization as somehow honorific.

Much as there are beings, there *are* questions. In raising a question about whether or not "the meaning of Being" is a question, one already utilizes the notion of *Being*. If I say *either* that there is a question or that there is not a question, I am making a claim about what *is*. Heidegger's question is precisely the following: What do I mean by this "is"?

It thus seems difficult to claim that there is no question about Being, at least where this means that there is nothing for us to ask about. In stating this position, we actually rely on the very thing we claim doesn't exist. Of course, Russell might have said, instead, "I do not see a question here." (This, of course, is another way something can fail to be a question—we can already understand something so thoroughly that there's nothing else to learn about it.) Do we know so much about Being that we're beyond raising questions about it? Are we simply incapable of seeing a question here?

To determine whether or not a question is *really* a question, it isn't enough to say we *think* the question is an illegitimate one (as Russell implies in the above quote). Heidegger begins *Being and Time* by pointing out that the very question he is asking has ceased *to be* a question for modern intellectuals: the question of the meaning of Being, he claims, has been forgotten (*BT*, 19). The aim of *Being and Time* is to pose this question once again. This task, Heidegger realizes, is far from easy: asking a question involves knowing what it might mean to answer the question one asks.[1] The irony of the modern age, for Heidegger, lies precisely here. We do not know what might count as an answer to the question of the meaning of Being. Forgetting this question, which had indeed been posed by the Greeks, also amounts to forgetting those things that would count as a possible answer to this question. Forgetting the question amounts to forgetting *Being* altogether.

But why has the question been forgotten? We can start by pointing out, as Heidegger does, that Being has come to be interpreted variously as the emptiest of concepts (it says nothing!), the most universal of concepts, and something that cannot be defined. Each of these ways of viewing Being effectively eliminates raising any serious questions about its meaning. As Plato made clear in the dialogue *Meno*, we can raise questions only where we think we don't already understand what we're questioning. Our very assurance that we understand Being prevents us from taking seriously questions about it. Thus part of Heidegger's task, much like Socrates' before him, is not so much to *answer* the question he poses, but to get us to see that *there really is a question*.

For anything we can describe, we can additionally say that the thing *is*. The particular descriptive terms we use when speaking about a given thing are called predicates. Any predicate you can apply to a subject (the thing being described) relies on the fact that the subject in question has some type of existence. This doesn't mean that the subject exists in the spatio-temporal world. It means, rather, that to say something about x *presupposes* x. Both sentences "The chair is red" and "The king of France is bald" assert a *being*, though the type of being in question is radically different. The king of France is a fiction—there is no king. Nonetheless, the phrase "The king of France" picks out something—a sort of fiction, or a thought-experiment, or a playful joke. Jokes, fictions, and thought-experiments have Being. They *are*. They don't have Being in the same way that, say, a desk in a classroom has existence, but they exist nonetheless.

But what are we saying here? Isn't it just nonsense to say of things that they are? Have we said anything more than "thing"? Perhaps not. But this doesn't mean there's no issue here. If we think of Being as a genus or a species—as a category into which things fall—we're no doubt involving ourselves in nonsense. To say "A thing falls into the genus of Being insofar as it is" is a piece of nonsense. The problem here isn't that we are talking about the Being of things. The problem is that we're talking about the Being of things *as though Being were a predicate or a property*—as though an existing thing could *fail* to have it.

> The "universality" of Being is not that of a class or genus. The term "Being" does not define that class of entities which is uppermost when these are articulated conceptually according to genus and species. (*BT,* 22)

We are thus not concerned with the type of predicate Being is (when we construe this in the traditional subject/predicate relation). Our concern is not with predicates at all: Being is not the same thing as "mammal" or "arachnid" or "bald." Rather, we're concerned here with what it means for something *to be a subject*—with what it means for something to be a possible *object* of predication. And this, of course, is just another way of inquiring about what it means for something *to be*.[2]

But isn't the meaning of Being transparent? We utilize the notion of Being in everyday interaction, as evinced by the constant use of the verb *to be* (e.g., "The sky *is* blue," "I *am* reading," and so on). There's an obvious sense in which we do understand the meaning of Being. If we didn't have some understanding of it, we couldn't employ it so unproblematically (as we do continuously every day). As Heidegger notes, however, "here we have an average kind of intelligibility, which merely demonstrates that this is unintelligible" (*BT*, 23). Moreover, "the very fact that we already live in an understanding of Being still veiled in darkness proves that it is necessary in principle to raise this question again" (*BT*, 23).

This claim is a central theme in Heidegger's *Being and Time*, as well as in his later work. Heidegger thinks that we have a general understanding of the world. This understanding is that in virtue of which the world is intelligible to us. Moreover, he thinks that this general understanding of the world is a public one. We can engage with one another in a public world in virtue of the fact that we share an understanding. The dark underbelly of this is that our understanding is frequently forced into submission by this public world. We all have an understanding of, for example, democracy—and we share this understanding. We take the vague generalities that we share as adequate to the phenomenon in question—and we do this *because* we all agree on these generalities. "Rule by the people" probably captures what we collectively understand by the term *democracy*. But this understanding, although it allows us to understand each other, has virtually no depth. It remains right on the surface of the phenomenon, and probably has to if we're going to understand one another. Any genuine inquiry must move beyond this general (and hence vague) understanding of a given phenomenon.

We're in a similar position in regard to Being. This is an unproblematic notion in everyday life. No one gets confused when someone says, "I am fine." We know what it means for someone to be fine, at least in the most general terms (in more Heideggerian language, we know what it means for someone to have the sort of Being we call "fine"). But we should not think that this general and frail understanding is the end of the analysis. Its publicity (or public-ness) is just an indication of its inadequacy—of the vagueness and imprecision that characterizes *all* public understanding. We thus have reason to pose again the question of the meaning of Being.

BEGINNING TO QUESTION BEING

But where do we start? Everything we can name *is*. It has *Being*. How are we to investigate the question of the meaning of Being, given the near-infinite range of possible starting points? Do we start with regular objects, such as cups and radios? Or do we take more abstract kinds of beings, such as dreams and jokes, as our point of departure?

Since we're engaged in questioning, Heidegger cleverly begins with *questioning itself*. What does it mean to ask a question (in other words, what is the meaning of the Being of a question?). This manner of proceeding is typically Heideggerian: Heidegger takes a given phenomenon, explores its structural features, and then applies these features to a particular case. The phenomenon we're considering here is that of asking a question. Heidegger points out that this phenomenon has its own type of Being (yes, that's right, the Being of inquiring, of asking a question—and it is a form of "seeking"), and this sort of Being admits of certain structural features: there is something that one interrogates (an object of analysis), there is what one is asking about (what is "asked after"), and there is that which one finds out after asking. As should be clear, this means that the very asking of a question sets the inquirer in a space of concerns—it provides one with an orientation. As Heidegger puts it, "inquiry, as a kind of seeking, must be guided beforehand by what is sought" (*BT*, 25). Our understanding of Being, then, makes it possible to know what we should interrogate—at least in a general form, and subject to revision. This understanding orients our investigation. Indeed, it makes an investigation *possible*.

The kind of "guiding" that occurs in questioning is always situated historically. Heidegger makes this point in his lecture course of 1927, *Basic Problems of Phenomenology*.

> The consideration of Being takes its start from beings. The commencement is obviously always determined by the factual experience of beings and the range of possibilities of experience that at any time are peculiar to factical Dasein, and hence to the historical situation of a philosophical investigation. It is not the case that at all times and for everyone all beings and all specific domains of beings are accessible in the same way. . . . Because Dasein is historical in its own existence, possibilities of access and modes of interpretation of beings are themselves diverse, varying in different historical circumstances. (*BP*, 22)

Heidegger is thus well aware that our understanding of Being is located in a context and influenced by that context. In fact, it is a little misleading to say that Heidegger is "well aware" of this, for in some respects it pervades all of his thinking about human existence as well as philosophical inquiry: to be Dasein (a human being[3]), as we will see, is to exist within a tradition and to take one's general point of departure in *all* understanding from this tradition. This point will mark a central concern in understanding Dasein's everydayness, but also the structure and possibility of authenticity (which we will discuss primarily in chapter 6).

So we must interrogate individual entities in order to seek the meaning of Being, but we must begin with the everyday understanding of

Being already in our possession. This understanding is necessary for us to raise questions at all, but it also enables us to populate our understanding with a range of possible answers—the interpretation of which must be worked out as we investigate the question we are considering.

As we mentioned before, we do have a particular orientation: we have a general understanding of Being, and it is here that we must start if we are to investigate the meaning of Being. As Heidegger puts it,

> the meaning of Being must already be available to us in some way. As we have intimated, we always conduct our activities in an understanding of Being. Out of this understanding arise both the explicit question of the meaning of Being and the tendency that leads us towards its conception. We do not know what "Being" means. But even if we ask "What is 'Being'?," we keep within an understanding of the "is," though we are unable to fix conceptually what the "is" signifies. We do not even know the horizon in terms of which that meaning is to be grasped and fixed. But this vague average understanding of Being is still a Fact. (*BT*, 25)

So we do have a place to begin. We must flesh out our understanding—we must begin where we all are, and probe the depths of the understanding that allows us all to understand one another (and to interact) on an everyday basis. That our everyday understanding of Being is "dim" provides yet another series of problems: Why is it dim? Why have we forgotten the meaning of Being? Why are we divorced from this question?

Although Heidegger doesn't think that our current understanding of Being is sufficient for raising anew the question of the meaning of Being, it is nonetheless necessary. Our everyday understanding of Being is where we must start. Our "seeking" is after the meaning of Being, and our everyday understanding provides an idea of what it is that we seek—albeit one that is only meant to get our inquiry going. The structure of the Being of a question, then, is filled out by Heidegger's own project. What orients our understanding—our projection of an answer—is the everyday understanding of Being that we all already possess. But where do we look? Heidegger maintains that "in so far as Being constitutes what is asked about, and 'Being' means the Being of entities, then entities themselves turn out to be *what is interrogated*" (*BT*, 26).

This methodological move is both instructive and unhelpful, at least initially. It's instructive in that it reveals that Heidegger isn't attempting to reify the meaning of Being into something that exists in some Platonic heaven—a move that, as we shall see, would be anathema to the battle cry of phenomenology ("To the things themselves!"). Insisting that we can only investigate entities thus clarifies the kind of answer Heidegger is seeking, as well as the point of departure that the inquiry takes. In this respect, pointing out that entities (beings, construed broadly) are what must be interrogated is instructive. It allows us to further frame the question at hand.

But the remark is also unhelpful when we think about those things that count as "entities" or "beings." The terms denote anything that has Being—anything that *is*. Thus, while it might initially seem that we have substantially limited our domain of inquiry, on reflection it's easy to see that we haven't—at least not yet. Every thing *is*. Mathematical equations, jokes, dreams, unicorns, trees, horses, people, sciences, and so on. They *are*. Being is not something that is independent of beings. It is not a category, a genus, a species. It subsists in actual *beings*. To investigate the meaning of Being in general, then, we must look at *beings*.

But this really isn't all that helpful. Anything you name is a being that *is*. We must still decide which entity we ought to investigate, otherwise we'll never get anywhere. (We might continuously examine beings that don't help us much in answering the question we're posing.) It's essential, if we're to answer the question of the meaning of Being in the appropriate way, that we start at the appropriate place.

Heidegger proposes a solution to this methodological quandary: we start with that being who asks the question "What is the meaning of Being?"; we start with *Dasein*: "this entity which each of us is himself" (*BT*, 27).

> Looking at something, understanding and conceiving it, choosing, access to it—all these ways of behaving are constitutive for our inquiry, and therefore are modes of Being for those particular entities which we, the inquirers, are ourselves. Thus to work out the question of Being adequately, we must make an entity—the inquirer—transparent in his own Being. The very asking of this question is an entity's mode of Being; and as such it gets its essential character from what is inquired about—namely, Being. This entity which each of us is himself and which includes inquiring as one of the possibilities of its Being, we shall denote by the term "*Dasein*." (*BT*, 27)

Heidegger's methodological move here is quite clever. Of the perhaps infinite number of things that are, any of these could be investigated in order to address the question of the meaning of Being. To narrow down the range of possible entities to be interrogated is thus crucial for any viable enquiry to be carried out. Heidegger takes a step back, acknowledges that seeking an entity to interrogate is *itself* a kind of Being that is concerned with Being. This provides a clue for how to proceed: we ought to investigate that Being who has concerns about Being—that Being, as Heidegger often remarks, for whom Being is an issue—namely, *us*.

THE ONTIC AND ONTOLOGY

Heidegger frequently offers stunning insight into topics he doesn't explore in detail. For example, in the introduction to *Being and Time*, Heidegger claims that

> the real "movement" of the sciences takes place when their basic concepts undergo a more or less radical revision which is transparent to itself. The level which a science has reached is determined by how far it is capable of a crisis in its basic concepts. In such immanent crises the very relationship between positive investigative inquiry and those things themselves that are under interrogation comes to a point where it begins to totter. (*BT*, 29)[4]

Every particular science is distinguished by the kind of entities it investigates. This means, at bottom, that every science presupposes an ontology—a conception of what it means *to be*. Even the names of our sciences bear this out: biology studies *bios* (life), psychology studies *psyche* (mind), geology studies *geos* (earth), anthropology studies *anthropos* (human beings), and so on. What distinguishes these sciences is precisely the things they study—that is, the domain of beings that they presuppose and attempt to analyze.

Heidegger's aim is *not* to criticize the sciences for presupposing an ontology. There's nothing particularly problematic in such presupposition. In fact, all inquiry *requires* such presuppositions. Heidegger's aim is thus not to "correct" science—a fool's errand, in any case. His aim, rather, is to investigate the very thing that the sciences take for granted—namely, the meaning of Being in general.

As we can see, then, it's possible to distinguish the investigations of a particular science, on the one hand, from the ontology of that science, on the other. There's a difference, in other words, between the results of investigating a set of entities (like living things) and our basic presuppositions about what entities there are. A crisis in the sciences occurs when scientists are no longer sure they're investigating the right *kind of thing*.[5] Questions of the latter sort bring into doubt the very enterprise of any science by calling into question the domain of that science.[6]

As this hopefully makes plain, ontology is *always* prior to investigation. In order to investigate something at all, one must know what it is that *is to be investigated*. It is thus the case, says Heidegger, that "basic concepts determine the way in which we get an understanding beforehand of the area of subject-matter underlying all the objects a science takes as its theme, and all positive investigation is guided by this understanding" (*BT*, 30). The idea of presuppositionless inquiry, then, is unintelligible. To inquire about something, one must have some idea of what that thing is, otherwise inquiry can never begin.[7] One begins, as it were, with an ontology.

The difference between Being and beings is what Heidegger calls "the ontological difference." This difference marks the distinction between Being itself, on the one hand, and particular entities (beings), on the other. To ensure conceptual clarity, Heidegger uses different terminology to distinguish these two domains: the *ontic* (concerns particular beings) and the *ontological* (concerns things in their Being). Ontology can investigate Being in general (in which case it's fundamental ontology), or it can investigate the Being of particular kinds of things (in which case it's regional ontology). Importantly, we must remember that the ontic is itself ontological: every ontic investigation presupposes an ontology. To engage in ontic inquiry, then, is to engage in an inquiry that involves an ontology that makes it possible, but that it does not examine.

Any science presupposes an ontology and operates ontically with that ontology. It takes for granted the types of beings in its ontology (for example, anthropology takes for granted that there are beings called "human") and says things about the entities it presupposes (for example, that humans are evolutionarily related to other species, are tool-using, language-using, rational, and so on). The domain of objects taken for granted is a science's ontology. What is said about these entities *after* taking an ontology for granted is the ontic.[8]

This distinction allows Heidegger to spell out in what sense the ontological has priority. His view is not that the ontological is primary because it was, to put it crudely, "there first." The ontological is primary because it is a condition for the possibility of ontic inquiry. To truly understand an ontical investigation involves understanding the sorts of beings it presupposes and examines, and hence involves understanding the ontology it takes for granted. The fact that we can engage in distinct sciences suggests that there is an even more basic conception of Being that the ontologies of the sciences presuppose (a general conception of Being). The question of the meaning of Being in general, then, is logically prior to any assertion in the sciences as well as any specific ontology presupposed in the sciences. As Heidegger puts it,

> The question of Being aims therefore at ascertaining the *a priori* conditions not only for the possibility of the sciences which examine entities as entities of such and such a type, and, in so doing, already operate with an understanding of Being, but also for the possibility of those ontologies themselves which are prior to the ontical sciences and which provide their foundations. (*BT*, 31)

This fact also presents us with a philosophical task:

> Basically, all ontology, no matter how rich and firmly compacted a system of categories it has at its disposal, remains blind and perverted from its innermost aim, if it has not first adequately clarified the meaning of Being, and conceived this clarification as its fundamental task. (*BT*, 31)

We are to investigate the meaning of Being by investigating one being in particular—that being for whom being is an issue; that being who has an understanding of its Being. Although Heidegger uses the term *Dasein*, he reminds us once more (for the third time) that "we *are* it, each of us, we ourselves" (*BT*, 36).

INTERPRETING DASEIN

One of the essential features of Dasein is that we *misunderstand ourselves*—and we do so *ontologically*, both in the sense that (1) we do not understand the kinds of beings we are, and in the sense that (2) we *are the kinds of beings* who are prone to misunderstanding the kinds of beings we are. Obviously, then, we can't simply take our current understanding of Being for granted.

It is the proximity we bear to our own existence (our own Dasein, which literally means "being-there" in German) that marks it as ontologically farthest from us. We might call this "the obscurity of the familiar": those things we know unreflectively—nondiscursive background practices—are the most difficult for us to grasp conceptually. It is easy to see this point in everyday activities: we are quite adept at walking, talking, not bumping into things, and so on, but we would be hard-pressed to give a full-fledged account of these things. We do them so effortlessly— we are so painlessly competent in our everyday dealings with the world—that we don't give such matters any thought. When we are provoked to do so, it is thus quite difficult. Our understanding of these things is nonconceptual, and we must thus force them into conceptual form. Our everyday action is effortless. We operate in the world "as if its Being has been interpreted in some manner" (*BT*, 36). This manner, as Heidegger claims, is one that reflects what is "proximally closest" to Dasein. This is the world. Dasein's pre-ontological understanding (its everyday, proximal understanding) is bound up with the world in which Dasein exists.

This is not to say that everyone's understanding of Being is identical, nor that one understanding of our Being has existed across historical epochs. As Heidegger claims, "this understanding develops or decays along with whatever kind of Being Dasein may possess at the time; accordingly there are many ways in which it has been interpreted, and these are all at Dasein's disposal" (*BT*, 37). As we will see, our understanding of our Being is related to the world in which we exist—but this world is not simply a world of physical objects that we can either understand or fail to understand. In fact, it is not even this fundamentally or usually. The world in terms of which we understand ourselves, as Heidegger plans to spell out in some detail, is a social one.

The varying interpretations of Dasein's Being are evidenced by the robustly different interpretations we can find in biology, art, philosophy, and other disciplines. Each discipline excavates an aspect of our understanding and of our relationship to the world in which we find ourselves. By Heidegger's lights, all of these interpretations presuppose a more basic one. It is this which Heidegger is after: he wants to excavate the basic structural features of Dasein. It is this at which his "existential analytic" aims.

Heidegger thus explores, in a preparatory way, the everyday understanding of Being that we always already have. He does this in order to examine the essential structural features of Dasein's Being. But this is only an orienting point, a place to begin an inquiry into the fundamental question of Being; it is not enough to simply display this understanding in its average everydayness, we must also probe its depths, seek its implications, and excavate its ontology. This excavation of everydayness, to reiterate, is provisional. It is a point of departure. Heidegger is here laying out the basis of a methodological departure from the philosophical tradition. It is called "hermeneutics."

HERMENEUTICS

Hermeneutics is a method of interpretation that aims to understand something (a text or a text-analogue) in terms of its constituent parts and the relation of these parts to the whole. Perhaps the best example of this view is to be found in the novel. Imagine picking up a novel you know nothing about. You turn to the first page and begin reading about a murder scene. Your initial suspicion is that the novel in question is a mystery. You project this possible meaning onto the rest of the text in order to understand what it is that follows. You have understood the first page in terms of a possible context: the genre of the entire novel. You can understand the rest of the text in light of this provisional understanding.

Now imagine that, as you read on, a very strong love story emerges. The strength of this element makes your initial suspicion about the nature of the text seem suspect. You begin to revise your overall take on the novel. You understand the opening pages, as well as the pages you are now reading, in a new way. This is the core of hermeneutics: we understand part in terms of whole and whole in terms of part. We project a provisional meaning on a text or text-analogue in order to understand, in order to orient our investigation. This initial projection is revisable in light of what our investigation yields.

It is precisely this method that Heidegger invokes and that he thinks marks all human understanding. We understand ourselves, the world, and ourselves in the world in terms of a projection upon the whole. We can revise this projection in light of new discoveries (or simply refine it).

Likewise, the way we understand a particular thing will be determined to some extent by the overall projected meaning we have made.

Heidegger's inquiry into the meaning of Being follows suit. He makes a provisional projection that the key to understanding the meaning of Being will lie in Dasein's average everydayness. Likewise, he projects that the meaning of Dasein's Being will be found in the everyday understanding of Dasein. This is the first projection Heidegger makes. He then notes, as is only appropriate, that the understanding of Being present in Dasein will also be a projection. This is not an infelicity. We must do this. Interpretation, Heidegger thinks, cannot begin without such an orientation—without taking some things for granted.

This point can be made via a famous metaphor—the metaphor of Neurath's boat. Imagine being out to sea on a small boat. You have enough wood to build an entirely new boat, but you're already out to sea. As planks give out, you can replace them—but you can only replace them one at a time. The reason for this is simply that something must support your weight as you work. You can change any part of your boat, resting your weight on the other planks, but you cannot change them all at once. This, to put it metaphorically, is the hermeneutic situation—and because it is characteristic of human understanding, it will also play a constitutive feature in philosophical inquiry. This raises perplexities that simply are not present for traditional epistemology. The power of a projection lies in what it allows us to understand. If an overall understanding will make our everyday lives transparent, then it is justified. This is obviously a far cry from justification by correspondence—where a claim about the world is made and then we see whether or not it maps onto some state of affairs. There is no final justification for a hermeneutic projection. There is no definitive way of saying whether or not it maps onto some type of "fundamental reality." We are condemned, as it were, to interpretation. We must start with interpretation and see how well our initial projection allows us to understand that which we will interpret.

The projection Heidegger makes is that the Being of Dasein is constituted by temporality, and that the meaning of Being in general is time. It is his view that this initial projection will make the meaning of Dasein's Being intelligible to us.

PHENOMENOLOGY

As should at this point be clear, investigating the meaning of Being through Dasein will involve exploring the way that Dasein *experiences* the world around it. The method Heidegger employs is phenomenological—and phenomenology is concerned with examining the objective structures of our experience of things. Phenomenology, as Heidegger conceives it, proceeds by paying close attention to the way the world is

disclosed to us. This emphatically does *not* mean simply the way things
seem to be when we experience them (which can certainly be misleading).
Rather, phenomenology aims to get at the *essence of things* as they present
themselves to us. In the final section of this chapter, we'll flesh out Heidegger's particular reconstruction of phenomenology in *Being and Time*.

Heidegger's Analysis of Phenomenology in Section 7 of Being and Time

There are two quite distinct meanings that we can attach to the notion
of a phenomenon. The first is found in expressions like "He appeared at
my door out of nowhere" or "It appears I was right." What we designate
in these expressions is something *actual*—an existing thing (Heidegger
calls this "the manifest"). There is *in fact* someone at my door. He is
obviously there; he is present; he *shows himself*. This is obviously quite
different from what Heidegger calls *semblance*. Perhaps the best example
of semblance is in the famous Rorschach ink blots. Persons are asked to
look at the ink blots and describe what it is they see *in* the ink blots—that
is, they're asked to describe what the ink blot *resembles*. If someone were
to say, "I see ink all over the page," she would miss entirely the point of
the exercise. Here the thing that presents itself does so by *resembling
something* that it *isn't*. If I see a spaceship in the ink blot, I'm claiming that
the arrangement of ink *presents* a spaceship to me. I'm not saying that all
spaceships are really made of ink. Likewise, if I notice that a person I see
at the movies looks like my brother, I am encountering this person in a
particular way: the phenomenon in question is one in which what I see
resembles something else that I *do not* see. I encounter this person as
looking like something else.

Both of these notions of "phenomenon" are to be distinguished from
what Heidegger calls *appearance*. The notion of appearance itself is an
ambiguous one. The first meaning associated with calling something an
"appearance" can be seen in expressions like "It appears that you have a
cold." In this case, the notion of appearance captures a *relation* between
what is seen and something else that is not seen. The symptoms of a cold
appear, and the appearance of these symptoms "announces" that the
person with the symptoms has a cold. Interestingly, this notion of appearance is very common when dealing with friends and family. A
friend's bad mood presents itself to us in harsh words or a grimace; our
neighbor's boredom shows itself in his listless foot-tapping; a family
member's depression reveals itself in his not eating, choosing isolation,
and so on. In all of these cases, the appearance in question announces
something that it itself is not: the cough is not the cold, the grimace is not
the mood, the foot-tapping is not the boredom, and so on. It is this relation that Heidegger has in mind when he talks about "*appearing*, in the
sense of announcing-itself, as not-showing itself." The cold, much like the
mood, announces itself without showing itself.

The expression "Appearances can be deceiving" captures another significance of the term *phenomenon* (φαινομενον) as appearance. Here, to
say that something appears to be the case is to say that the appearance
itself is not to be trusted—it is *merely* an appearance—it does not even
represent something real. The contrast here is "reality." In this particular
understanding of phenomena, we understand the phenomenon as *distinct from* reality. We regard the appearance as a chimera—something
experienced, but that announces nothing.

With these distinctions, we can refine our discussion. Heidegger has
enabled us to see differences among

1. phenomenon (something showing itself; the manifest);
2. semblance (something resembling another thing, as in the Rorschach ink blots);
3. appearance (something announcing itself, as in the symptoms announcing the presence of a cold); and
4. mere appearance (something illusory, as in a mirage)

Heidegger insists that 2 through 4 are in fact dependent on 1. The notion
of the phenomenon as that which shows itself is a necessary conceptual
precondition for semblance, appearance, and mere appearance. It is this
central notion of phenomenon—that which shows itself in itself (where
this is understood as distinct from 2 through 4, above)—that concerns the
phenomenologist. To get clear about the task of a phenomenology, however, we must still investigate the meaning of "logos" (λογος).

Heidegger laments the various versions of "logos" that exist in the
history of philosophy. The term has been translated as reason, language,
principle, speech, order, and discourse, among other things. Without
much ado, Heidegger claims that all of the standard representations of
this Greek notion are either wrong or unhelpful. Simply paraphrasing the
term with another, equally opaque term does not advance the philosophical conversation. Likewise, translating the term in multiple ways only
promotes confusion. To get clear about this word, we need to investigate
it afresh.

As "discourse," Heidegger claims, "logos" means "to make manifest
what one is talking about in one's discourse" (*BT*, 56). This "making
manifest" Heidegger characterizes as "letting something be seen" (the
Greek term φαίνεσθαι is also the root of phenomenon). Logos pulls
things out of obscurity into focus; it enables us to *see* what is under
consideration. In this sense, speaking about something is also a way of
letting something be seen: speech directs our attention to the thing that is
spoken about. Hence, it is a way of making things manifest. This is the
sort of thing we often mean when we talk about a description being
"illuminating" or "bringing something to light."[9]

The notion of logos as making manifest has implications for the way
we understand truth—a topic we will return to later (in chapter 5). Typi-

cally, people think of a sentence (or a proposition) as true. We can say that a sentence is true if that sentence corresponds to a state of affairs in the world. Heidegger claims that this way of conceptualizing truth is in fact derivative (this *does not* mean that it's false!). The more fundamental notion of truth, on Heidegger's view, is closely linked to logos (construed as letting something be seen). The most ontologically basic conception of truth is truth as *aletheia*: a form of seeing (*noein*) things for what they are. The basic form of truth thus has nothing to do with sentences. Rather, it has to do with seeing things that *make themselves* manifest.

Heidegger thinks that the idea of a phenomenology ultimately amounts to the dictum "To the things themselves!" It is, in this respect, unlike other disciplinary terms with the root 'logos' (psychology, biology, and so on). The task of phenomenology is not to construct a science of phenomenon. Rather, the task is to capture that which shows itself in the very way that it shows itself. To take phenomenology seriously is to take seriously the proposition that our experiences matter, that they cannot be brushed aside. All analysis and inquiry presupposes our experience. Moreover, phenomenology demands that we recognize the fundamental relationship between our experience and the world around us: it is in our experience that things reveal themselves to us. To do phenomenology is to try to capture the manner in which things present themselves to us.

It is this that leads Heidegger to claim that the phrase *descriptive phenomenology* is a tautology: phenomenology's only task is to be descriptive; its aim is to describe what shows itself in-itself *as* it shows itself in-itself. It is in the very nature of phenomenology that we find a clue as to how any *ontology* will proceed. Because the task of phenomenology is to describe how beings present themselves to us, Heidegger claims, "only as phenomenology, is ontology possible" (*BT*, 60). In other words, only by systematically describing the way things present themselves to us in their Being (phenomenology) will we ever be able to investigate Being (ontology).

NOTES

1. The logical positivists of the analytic tradition were fond of making precisely this point. Likewise, Wittgenstein, both early and late, insisted that a question was only sensical if it admitted of an answer that, in some sense, involved more than a positive restatement of the question posed. See, for example, Wittgenstein, *On Certainty*.

2. This formulation is slightly misleading. The very locution of subject/predicate is one that Heidegger thinks we must move beyond.

3. There's obviously much more to Dasein than the paraphrase "human being" suggests. We'll spend a good deal of time exploring what it means to be Dasein throughout this book.

4. The passage certainly anticipates the work of Thomas Kuhn.

5. It is this same distinction that marks the boundaries of Kuhn's normal and revolutionary science split in *The Structure of Scientific Revolutions*.

6. Whereas Aristotle engaged in physics by looking toward the natures of individual objects, Newton looks to force and motion. Newton effectively cast doubt on the entities to be examined in an appropriate physics.

7. Plato, of course, raised precisely this concern in *Meno*.

8. I find it relatively harmless, in this context, to call the ontic the empirical. This will not work in every case, however, as the assertions we make based on the ontologies we take for granted will not always aim at saying something about the world.

9. My thanks to Dorothy Wisnewski for bringing these examples to my attention.

THREE

Being-in-the-World

We've introduced the general question Heidegger wants to pose in *Being and Time* (What is the meaning of Being?), as well as the method Heidegger will use to investigate this question (a phenomenological ontology of Dasein—that being for whom being is an issue). The point of this chapter is to explore the notion of "Being-in-the-world," which is one of the first characterizations Heidegger offers of the Being of Dasein—of those beings *we ourselves are*.

Heidegger insists that we should not understand Being-in-the-world as a sum of several elements put together. (Heidegger hyphenates this expression to emphasize that the world is an essential part of the being in question—it cannot be separated out.) The notion of Being-in-the-world, Heidegger insists, is a "*unitary* phenomenon. This primary datum must be seen as a whole" (*BT*, 78). This does not entail, however, that we cannot explore *aspects* of Being-in-the-world in our attempt to understand this phenomenon. As Heidegger notes, although "Being-in-the-world cannot be broken up into contents which may be pieced together, this does not prevent it from having several constitutive items in its structure" (*BT*, 78).

WHAT IS DASEIN? SOME PRELIMINARY CONSIDERATIONS

Dasein is not to be construed as one more object in a world of objects. Dasein is separated from other objects by what Heidegger calls its "mineness." "The Being of any such entity is *in each case mine*. These entities, in their Being, comport themselves towards their Being" (*BT*, 67). This manner of Being is to be sharply distinguished from what Heidegger calls the "present-at-hand." A *present-at-hand* object does not involve *mineness*; it does not involve a concern on the part of the object about its Being. A

31

table does not ask, "Am I being the table I want to be?" A table simply is what it is, and no more. Everything about the Being of a table lies easily available—present to us, immediately at hand. Its Being *is* present-at-hand.[1] Dasein is not like this.

Heidegger isolates two theses about Dasein to be explored in the analysis of Dasein's Being.

1. "The essence of Dasein lies in its existence" (*BT*, 67).[2]
2. The Being of Dasein is *authored* by that Dasein: Dasein is constantly living out its possibilities, and the possibilities Dasein is living out are (in a mitigated sense at least) products of *choice*.

Dasein, because it is in each case mine, admits of modes of existence: we can exist as having chosen ourselves, as being masters of ourselves (authenticity), or as not having chosen ourselves, as not "owning" our own existence (inauthenticity). These two things are to be viewed as equally basic modes (or possibilities) of Dasein's Being.

Heidegger insists throughout *Being and Time* that the distinction between the authentic and the inauthentic is not meant to be evaluative. The terms themselves (*authenticity* and *inauthenticity*) nevertheless seem to have clear evaluative content. Who, after all, would *want* to be inauthentic, and who *wouldn't* want to be authentic? While the German terms are not without their own evaluative connotations, these connotations are less striking in the original German. The term translated as *authenticity* is *Eigentlichkeit*; the term translated as *inauthenticity* is *Uneigentlichkeit*. The significance of the German, however, is not simply that it is less evaluative than the English. The German terms themselves provide us with a clue to the meaning of the concept Heidegger is trying to articulate. The German *eigen*, used as an adjective, specifies that a thing is *yours*—it belongs to you; it is your own. The term *Eigentlichkeit* (authenticity) is rooted in this term (*eigen*). One can thus see that to be authentic, in Heidegger's sense, is to *own oneself*. By contrast, to be inauthentic is *not* to own oneself. These are the two basic modes of Dasein's Being.[3]

Dasein can either own itself or not own itself—and this is simply a feature of what it means to be Dasein. The choice of being ourselves (or not) marks the boundaries of our existence, and hence our essence. We *are* this possibility. Inauthenticity and authenticity are the basic modes of being Dasein. The way we operate—the way we live out these possibilities—is determined by the understanding of the world that we already have—one which, in turn, will be shaped by the choices we make, by the possibilities we actualize.[4]

In relation to the question of authenticity—and to the question of Dasein's Being itself—we are also introduced to the notion of average everydayness. For the most part, Heidegger claims, we are inauthentic. We tend to flee in the face of our own existence—and this constitutes a basic mode of our Being as Dasein. We exist, firstly and mostly, in average everydayness. This mode of Being (average everydayness), Heidegger claims, has been passed over by the intellectual tradition. We haven't paid much attention to Dasein as we find it in the workaday world: pumping gas, watching television, relaxing on the beach, and so on. Heidegger points out that this mode of Being is in fact *essential* to Dasein—it constitutes a part of the ontological structure of Dasein; it is an integral part of being what we are. Equally importantly, "the inauthenticity of Dasein does not signify any 'less' Being or any 'lower' degree of Being" (*BT*, 68). In other words, we are not to understand authenticity as in some sense a "higher" way of being than inauthenticity. The two modes of Being are both basic to Dasein—they are possible ways in which Dasein *is* in the world; they are possible ways in which Dasein *is* itself.

Heidegger insists that most of us, most of the time, are inauthentic. It's tempting for many readers of *Being and Time* to regard this as a *criticism* of our basic modes of existence, despite Heidegger's protests to the contrary. We should fight this temptation—at least as much as the evidence allows. As we will see, Dasein's inauthenticity is a kind of *foundation* for Dasein's Being-in-the-world. Without our everyday understanding, we will see, there would be nothing out of which we might *become* authentic. Indeed, as Heidegger remarks later in *Being and Time*, authenticity is simply a way of "taking up" or "appropriating" inauthenticity. Moreover, as Heidegger suggests, the general ontological structures that constitute Dasein in its mode of average everydayness "may be structurally indistinguishable from certain ontological characteristics [*Bestimmungen*] of an *authentic* Being of Dasein" (*BT*, 70). This, of course, stands to reason, as authenticity and inauthenticity are rightly understood as modes of Dasein's mineness (that is, these are two ways that Dasein can *be* Dasein).[5]

Heidegger distinguishes between existentialia/existentiale and categories. This terminological distinction actually marks a more important *on-*

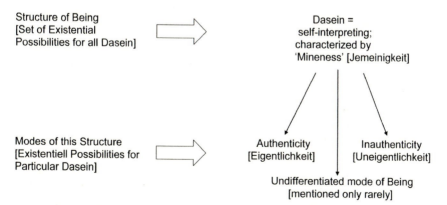

Figure 3.1. Dasein's Existential and Existentiell Possibilities

tological one. When investigating Dasein, we are not merely investigating some object with particular properties. Rather, we are interested in a *mode of Being*. So we will attempt to get clear about what is involved in being what Dasein is. Investigating the structure of Dasein's Being will yield existentialia, or "existential structures." Because Dasein's essence lies in its existence, doing ontology (investigating this type of Being) requires examining these structures.

An investigation of objects possessing properties involves, on the other hand, specifying categories into which objects fall, and is rather far removed from the investigation of the Being of a thing. In fact, it presupposes regarding the Being of the thing in a particular way. Heidegger distinguishes the two sorts of investigation by noting that they involve asking different questions. An analysis of Dasein asks "Who?" while an investigation of present-at-hand objects asks "What?"

We've introduced some crucial distinctions here, even if only in a provisional way. The fundamental distinction, of course, is between the kind of Being that Dasein has, on the one hand, and the kind of Being that objects have, on the other. Some of the basic distinctions we have introduced are captured in table 3.1.

Once we have recognized that Heidegger is not interested in investigating the "what" of Dasein, we are also in a position to see how an inquiry into the *Being* of Dasein will necessarily be distinct from the ontical sciences: anthropology, psychology, and biology, for example. As Heidegger notes, those sciences that have aimed at investigating Dasein as one more entity with the same character as other entities that are present-at-hand "have missed the real *philosophical* problem notwithstanding their objective fertility" (*BT*, 71). Importantly, Heidegger is *not* criticizing the normal scientific investigation of Dasein here. As he readily acknowledges, such inquiry has "objective fertility"—there is much to be learned in psychology, anthropology, and biology (as well as in other

Table 3.1. Dasein and the Present-at-Hand

	Dasein	**Present-at-hand object**
Essential characteristic	Characterized by "mineness"	Characterized by possession of impersonal properties
Ontological structures	Existentiale [structures of Dasein]	Categories [structures of the present-at-hand]
Mode of interrogation	"Who?"	"What?"
Modes of Being	Authentic/inauthentic	Discovered/undiscovered
Relation of existence and essence	Essence is existence	Essence is given prior to existence

theoretical attempts to understand human existence). So Heidegger is not claiming that the ontic sciences can make no claims about entities without first working out an ontology. Indeed, the ontic sciences have *always already* presupposed a particular ontology, and in one respect all ontic investigation is exploring the logic of the particular ontology it takes for granted. The task of phenomenology is not to *prevent* this; rather, phenomenology wants to make our ontological presuppositions more transparent—and, in a way, more problematic. To be forgetful of Being, as we've seen, is to fail to recognize that there is even an issue regarding the kinds of beings that we take for granted in the workaday world (and their significance). Phenomenological investigation will enable us to see that there is an issue involving Being, as well as the meaning of the beings that populate our ontical inquiries. Thus, as Heidegger concedes, "ontology can contribute only indirectly towards advancing the positive disciplines as we find them today. It has a goal of its own, if indeed, beyond the acquiring of information about entities, the question of Being is the spur of all scientific seeking" (*BT*, 77).

TRADITIONAL INVESTIGATIONS OF HUMAN BEINGS

What is missing in scientific attempts to understand humanity is a prior investigation into what it *means* to be a Dasein—what it means to be the sort of thing that could be examined in such subject areas.

What does it mean to be "anthropos," or a being with "psyche," or "bios"? These questions are unavailable within those disciplines that are grounded on their study. These notions must be taken for granted if any interrogation of them (and logos concerning them) is to be possible at all. The traditional "ologies" have not adequately established their points of departure. Heidegger attempts to capture this by examining Descartes's famous "cogito sum" ("I think [therefore] I am"). As Heidegger points out, although Descartes offers some analysis of the "ego" of the "cogitare" (of the "I" that engages in thinking), "he leaves the '*sum*' [Being] completely undiscussed, even though it is regarded as no less primordial than the *cogito*." (*BT*, 71). Heidegger's aim is to raise "the ontological question of the Being of the '*sum*'" (*BT*, 72).

But as Heidegger quickly goes on to explain, the problem is actually deeper than this challenge to Descartes suggests. *Any* philosophy that posits an "I" prior to investigating Being inevitably begins with an ungrounded ontology. To posit an "I" prior to an investigation of Dasein is to

> completely miss the phenomenal content [*Bestand*] of Dasein. *Ontologically*, every idea of a "subject"—unless refined by a previous ontological determination of its basic character—still posits the subjectum (υποκειμενον) along with it, no matter how vigorous one's ontical

protestations against the "soul substance" or the "reification of consciousness". The Thinghood itself which such reification implies must
have its ontological origin demonstrated if we are to be in a position to
ask what we are to understand *positively* when we think of the unre-
ified *Being* of the subject, the soul, the consciousness, the spirit, the
person. All these terms refer to definite phenomenal domains which
can be "given form": but they are never used without a notable failure
to see the need for inquiring about the Being of the entities thus designated. (*BT*, 72)

The philosophy of the subject has dominated much of our thinking about
humanity and our forays into ontic investigations. The "human" sciences
are possible, after all, precisely because we presuppose there is a thing
called the "human," the Being of which is transparent enough to distinguish it from other types of entities. When philosophers attempt to deny
the existence of certain properties (when one denies, for example, that
human beings have a "soul"), one still presupposes the existence of human beings as particular entities. This kind of protestation, it seems,
comes too late, as it presupposes the very thing that requires analysis.

Drawing on Scheler, Heidegger articulates very concisely that which
distinguishes personhood from thinghood: "the person is no thinglike
and substantial Being. Nor can the Being of a person be entirely absorbed
in being a subject of rational acts which follow certain laws. The person is
not a thing, not a substance, not an object" (*BT*, 73). A person, in other
words, has a completely different character from anything with which
traditional sciences—human or not—have been concerned. The idea of a
person as a body put together with a mind has been the fundamental
mistake of ontology prior to Heidegger. On Scheler's view, "Essentially
the person exists only in the performance of intentional acts, and is there-
fore essentially *not* an object" (*BT*, 73). Heidegger accepts this, so far as it
goes, but insists that it does not yet go quite far enough.

In attempting to understand the Being of humanity, we cannot proceed by addition, as it were. That is, we cannot simply compile all of the
intentional acts that one engages in, looking at the result as a definition of
the person. Indeed, to compile parts into a coherent whole *presupposes*
that there is a whole into which the set of parts will fit. In the same way,
"some idea of the Being of the whole must be presupposed" (*BT*, 74). The
whole that is typically presupposed, Heidegger contends, is captured in
two basic theses—theses central to both Christianity and the ancient traditions of the western world:

1. "Man" is an animal with logos (reason/speech) (ζωον λογον εχον).
2. "Man" has been conceptualized as existing in the image of God.

These particular presuppositions have infiltrated both anthropology and
psychology. Likewise, this particular conception of humanity is, in certain respects, presupposed by biology. As Heidegger claims, "biology as

a 'science of life' is founded upon the ontology of Dasein, even if not entirely. Life, in its own right, is a kind of Being; but essentially it is accessible only in Dasein" (*BT*, 75). From this vantage point, Heidegger claims that we must keep separate the investigation of ontic entities, on the one hand, and the investigation of Dasein—that being through which ontic entities reveal themselves and are understood as they are—on the other. As Heidegger puts this point: "these ontological foundations can never be disclosed by subsequent hypotheses derived from empirical material" (75).

The importance of this point should not be underestimated. It is crucial for understanding, again, the priority of the question of Being in general and the question of Dasein's Being in particular: ontic (empirical) investigations can *never* justify an ontology, as one cannot get *results* in ontical inquiry unless one has already presupposed an ontology. Recall that ontic inquiry is only possible given a prior understanding of what sorts of things there are (thus, psychology must presuppose a "psyche," anthropology must presuppose the "anthropos," and so on). If these very things are assumed prior to any investigation, the results of such an investigation will obviously not justify the very ontology they presuppose.[6]

DASEIN AS BEING-IN-THE-WORLD: A PRIMER

The notion of "Being-in" has two significantly different senses. The first sense is captured by claims like "I am in the philosophy department," where this is construed in the sense of spatial location. This, for Heidegger, is a derivative, ontic sense of Being-in. The very same sentence, however, has a remarkably different sense when construed ontologically: "I am in the philosophy department" also signifies an *involvement*. This second, existential sense of Being-in is what Heidegger wants to capture in the notion of Dasein's Being-in-the-world. Heidegger is not claiming that Dasein is fundamentally an extended substance.

> A person [Dasein] is not a Thing, not a substance, not an object. . . . Essentially the person exists only in the performance of intentional acts, and is therefore essentially not an object. (*BT*, 73)

> Being-in . . . is a state of Dasein's Being; it is an existentiale [structure of Dasein]. So one cannot think of it as the Being-present-at-hand of some corporeal Thing (such as the human body) "in" an entity which is present-at-hand. (*BT*, 79)

Rather, Dasein's Being is one of *involvement*, where involvement is construed as "concern." We are "in" the world in this ontological (as opposed to ontic) sense: the world is that context of significance with which we are always already involved. Something close to this sense of world surfaces in everyday speech when we speak of "the business world" or "the world of fashion." There is no Dasein independent of a world of significance, independent of a world of concern. "Being-in is thus the formal existential expression for the Being of Dasein, which has Being-in-the-world as its essential state" (*BT*, 80).

The two fundamental senses of "Being-in" we have been discussing are represented in figure 3.2. We're in a world, fundamentally, in the sense that we're *involved in* and *concerned about* a web of meaning. It is Dasein's existence as involved in the world that separates Dasein fundamentally from objects that are in the world in the merely ontic, spatial sense. It is for this reason that Heidegger claims that "there is no such thing as the 'side-by-side-ness' of an entity with another entity called 'world'"(*BT*, 81). Dasein is thus not to be construed as an object, standing apart from other objects, each with their own particular properties. To think of Dasein as akin to, say, a stereo or a tree is to miss the fundamental nature of Dasein as a being that is not merely present-at-hand but one that is concernfully absorbed in its world (where "world" is construed phenomenologically). Being-in-the-world is being in a world disclosed to us. Dasein is such that it always has an understanding of the world: the world is just that which is disclosed to us in our Being-in. This way of understanding our existence thus challenges some major philosophical assumptions.

> When Dasein directs itself toward something and grasps it, it does not somehow first get out of an inner sphere in which it has been proximally encapsulated, but its primary kind of Being is such that it is always "outside" alongside entities which it encounters and which belong to a world already discovered. (*BT*, 89)

> Whenever we encounter anything, the world has already been previously discovered, though not thematically. (*BT*, 114)

> Dasein, in so far as it is, has always submitted itself already to a "world" which it encounters, and this submission belongs essentially to its Being. (*BT*, 121)

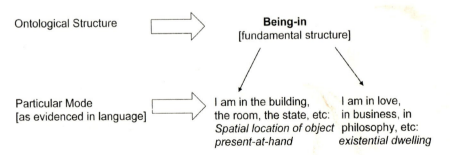

Figure 3.2. Being-in

Dasein's Being-in-the-world thus acts as a riposte to a philosophical tradition that has consistently separated mind and world with a veil of perception. For Heidegger, mind is dispersed in world. There is no thing "mind" that is to be viewed as fundamentally distinct from a world that is known. Our very mode of Being is one of knowing the world, is one of the world being disclosed to us in different ways.

Moreover, what we standardly call "objective knowledge" is based on one particular way in which the world is disclosed—a way that, as Heidegger goes on to claim, is derivative of the basic context of concern through which we usually understand the world.

> Being-in-the-world, as concern, is *fascinated by* the world with which it is concerned. If knowing is to be possible as a way of determining the nature of the present-at-hand by observing it, then there must first be a *deficiency* in our having to do with the world concernfully. (*BT*, 88)

To round out our preliminary conception of Being-in, it will be worthwhile to consider the sense of "world" that Heidegger employs when talking about our Being-in-the-world. A general sense of the notion of "world" should already be clear from the above reflections. The world is a totality of significance—a way of understanding, a mode of disclosure. The world is given prior to particular things within the world. Before we can examine a particular object, we must already be involved in the world in a certain way. By and large, this happens when our "circumspective concern" (our absorption in the projects we have) is interrupted. I notice that a hammer has certain physical characteristics, for example, when it breaks: I am forced to see it as an object present-at-hand when I can no longer simply use it to build something.

Of course, this does not mean that viewing the world present-at-hand is useless. Quite the contrary, the empirical sciences do precisely this. We only run into error when we think of this way of understanding the world as in some sense fundamental. When we do this, we mistake one mode of the Being of objects for their Being in general—we mistake one aspect of a thing for its entirety.

> As long as we take our orientation primarily and exclusively from the present-at-hand, the "in-itself" can by no means be ontologically clarified. (*BT*, 106)

The key to understanding worlds of disclosedness, if Heidegger is correct, lies in the Being of that being who exists fundamentally and existentially "in-the-world," that is, in Dasein.

> Dasein, in its familiarity with significance, is the ontical condition for the possibility of discovering entities which are encountered in a world with involvement (readiness-to-hand) as their kind of Being, and which can thus make themselves known as they are in themselves. (*BT*, 120)

THE READY-TO-HAND

Being-in-the-world offers a point of departure for understanding anew some of our central philosophical prejudices concerning subjectivity, objectivity, knowledge, and what it means for a thing to be "real." As Heidegger makes clear,

> The kind of dealing which is closest to us is as we have shown, not a bare perceptual cognition, but rather that kind of concern which manipulates things and puts them to use; and this has its own kind of "knowledge." (*BT*, 95)

In Being-in-the-world, we're interested in "those [entities] which show themselves in our concern with the environment" (*BT*, 95). Heidegger distinguishes this from the philosophical tradition that he thinks has proven so misleading—a tradition attempting to capture the world as a set of material objects.

> Such entities [i.e., those encountered in our everyday dealings (*Umgang*)] are not thereby objects for knowing the "world" theoretically; they are simply what gets used, what gets produced, and so forth. . . . The phenomenological interpretation is accordingly not a way of knowing those characteristics of entities which themselves are; it is rather a determination of the structure of the Being which entities possess. (*BT*, 95–96)

The way we encounter and operate with entities on a daily basis is not captured by our theoretical descriptions. When we *reflect* on our basic activities in the world, we burden our perception with the theoretical weight of a tradition that demands we view objects as present-at-hand. Even simply claiming that we encounter "things" in "reality" can mislead us into a traditional ontology of substantiality, materiality, extendedness, and so on.

To avoid this confusion (or, at any rate, to attempt to avoid this confusion), Heidegger uses the term *equipment*. Equipment is a mode of being we find when comporting ourselves to the world: we are engaged in concernful dealings with the world, and within these concernful dealings we are engaged in a world that facilitates our undertakings. In this everyday bumping around, we encounter a totality of equipment: we don't understand one tool at a time, each independent of all the others. Rather, we're involved in a pragmatic mode of viewing the world—as serviceable and manipulable for our current projects. To experience equipment is always to experience it as embedded in the context of other equipment. Singular pieces of equipment can't be isolated when we experience them *as equipment*. To isolate a piece of equipment is to cease viewing it as something ready-to-hand—it is to divorce it from the context in which equipment is and must *be*.

This claim isn't as strange as it might initially appear. The way we experience things depends crucially on what *we're doing*. When we're trying to describe things, those things appear to us in a way *different from* the way they appear when we're engaged with them. A typical philosophical mistake, according to Heidegger, is to think that our descriptions of things capture our *experience of them*, and this just isn't so. When we're busy with particular projects, we don't reflect on those things we're using to complete the project. When we drive on a freeway, we needn't think of the properties of the gear shift in order to use it. We simply operate with the equipment as it is—bound up with other equipment that is useful to us in engaging in the projects that mark the space of our concern. I don't contemplate the properties of a pen when I use it to write a quick note to my wife. I simply grab the pen and begin to write. The "equipmentality" of the pen is tied up in a context of significance generated by the project I have. I want to write a note. I perceive the pen, not as an isolated object with particular properties but as a tool I can use to accomplish my task. I see the pen in conjunction with the other tools necessary to complete the project I have: the paper I will write on, the magnet I will use to hang the note, the refrigerator I will put the note on, and so forth.

The sort of being we perceive in our projects isn't the sort of being we perceive when we're engaged, for example, in disinterested description. One way of capturing this distinction is in the notion of "know-how."[7] Knowing how to use a pen or drive a car or walk down the street is not the same as knowing the properties and characteristics of a pen, a car, or walking. In the first case, I am engaged in the world in such a way that knowing particular propositions such as "One must shift to third gear at x rpms" or "A pen is a small implement used to write" simply does not come up. I have a competence. I understand the world, and I understand it in terms of the projects I hope to accomplish. This requires no conscious cognitive activity. I know how to do what I am doing. It's only when this know-how breaks down, Heidegger claims, that we resort to knowing-that, to conscious deliberations about what might have gone wrong given what we know (and can articulate) *about* those things with which we're concerned.

Take Heidegger's own famous example. Imagine you are using a hammer to build something. You are pounding in nails. You're engaged in a project. You aren't thinking about the properties of a hammer—that it's made of wood and metal, that it is eighteen inches long, and so on. Rather, you're absorbed in an activity that requires no reflection: the hammer is that which you can use to complete your project, albeit with the rest of the equipment necessary to this task.

Now say your hammer breaks. Your absorption in activity is disrupted: there's an impediment to completing your project. You now see the broken hammer as an object present-at-hand—as an object with properties that don't allow you *to be* concernfully absorbed in an activity. Viewing objects as present-at-hand depends on a more primordial under-standing—on a more primordial knowing-how. It's this more primordial mode of coping with the world that Heidegger attempts to capture with the notion of the ready-at-hand.

> The less we just stare at the hammer-Thing, and the more we seize hold of it and use it, the more primordial does our relationship to it become, and the more unveiledly is it encountered as that which it is—as equip-ment. . . . The kind of Being which equipment possesses—in which it manifests itself in its own right—we call "readiness-to-hand." (*BT*, 98)

The way of seeing the world that is typical of the ready-to-hand Heideg-ger calls "circumspection" (*BT*, 98). The term *circumspection* translates *Umsicht*, which literally means something like "seeing-around"—it is, in other words, quite *literally* a kind of seeing. Circumspection is a way of comporting ourselves to entities, one that places us in a relation of con-cern to these entities as opposed to one of so-called disinterest, in which we try to specify the properties of a particular occurent (present-at-hand) object.

Circumspection is a mode of Dasein's Being through which the world is disclosed. We encounter objects in a pretheoretical manner as useful to our endeavors. This is not to say that we see an object and reflect to ourselves, "That's the tool I need." The encounter of the ready-to-hand is prereflective. We encounter the world as ready-to-hand when we *do not* reflect about it, when we are engrossed in activity.

But what, exactly, is disclosed when we are so engrossed? What is the "sight" of circumspection? In one sense, *everything* is disclosed. Circum-spective concern, as a mode of Dasein's Being, is a form of knowing the world. Of course, when we discuss it in this manner, laying bare its properties, we make it into a set of objects present-at-hand. In represent-ing the ready-to-hand, we necessarily misrepresent it. In thinking through the ready-to-hand in a reflective manner, then, we must be care-ful never to mistake it for something that is itself reflective.

Viewing our hammer as a piece of equipment in the totality of equip-ment is a mode of disclosure: we know the world, in this case, in relation to the projects we have. This way of understanding the world (this "mode of disclosure") can be thwarted by the world: the hammer can break, get stolen, be missing, or any other number of things. When this occurs, Heidegger thinks, we experience a deficiency. That which we need in order to engage in our projects (building a chest of drawers, say) becomes apparent to us the moment it ceases to be ready-to-hand. We are forced to reflect on the object when it no longer suits our needs. I needn't think about the hammer when it's in my hand and I'm using it to pound nails into the chest of drawers. I am simply using it. When it flies out of my hand and smashes into the wall, or when I misplace it during a bathroom break, I *do* think about the hammer explicitly. My concernful absorption is broken by the presentation of an object present-at-hand. Instead of using the hammer, I must ask, "Where did I put that hammer?" It becomes, as Heidegger says, *obtrusive* (*BT*, 103)—it obtrudes into my concernful absorption, forcing me to recognize that there is a particular thing that I am missing. This "brings to the fore the characteristic of presence-at-hand in what is ready-to-hand" (*BT*, 104).

Objects in the world are what they are—have the mode of Being they do—in virtue of the fact that they are disclosed to us in a certain way. Being is disclosed to us in our Being-in-the-world. We must be on guard here, however, not to invoke another appearance-versus-reality split. What a thing *is* is revealed to us in our modes of comportment. There are different modes of disclosure, it is true—different ways in which the world is made known to us—but each disclosure is a disclosure of the thing itself, is a disclosure of a mode of Being.

When our concernful absorption breaks down, the world is disclosed in a new way. It is disclosed as something present-to-hand. We recognize the totality of equipment *as* a totality of equipment, as present-at-hand: we needed the hammer in order to build the chest of drawers, and we wanted to build the chest of drawers for a friend, who could use it in order to store clothes made in Taiwan.

What becomes evident in our reflections on our projects, then, is that each piece of equipment in effect references a *world*—a web of significance in which things make their appearance, have significance, and so on. In this respect, every piece of equipment signifies (and makes reference to) a context in which that piece of equipment is intelligible as equipment. Equipment functions as a sign of a world.

The sort of sign Heidegger has in mind is exemplified, he thinks, by the signaling of an automobile. When an automobile signals to change lanes or turn, there isn't a reference in the strictest possible sense (there isn't a *Bedeutung*, in Frege's sense of the term). Rather, a sign is something that provides us with an orientation: we now know what the car will do. We have an understanding of the situation in which the sign indicates.

This is not an entirely unfamiliar use of the term *reference* even in English. If I say, "In reference to your recent request to . . . ," I am providing you with an orientation for the speech that will follow. It is this sort of "indicating" or "showing" that Heidegger has in mind. A sign indicates what to expect. It indicates an orientation to take up in the world.

> Signs of the kind we have described let what is ready-to-hand be encountered; more precisely, they let some context of it become accessible in such a way that our concernful dealings take on an orientation and hold it secure. A sign is not a Thing which stands to another Thing in the relationship of indicating; it is rather *an item of equipment which explicitly raises a totality of equipment into our circumspection so that togeth-*

er with it the worldly character of the ready-to-hand announces itself. . . .
Signs always indicate primarily "wherein" one lives, where one's concern dwells, what sort of involvement there is with something. (*BT*,
110–11)[8]

The example of a wedding ring is useful here. A wedding ring indicates
something. It is a sign for something, but not in the sense of signification.
When you see a wedding ring on the finger of someone in a bar, this sign
indicates to you a certain context: the person in question has tied his or
her life to another, has made a set of commitments, and so on. While this
might not change your mode of interaction in any empirically obvious
sense, the sign nevertheless creates a context in light of which what you
do will have significance. If you end up having a relationship with the
married person, you will be engaged in infidelity. This is only possible in
virtue of the fact that the person in question is married. The ring is a sign
that indicates an orientation to you. Even if you do not change what you
do, you are nonetheless aware of a context of significance indicated by
the wedding ring.

> A sign is something ontically ready-to-hand, which functions both as
> this definite equipment and as something indicative of the ontological
> structure of readiness-to-hand, of referential totalities, and of world-
> hood. (*BT*, 114)

This discussion of signs enables us to understand what we might call the
"holism" of the ready-to-hand. When we understand the ready-to-hand,
we do not understand it in terms of individual objects with specific properties. Rather, our involvement is an involvement in a web of connections
(a referential totality, as Heidegger says), where each thing is what is
only in reference to other things within this web. Heidegger introduces a
series of terms meant to capture this referential feature of the ready-to-
hand: the with-which, the toward-which, the for-which, the from-which,
and the for-the-sake-of-which.

It's easy to get distracted by the constant use of new jargon. Indeed,
some readers often feel as though they are adrift on the seas of language
when they encounter such sets of new terms. The core point Heidegger is
making, though, arguably *requires* new terminology. Our standard mode
of describing things is in terms of objects and their properties—that is, it
is fundamentally present-at-hand. In introducing new terminology, Heidegger is emphasizing that what we are discussing here is *not* this standard way of understanding the world around us. The new terminology is
meant to emphasize that, while we are absorbed in the ready-to-hand, the
world presents itself as a whole, as intimately interconnected. In any
instance where we break these connections, we find ourselves changing
our phenomenological perspective from the ready-to-hand back to the
present-at-hand. While there is nothing wrong with viewing things as
present-at-hand (indeed, it can be quite useful), we don't want to simply

ignore other ways in which the world presents itself to us (namely, the way it presents itself when we are fully engaged in some project, as opposed to simply detaching ourselves from immediate involvement).

The toward-which and the for-which of the ready-to-hand constitute a type of reference—it is precisely the reference of involvement. When we view x as equipment, it is equipment "with y for z." When we are circumspectively concerned in the world, we are engaging in projects: rebuilding engines, writing papers, reading, putting down carpet, and so on. We do this with an end in view: to have a better car, to get an insight, to have a nicer living room, and so on. The end in view is the toward-which of our projects. In engaging in these projects, the tools we use are tools for the completion of the project: the hammer is a tool for getting the carpet down, the glasses are a tool for reading the book, the laptop is a tool for writing a report. The tools are for something that we are working on, and what we are working on fits into a larger project—a goal we have in view. The entire project itself, of course, refers back to that very being who engages in it: Dasein. In this respect, Dasein is the for-the-sake-of-which of any project.

Figure 3.3 is meant to capture what I called above the holism of the ready-to-hand. Using a simple action—making coffee—we can see how an entire world is both disclosed and presupposed by our activity. As we put our coffee into a coffeemaker, we inhabit a world already populated by other Dasein and much richer than any list of the objects in front of us would suggest. The coffee beans themselves, we understand, did not materialize out of thin air: they were grown by other Dasein, processed in a factory, packaged and shipped to various locations, and then sold. Even *having* coffee in the kitchen already discloses an entire world (what Heidegger calls the from-which). In making coffee, I prereflectively understand that coffee comes *from somewhere*. If we tried to fully articulate everything about the process by which we get coffee, we would find ourselves on an endless quest: after we specified that it was grown on a farm, after all, we'd need to say who grew it, what tools were used, what kinds of techniques, and so on. But each of these further specifications would point to still others: some Dasein used a tractor to till the fields, but this tractor itself comes from some other Dasein, who used materials extracted from the earth by another Dasein, who used tools produced by another Dasein, and so on. So the things we use to make coffee (water, coffee beans, perhaps a coffeemaker) fit into a much larger context than simply some discrete set of objects with particular properties. The with-which, to put it in Heideggerian language, already suggests the from-which.

But this is really only the beginning. After all, we make coffee with a particular purpose—namely, to drink it. But we also drink coffee for a particular purpose—perhaps to have a shot of caffeine that will allow us to have a productive morning. Whatever the reasons one has for making

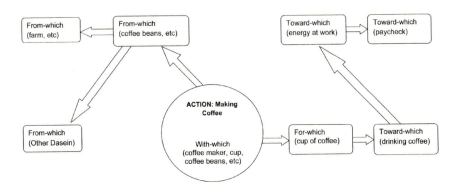

For-the-sake-of which: Dasein

Figure 3.3.   The World of the Ready-to-Hand

and drinking coffee, this much should be clear: one's activities always point toward something. One engages in a project in order to accomplish some end. This is precisely the toward-which of the ready-to-hand. As in the case of the with-which and from-which, though, the toward-which seems to go on indefinitely. I make coffee in order to drink it; I drink coffee in order to get the caffeine; I get the caffeine in order to feel more awake and energized; I want to feel more awake and energized in order to be productive at work; I want to be productive at work in order to get a raise; I want to get a raise so that I can make more money and feel more satisfied with my laborious activities; and so on. One can keep chasing the toward-which into the future, much as one can chase the from-which into the past. At the bottom of the entire project, of course, is one's own Dasein itself: Dasein is the for-the-sake-of-which—the reason one is engaging in any projects at all.

Characterizing the world in terms of separate, independent objects, each with their own properties, certainly captures *one way* in which we understand the world (namely, as present-at-hand). But, Heidegger insists, this is not the way we understand things for the most part. The ready-to-hand, by contrast, *does*. Indeed, on Heidegger's account, it is precisely when our projects are frustrated—when, for example, we run out of coffee, or the coffeemaker breaks, or the water is shut off—that we see things in terms of individual objects with particular properties. When everything is functioning smoothly, I am simply absorbed in my activities, unaware and unconcerned with how one might describe the world from a perspective of detached observation.

HEIDEGGER'S REJECTION OF THE CARTESIAN WORLD

The fact that we are sometimes absorbed in projects, of course, does not entail that the world is not *in fact* composed of individual objects, each with specific properties. One might object to Heidegger's analysis so far on precisely this point. Yes, someone might say, we do not always pay attention to individual objects and their properties. But the world is composed of such things *regardless* of how we experience them.

To understand Heidegger's response to this objection, we should emphasize that Heidegger *does not* claim that the experience of things as present-at-hand is somehow illegitimate. We *do* experience things in this way very frequently. When our hammer breaks, for instance, we notice that it is composed of a certain material and that it has particular properties (it's breakable, for example). What Heidegger wants to emphasize, though, is that this is only *one way* in which the world presents itself to us. To claim that this way is *the right way*, moreover, requires argument—not simply assertion.

Why should we think that things are fundamentally present-at-hand rather than ready-to-hand? This question, it soon becomes apparent, is difficult to answer without reasoning circularly. One might claim that it is more intuitive to think of things as present-at-hand, but this hardly passes for persuasive argument. After all, what one finds intuitive is very often the product of a conceptual familiarity with one way of thinking about things. Because our experience of things as ready-to-hand is not *conceptual*—and even defies discussion in terms of concepts (concepts, after all, *presuppose* that things are distinct and independent)—it is hardly surprising that our intuitions lean toward the present-at-hand. Appealing to intuition, then, can't carry much argumentative weight. The challenge then is to see why we shouldn't advocate a kind of ontological pluralism. The ready-to-hand might well be in certain respects more basic than the present-at-hand.[9] In fact, Heidegger hopes to show precisely this by examining one famous conception of the world as constituted by present-at-hand objects—the conception of the world found in the work of Rene Descartes.

We experience things in various ways—as both present-at-hand and ready-to-hand, for example. Our understanding of Being manifests itself in both of these ways. The philosophical tradition, however, has made one such way (the view of things as present-at-hand) seem to be the "more natural" way of conceptualizing agents and objects, persons and things. This is a part of our phenomenology when we engage in certain sorts of behavior—philosophical theorizing, for example. As a part of our understanding of the world, the overall projection of the meaning of Dasein's Being needs to be able to provide an account of this part of our understanding if it is to be at all adequate. By offering an account of the

Cartesian conception of the world, Heidegger will test the adequacy of his analysis.

Heidegger hopes to show that the ontological sense of the world as a nexus of significance, as a web of involvement, is prior to Descartes's conception of the world as a container of substances that exist in space (what Descartes calls "extended" substance). If Heidegger really is operating from the understanding of the world that we already have, he should be able to give an account of the view of the world familiar to philosophers in light of his alternative. One such view is captured by the phrase *Cartesian worldview*.[10]

The view of the world in Descartes (the source of the term *Cartesian*), the view Heidegger wishes to contest, is one of essence and accident. Things are fundamentally extended (that is, they exist as three-dimensional objects in space). These extended things manifest certain secondary properties as modes of their extension. A gumball is round, has a certain shape, smell, and so on. These features are modes of an extended thing. If we changed these modes—if, say, we chewed the gum—we would alter those secondary properties that make a thing appear as it does, but that thing would still be extended. A piece of chewed gum still exists in space, even if it is no longer round, no longer has a taste, no longer smells the same, and so forth. This isn't to say that extended things are the only things that exist in Descartes's ontology. Indeed, Descartes is famous for the view that the mind and body are distinct—that mind is immaterial, and hence marks a fundamentally different substance than that which we find in extended items. It turns out, for Descartes, that substantiality is the fundamental feature of things in the world—though we must be careful not to conflate the notion of substance with the notion of extension: extended things (*res extensa*) are but one type of substance.

In the standard (theoretical) view of the world, "the Being of a 'substance' is characterized by not needing anything," Heidegger notes (*BT*, 125). Substances can be infinite (God) and finite (*res cogitans* [minds] and *res extensa* [things/bodies]). God is the only thing that is not an *ens creatum* (created being). The other two substances, mind and bodies, are both finite, created things. Here we end up with a taxonomy of beings that fails to address the meaning of Being. The reason for this, Heidegger thinks, is that Descartes assumes that the meaning of Being is self-evident (*BT*, 127).

> Thus the ontological grounds for defining the "world" as *res extensa* have been made plain: they lie in the idea of substantiality, which not only remains unclarified in the meaning of its Being, but gets passed off as something incapable of clarification, and gets represented indirectly by way of whatever substantial property belongs most pre-eminently to the particular substance. (*BT*, 127)

In Heidegger's view, this standard conception of the world as a container of extending things presupposes (and thereby ignores) a more fundamental way of understanding the world. As Heidegger claims, Descartes passed over "both the phenomenon of the world and the Being of those entities within-the-world which are proximally ready-to-hand" (*BT*, 128). Indeed, Heidegger thinks Descartes begs the ontological question; he presupposes an ontology. Descartes begins with a certain conception of what it means to be an object, and he imposes this conception on the world. Instead of allowing that which manifests itself to show itself for what it is, Descartes

> prescribes for the world its "real" Being, as it were, on the basis of an idea of Being whose source has not been unveiled and which has not been demonstrated in its own right—an idea in which Being is equated with constant presence-at-hand. (*BT*, 129)

In brief, the problem with Descartes is that he assumes that only one way in which Being reveals itself is the right way. He thinks it is only when we perceive objects present-at-hand that we get what they "really" are. When one approaches the world in this way, we are led to simply ignore the other ways in which the world is disclosed to us (in engaged activities, such as making coffee, competently playing a musical instrument, or rebuilding an engine, for example). We can understand a tree as an extended thing, with definite properties, or we can understand it as lumber, as a poetic object, as an instance of life, or whatever. When we impose a particular view of what objects must be in order for them to be real, we have failed to pose Heidegger's fundamental question. We have ignored the way we experience the world proximally and for the most part (first and mostly, by and large)—we have failed to do justice to phenomenology.

This, in turn, leads Descartes to think of objects as extended, and of Dasein as just another type of substance that has access to these extended things. He posits a *res cogitans* (a thinking thing) that can grasp the *res extensa* (the extended thing), imposing a view of them both as objects present-at-hand. Once we've conceived of things this way, however, we've already blinded ourselves to the kind of being that is characteristic of Dasein: Dasein becomes one more object with properties; its mineness and Being-in-the-world disappear from view.

AN OBJECTION TO HEIDEGGER'S "WORLD"

Even if Descartes presupposes his ontology of objects present-at-hand, isn't this an entirely reasonable thing to do? If we sometimes experience the world as equipment, doesn't this presuppose things that themselves are suited (given their material nature) to certain ends? A hammer can be used as we use it precisely because it's made of certain materials (of metal and wood, for example). If a hammer were made out of certain other materials, it couldn't be a tool at all (for instance, if it were made out of sponge and cotton). When we use and understand our environment as equipment, aren't we presupposing a present-at-hand nature that makes such use possible?

To put the worry in a more general way: Assume that we can and do understand the world in various ways. Shouldn't there be a substance—a substratum—that presents itself in various ways? Indeed, couldn't we simply posit present-at-hand things, and then add to these things properties that account for their utility? There is an object made of wood and metal. This object has the property of being suitable to pounding nails. We add a predicate to the substance that captures and references the utility we attach to the thing.

While this initially sounds like a plausible way of getting at the ready-to-hand from the present-at-hand, it is a way Heidegger rejects. He does not reject this view because it is entirely implausible. Rather, he rejects it because it cannot answer the question he wishes to pose about the Being of beings.

> Adding on value-predicates cannot tell us anything at all new about the Being of goods, but would merely presuppose again that goods have pure presence-at-hand as their kind of Being. (*BT*, 132)

Undoubtedly, this answer will prove unsatisfactory to many. What's important to keep in mind here is that Heidegger is not after an absolute refutation of the notion that things are present-at-hand. What he wants to do, rather, is show that there is another way in which we understand the world that is a candidate for considering the Being of beings and which matches our phenomenology. There's no way to show that the present-at-hand is fundamental without *presupposing* the present-at-hand. Heidegger's task is thus to show that such a presupposition is unwarranted, and that such a presupposition would fail to ask the question, "What is the Being of objects?" (That is, it would beg this question by presupposing its answer—namely, that the Being of objects is the Being present-at-hand of entities.)

As Heidegger explicitly notes, to show that the ready-to-hand is more primordial, he must also be able to give an account of the present-at-hand that does justice to our obsession with it. If he fails in this task, he fails to adequately interpret parts in terms of whole—and hence he must reject his initial hermeneutic projection.

Heidegger's aim is thus to spell out the more primordial view of existing in space that can make sense of Descartes's (and our) intuitions about the world as a set of present-at-hand and extended objects. His strategy for this should by now be familiar: Heidegger wants to show that our ontic notions of space and spatial location presuppose a more basic, existential one. Beneath our discussion of objects as existing in a spatial grid, there is a more fundamental notion of existential space—the space of concern—and it is in virtue of this space of concern that it becomes possible to see things in terms of "objective" space.

A quick access point to this general theme can be seen in our everyday talk about spatiality. When someone says, "It is close," we might take them to mean that some object (a building, say) is a few blocks away. In this case, we construe "close" in a literal (i.e., ontical) way. We might analyze this as asserting the following: "There exists an object that exists in a particular spatial location and that stands in a (spatial) relation of proximity to another object in another particular (spatial) location." There is nothing wrong with construing the sentence in this way. We only run into trouble when we take this "literal" notion of space as the fundamental one and construe other (metaphorical) uses as derivative ones. For example, it is easy for us to think of the sentence "She is close to my heart" as primarily figurative. We think this because we assume that the ontic view of space is the primary one, and the sentence clearly does not mean "There is an object x (some person) that stands in this spatial relation to another object y (my heart)."

Heidegger wants to call these intuitions about the literal and the metaphorical into question. Indeed, the so-called metaphorical sense of "close" is, for Heidegger, ontologically prior to the literal sense. Proximity relations, for Heidegger, are phenomenological. They pick out something about the way a Dasein experiences the world. "She is close to my heart" means I stand in a relation to her—she provides me with an orientation. This sort of orientation, for Heidegger, is more primordial, more basic. The "literal," quantifiable view of space is the derivative one—it relies on another notion of proximity that is itself not quantifiable.

> All "wheres" are discovered and circumspectively interpreted as we go our ways in everyday dealings; they are not ascertained and catalogued by the observational measurements of space. (*BT*, 137)

The underlying view here concerns the way Dasein understands the world. When the world is disclosed, it is disclosed in terms of use. Equipment belongs somewhere, and this follows simply given the projects in which we're engaged. The hammer belongs in my hand, the nail set in the wood, the screwdriver out of the way. These tools belong in these places not because of a Cartesian coordinate system, but rather because I am absorbed in the world in a specific way. Heidegger designates this "belonging-somewhere" of equipment as a "region."

The ready-to-hand always has a region. As peculiar as this may sound, it is perfectly in line with the notion of the ready-to-hand we have already explored. When we understand the world as a totality of significance, things are disclosed to us in terms of the projects that occupy our attention. The spatial aspect of this we call "region." A hammer is far insofar as it is not available for immediate use. This is defined by our need to use the hammer, not by pulling out a ruler and measuring the distance between ourselves and the hammer. Space, in the ontological sense, is not absolute space. It is not a grid that is independent of Dasein. Rather, space is the orientation we have to the world around us.

> A three-dimensional multiplicity of possible positions which gets filled up with Things present-at-hand is never proximally given. This dimensionality of space is still veiled in the spatiality of the ready-to-hand. The "above" is what is "on the ceiling"; the "below" is what is "on the floor"; the "behind" is what is "at the door." (*BT*, 136–37)

Having seen the ontological sense of spatiality Heidegger attributes to ready-to-hand objects, it is only appropriate to revisit the sort of spatiality that Dasein has. Obviously, since the ready-to-hand is a way in which Dasein understands its world, we needn't think of the spatiality of the ready-to-hand and the spatiality of Dasein as fundamentally distinct. Dasein's spatiality will be connected with the region of equipment just articulated.

Heidegger characterizes Dasein's spatiality with the use of two important concepts. It will be worthwhile to explore these for a moment. Those concepts are *directionality* and *de-severance*. *Directionality* amounts to the view that Dasein is oriented in its world. It has an understanding of this world that directs its attention to certain things—what it needs to engage in its projects, for example. *De-severance* is a term meant to pick out the type of spatial relation (in the existential sense) that Dasein has with other entities within the world. Dasein has the ability to make entities close to it, and it can do this precisely because it can turn its attention to those beings around it. In this sense, directionality goes hand in hand with de-severance.

Our understanding of ourselves in space involves our understanding of our own existence—our projects and our involvements. "Dasein understands its 'here' in terms of its environmental 'yonder'" (*BT*, 142). As Heidegger puts it, "circumspective concern is de-severance which gives directionality" (*BT*, 143). When we are absorbed in the world, we understand things as close or far in terms of our projects. They are drawn close (de-severed) insofar as they are that with which we are concerned. This concern gives us direction (less misleadingly, we can say that *it is* our direction)—it is that in terms of which the world of a Dasein is disclosed.

Lurking in the background here, once again, is the view that nothing is given independent of understanding. While we might be tempted to think of certain intuitions as given—for example, up and down—Heidegger insists that our "intuitions" on things are just as much the product of existing in a world as any other thing we might name.

The subject with a "mere feeling" of this difference [between right and left] is a construct posited in disregard of the state that is truly constitutive for any subject—namely, that whenever Dasein has such a "mere feeling," it is in a world already and must be in it to be able to orient itself at all. (*BT*, 143)

This view has significant implications for the philosophical tradition, ones which we have already seen in passing. The idea of an "innate idea," for example, must be rejected. Any such idea already presupposes a way of understanding the world—a mode of disclosure—which involves an orientation in understanding. "I necessarily orient myself in and from my being already alongside a world which is 'familiar'" (*BT*, 144). Moreover, "as Being-in-the-world, Dasein has already discovered a 'world' at any time" (*BT*, 145). It is this assertion that justifies the view that the ready-to-hand is ontologically prior to the present-at-hand. It is because we orient ourselves in existential space that we are able to regard space, in certain circumstances, as objectively measurable.

Obviously, there are many questions that naturally arise from this analysis. We will pursue some of these in more detail in chapter 5. Before examining in detail some of the implications of Heidegger's analysis of Dasein as Being-in-the-world for our traditional epistemological and metaphysical debates, we need to flesh out *who* Dasein is—a task with fascinating results.

CONCLUSION

We've examined Dasein as Being-in-the-world and as that Being who is capable of understanding other beings. As we've seen, Dasein encounters the world as both present-at-hand and ready-to-hand. While the philosophical tradition has given pride of place to the present-at-hand, Heidegger insists that we cannot ignore the other ways in which the world is disclosed to us. We must, above all, recognize the distinction in the modes of Being found in the present-at-hand, the ready-to-hand, and Dasein itself.

In examining the general features of Dasein's Being, we introduced the concepts of authenticity and inauthenticity. It is now time to take a closer look at these modes, as well as the implications of Dasein's Being-in-the-world for traditional philosophical questions.

NOTES

1. The term *present-at-hand* is an unfamiliar one to many English-speaking readers. This is unfortunate. The German word is *vorhanden*. As usual, Heidegger is taking up common German words and reappropriating them into his philosophical analysis. He is doing this presumably because he thinks that the language we speak has important

clues for an understanding of Being. The immediate connection between this mode of Being and our everyday speech is lost in this translation. Importantly, however, our everyday speech in English does represent objects in this mode, and in a variety of ways: we speak of the task at hand, the object at hand, and so on. We will return to this topic in more detail later.

2. This is an obvious anticipation of Jean-Paul Sartre's claim in *Being and Nothingness* that, for human beings, existence precedes essence.

3. Heidegger also occasionally mentions a third mode, one of "undifferentiation," where Dasein is neither authentic nor inauthentic. Hubert Dreyfus reads this third mode as Dasein in its childhood. I do not find this convincing for various reasons. As I will later argue, I think it is more plausible to think of Dasein as "undifferentiated" at the moment in which Dasein confronts its own condition—that is, when one sees one's own inauthenticity in the confrontation with anxiety and must decide whether to remain inauthentic or to resolve to become authentic. Obviously, there's a lot packed into this statement that we have not yet examined. For more on this, see chapters 6 and 7.

4. The issue of authenticity is a complicated one, and it will occupy our attention in much of the following discussion. See, in particular, chapter 6.

5. Heidegger also mentions the possibility that Dasein might be "modally undifferentiated." Initially, this is a rather perplexing remark, as Heidegger almost always speaks of Dasein as though it *must* be either authentic or inauthentic. It is thus understandable that these passages have produced so many headaches. Later, I will suggest that we should understand undifferentiated Dasein as Dasein at the moment in which it faces its mortality in a "moment of vision" when it decides whether or not to engage anticipatory resoluteness. See note 3 above and chapter 7.

6. Note that there is a methodological issue here that Heidegger must contend with: he himself begins with certain postulations based on our everyday understanding of Being. He also wants to vindicate his view by revealing its accuracy in the way it elucidates ordinary phenomena. Obviously, a practitioner of an ontic science could make a similar kind of argument. What distinguishes Heidegger's case will be considered later.

7. The term *know-how*, and its contrastive *know-that*, is frequently attributed to Gilbert Ryle. Interestingly, Ryle was familiar with Heidegger's work in *Being and Time*. Ryle was one of the first to review it for an English-speaking audience (see the bibliography). While not without criticisms, Ryle's review was largely positive. It would be easy to claim that Ryle simply lifted some of these ideas from Heidegger's work. This would be unfair, however, for several reasons. Ryle's discussion is situated in a rather different context, first of all. Second, if Ryle can be said to have "stolen" this distinction from Heidegger, then both Heidegger and Ryle can be accused of stealing the same distinction from Aristotle! (Heidegger interprets Aristotle in just this way in the lectures on him throughout the 1920s.)

8. There are remarkable similarities here between Heidegger and Wittgenstein. The signs of a language only make sense with a context, and they make sense precisely because they are part and parcel of Dasein's *Lebensform*. The signs of a language-game provide us with an orientation. Their significance lies precisely in their ability to allow us to know what to expect—what grammar they follow—not always (nor exclusively) in their ability to refer to (*bedeuten*) states-of-affairs in the world.

9. It's also worth remembering that Heidegger thinks ontology is only possible through phenomenology—that is, we must investigate Being through Dasein—and specifically through the way the world is disclosed to Dasein. By itself, this methodological claim already suggests that we cannot dismiss the ready-to-hand, given that Dasein *does* experience the world very frequently in precisely this manner.

10. *Cartesian* refers to texts by Rene Descartes, who used the name *Cartesius* for the texts he composed in Latin.

FOUR

Everyday Understanding and Inauthenticity

In this chapter, we'll examine Dasein's inauthentic existence. As we've seen, Dasein is not to be considered an object among other objects—Dasein has a distinct mode of Being. We'll begin by exploring how we are to understand *who* Dasein is, and develop our account by exploring the general notion of Being-with. Finally, we'll examine how these features of Dasein's Being manifest themselves in everyday understanding.

THE "WHO" OF DASEIN

The "who" of Dasein has already been sketched in a formal way: Dasein is characterized by "mineness." We are beings for whom Being is an issue—who are capable of owning ourselves or not owning ourselves. But what does this mean? What does it mean to say that Dasein is a who and not a what?

The most tempting thing to do in hashing out this formal structure of Dasein, at least initially, is to say that the mineness of Dasein represents the fact that Dasein is a self, or an "I." It is precisely here, Heidegger claims, that we need to be very careful about how we proceed, lest we pass over that which characterizes Dasein firstly and mostly. The problem in positing an "I" as that which can answer the "who" of Dasein is that one ends up reading the present-at-hand back into the Being of Dasein—a temptation to which the philosophical tradition has constantly fallen prey, as we have seen. Even if one does not read the "I" as a thing, or an object, one may still end up looking at it as a static entity set over and against other entities (or experiences), which it itself is not. While there is something intuitive about this view of Dasein as a self, we must be wary of allowing this intuition to inform our investigation. As always, we must view our intuitions as something that might fail to get at the nature of a thing, if only because of the social basis of our intuitions.

The traditional philosophical picture of the self Heidegger hopes to guard against can be captured visually. It is a view of the self as that unchanging thing that is subject to the ever-changing swarm of experiences.

I (constant) → realm of involvement (changing)

This is not an advance beyond the present-at-hand ontology of a subject/object relation. In fact, it reinscribes this very ontology into the nature of the self, into the nature of Dasein. If we postulate a continuous consciousness as that thing that is involved in a world, we have made Dasein unlike the very thing it encounters, and this merely by fiat. Why should we think of Dasein as the one constant thing that allows us to view the realm of involvement as changing? Indeed, why not view the "self" as something that also constantly changes?

Perhaps surprisingly, this is not Heidegger's position concerning the self. The problem with both accounts of the self—that it is either constant or changing—presupposes the very ontology Heidegger hopes to excavate. Our task in answering the question of the "who" of Dasein is not to presuppose either answer, even if we eventually come to the conclusion that the account provided by Heidegger is inadequate. Heidegger simply asserts that Dasein is not present-at-hand, but he thinks that he can validate this assertion if given enough time. In working out the picture of Dasein's Being he hopes to make explicit, we should thus allow him some leeway.

Heidegger is sensitive to the methodological issues involved in his phenomenological analysis. If it is "natural" to think of the "I" as that which can accompany all the ways in which the world is disclosed (i.e., if Kant's transcendental unity of apperception is indeed compelling, which it seems to be), with what license can Heidegger simply reject this position? Indeed, if his analysis is true to our phenomenology, it seems as though he has to acknowledge at least some truth in this picture of the "I." It is precisely this methodological concern—the worry that Heidegger himself is imposing too much on his analysis of Dasein—that prompts a series of suggestive rhetorical questions: "What if this kind of 'giving-itself' on the part of Dasein should lead our existential analytic astray and, in doing so, indeed, in the manner of Being of Dasein itself?" (*BT*, 151). This question is at the heart of the existential analytic. The idea lurking behind Heidegger's question is as follows: in our attempts at self-understanding, we inevitably fall into the common understanding of things that is prevalent among Dasein. It is this feature of our understanding—that it moves, where possible, to assimilation—that marks the danger of our intuitions concerning the self: "Dasein is in each case mine, and this is its constitution; but what if this should be the very reason why, proximally and for the most part, Dasein *is not itself?*" (*BT*, 151). While this remark may initially seem cryptic, Heidegger is managing to put an insight into the human condition in an extraordinarily succinct manner: it might turn out that part of what it means to be human is to turn away from an understanding of being human that is adequate to the phenomenon in question. Our very existence (mineness) might be such that we turn away from what we are fundamentally: thrown Being-in-the-world.

The "I" we easily postulate to talk about who we are must thus be held at arm's length. This intuition could itself be an instance of Dasein's ignoring what it is fundamentally (as could any intuition we have about the self). The fact that this intuition is a natural one does not speak in its favor. Indeed, one might say just the opposite. The "I" is a formal indication of Dasein's mineness, but it does not advance our inquiry into the question of the "who" of Dasein. The "I" is a way of talking about Dasein that is itself informed by something existential-ontological—something that stands above and beyond our everyday dealings, as a condition for their possibility. We are not after merely formal indicators of Dasein's mineness. We are after its existential conditions of intelligibility. It is at this point that Heidegger points to an alternative way of considering the "who" of Dasein, and this based on what has been discussed in the prior pages.

> Yet even the interpretation of Dasein which we have so far given, already forbids us to start with the formal givenness of the "I," if our purpose is to answer the question of the "who" in a way which is phenomenally adequate. In clarifying Being-in-the-world we have shown that a bare subject without a world never "is" proximally, nor is it ever given. And so in the end an isolated "I" without others is just as far from being proximally given. If, however, the Others already *are there with us* in Being-in-the-world, and if this is attained phenomenally, even this should not mislead us into supposing that the ontological structure of what is thus given is obvious, requiring no investigation. Our task is to make visible phenomenally the species to which this Dasein-with in closest everydayness belongs, and to interpret it in a way which is ontologically appropriate. (*BT*, 152)

One can here see a quite distinct feature of everyday phenomenology that the traditional philosophical notion of the self fails to discuss: that our Being is such that Others are there in the world with us.[1] Even noting this feature of Dasein's Being (that we are always already among other Dasein) does not spare us the need for investigation. Indeed, once we recognize that this feature of our phenomenology stands at loggerheads with our philosophical intuitions concerning the self (that mind is divorced from world, that there is a "problem" concerning our knowledge of other minds, etc.), we have an incentive to inquire further into the nature of who Dasein, in its mineness, *is*.

BEING-WITH

Other Dasein have already been discovered in the work-world of the ready-to-hand. Heidegger is quick to remind us, however, that Dasein is not to be seen as one more piece of equipment, nor as one more thing present-to-hand. As we know from the preceding chapter, we are to keep the ready-to-hand, the present-at-hand, and the Being of Dasein distinct. When other Dasein are disclosed to us, we are confronted with a Being like us—a Being-in-the-world—a Being who occupies the same world we do. The buyer of the cabinet we build, the distributor of the wood we use to build the cabinet, the manufacturer of the screws we use to hold it together—we all occupy a web of significance. We needn't posit an "I" over and against some set of "others" and then notice a gap between our knowledge of our own mind and our knowledge of theirs. Heidegger rules this out *by definition*.

> By "Others" we do not mean everyone else but me—those over against whom the "I" stands out. They are rather those from whom, for the most part, one does not distinguish oneself. . . . The world is always the one that I share with others. The world of Dasein is a with-world. Being-in is Being-with others. Their Being in themselves within-the-world is Dasein-with. (*BT*, 155)

While it's easy to accuse Heidegger of arguing circularly here, one should not make this accusation too quickly. A standard motivation for the problem of other minds is to notice that we know the contents of our own minds with an ease that *could not* characterize our knowledge of the minds of others. The intuition is forceful: my thoughts are mine in a way that yours simply couldn't be, and this in virtue of what it means to call something a "thought." What Heidegger is pointing out, however, is that before our reflection on the contents of our minds (or on the contents of other minds), there is no privileged access whatsoever. I don't know the contents of my own mind more than I know the contents of yours, and this is so because the sort of "knowing" in question derives from the bare disclosedness of a familiar world in which we both engage. In this world, I do not "know" myself in any significant sense. I am engaged in a project, and this project is related to other Dasein who share the world I inhabit. My knowledge of myself in this context cannot be more fundamental because there *is no* knowledge (know-that) to speak of: there's only my concernful absorption, with you, in a world of shared significance.

Heidegger claims that Dasein is essentially Being-with. But it remains to be seen how we're to construe this version of the notion that the human is a social animal. One alternative—and one which Heidegger will reject—can be captured in the notion of atomism: the view that human beings are fundamentally distinct beings with a capacity for autonomy, allowing them to stand independently from society, culture, history, and one another. On this view, society and the with-world of Dasein would be seen as construed out of component "atoms." We need merely to add up the atoms to get the sum of their parts; one could have a Dasein without other Dasein; there could be one atom without the many. Whether or not Dasein existed in a society, on the atomist view, would turn on whether or not other Dasein happened to exist who decided to *join* a society. If we construe Dasein's Being-with in this manner, Heidegger claims, we will miss a fundamental feature of Dasein's existential structure.

> The phenomenological assertion that "Dasein is essentially Being-with" has an existential-ontological meaning. It does not seek to establish ontically that factically I am not present-at-hand alone, and that others of my kind occur. . . . Being-with is an existential characteristic of Dasein even when factically no Other is present-at-hand or perceived. Even Dasein's Being-alone is Being-with in the world. (*BT*, 156–57)

It's Being-with, Heidegger claims, that can explain the phenomenon of *being alone*, as well as derivative modes of Being-with-others. What is designated by these notions is not the presence or absence of other "entities-like-us." What is signified is a part of the way Dasein exists in a world. We exist in a social context—with and among others like us, others who share the experience of significance we have. Only this existential reading of Being-with can account for phenomena like being alone in a crowd, being a member of a community in isolation, and so on.

The term which Heidegger uses to designate our concern for other Dasein, as opposed to our concern for equipment, is *solicitude* (*Fürsorge*) (*BT*, 157). For the most part, Heidegger claims, we operate in a deficient mode of solicitude: we ignore one another, pass each other without a nod or a handshake on the street, and so on. This sort of relation with others is unique to Dasein; one does not find such a relation among pieces of chalk side by side in a chalk box: "there is an essential distinction between the 'indifferent' way in which Things at random occur together and the way in which entities who are with one another do not 'matter' to one another" (*BT*, 158).

As with other concepts Heidegger has introduced, we want to be sure not to reduce the idea of Being-with to some idea of one thing present-at-hand in relation to other present-at-hand things. Likewise, we shouldn't think of Dasein's relation to other Dasein (solicitude) as something that Dasein can either take up or fail to take up. On the contrary, to be Dasein is always to be concerned for other Dasein. Heidegger puts the point succinctly and powerfully: "Thus as Being-with, Dasein 'is' essentially for the sake of Others" (*BT*, 160). This applies with equal force even to those who claim to have no need of other Dasein. As Heidegger says, "even if the particular factical Dasein does not turn to Others, and supposes that it has no need of them or manages to get along without them, it *is* in the way of Being-with" (*BT*, 160).

The primary point to take from this is that the world we inhabit—the with-world—is always one that we coinhabit. The understanding we have of things is always an understanding that is *shared* with others. Even the way I understand myself ultimately depends on the other Dasein with whom I exist. Here, too, we can see one respect in which looking at ourselves honestly *requires* others. Our self-understanding depends on others precisely because we *are* always in relation to other Dasein. To have any self-knowledge is to understand oneself in relation to those Dasein that share one's existence in the with-world. "Knowing oneself is grounded in Being-with, which understands primordially" (*BT*, 161).

We are, first and foremost, Being-in-the-world, and the world we live in is a with-world. Hence, Heidegger says, our being is essentially the being of other Dasein. It is this very point that gives force to Heidegger's analysis of the "who" of Dasein in its inauthentic mode: Dasein is no one and everyone—Dasein is *the "they"* (*das Man*).

The "they" is *not* the sum of all persons. It is, rather, that mode of Dasein where Dasein cannot be distinguished from any other Dasein—where a person is anonymous, faceless, and wholly like any other person. In our normal ways of encountering the world, as well as our normal understanding of the things around us, we *are* the "they"—an amorphous public self that lacks anything distinctive, individual, or precise. "They" always already understand everything, so no questions need to be asked.

We will return to the "they" again below. First, however, we will clarify in more detail what it means to say that Dasein understands its world, and that Dasein is a "*clearing*" in which things present themselves. Once we've got a better picture of what this means, we'll be able to better articulate what inauthentic Dasein is like.

DASEIN AS BEING-THERE: STATE-OF-MIND, UNDERSTANDING, AND DISCOURSE

We may well be satisfied with what's been gained in the analysis of Dasein as Being-in-the-World. Indeed, the implications of Heidegger's analysis are in many ways revolutionary. But Heidegger doesn't stop here. Having excavated Dasein's basic ontological structures, Heidegger pursues his investigation according to the demands of hermeneutics. We've got a good orientation for considering the *details* of Dasein's Being. What does it mean to be *in* a world? What does it mean to be "there"

(*Da*)? What does our view of Dasein tell us about language, understanding, and mood? What, moreover, do these things tell us about the nature of Being-in-the-world?[2]

Recall that the word *Dasein* can be literally translated as "being-there." The *da* of Dasein means "there," and *sein* is the verb "to be." Pursuing the analysis of Dasein's Being requires that we clarify what it means for Dasein to *be in* a realm of significance; we need to understand how a Dasein can be (-*sein*) there (*Da*-), in the world.

Heidegger begins to elucidate Dasein's "there-being" (*Da-sein*) by noting that "Dasein brings its 'there' [*Da*] along with it. If it lacks its 'there' it is not factically the entity which is essentially Dasein; indeed, it is not this entity at all. *Dasein is its disclosedness*" (*BT*, 171). Dasein cannot be separated from the understanding it brings to bear on things in the world. It is this understanding that "lights up" these things, that lets them be seen in their Being, for what they are. Dasein's understanding can capture the Being of a thing because (as we will recall) ontology is only possible as phenomenology. We've seen how Dasein encounters the ready-to-hand and the present-at-hand. It's now time to see how Dasein's disclosedness itself is possible. To do so, we'll explore three aspects of this disclosedness: state-of-mind (or attunement), understanding, and discourse.

State-of-Mind (Befindlichkeit)

As with many other terms in *Being and Time*, it's easy to be misled by the phrase *state-of-mind*. The German term is *Befindlichkeit*. It doesn't carry the same connotations as the English translation chosen by Macquarrie and Robinson (state-of-mind). Befindlichkeit suggests *how one finds oneself*—that is, how one is *attuned to the world*. For this very reason, some Heidegger scholars prefer to translate *Befindlichkeit* as "attunement." In certain respects, one's state-of-mind captures this—but it captures it at a price. After all, we find ourselves talking about "minds," which may suggest a misleading philosophical perspective (we might think that minds are not bodies, or are present-at-hand "in" bodies, and so on). The term also suggests that a state-of-mind is something somehow "inside" Dasein. Attunement, on the other hand, does a much better job of avoiding this traditional philosophical prejudice—and Heidegger certainly wants to avoid it! So long as we're cognizant of the dangers of state-of-mind as a translation, however, there's no harm in using the term (at least in my view). Given this, along with the continuing prevalence of the Macquarrie and Robinson translation of *Being and Time*, I will continue to translate *Befindlichkeit* as state-of-mind.[3]

A state-of-mind, in Heidegger's sense, is *not* a certain condition of a person's brain/mind; it is, rather, how we *disclose the world* in our interactions with it. *State-of-mind* designates an existential structure (a structure of Dasein, whose essence lies in existence); *mood* designates the particular manifestations of that structure in an individual Dasein. State-of-mind characterizes the Being of *all* Dasein (it is part of Dasein's essential structure); mood characterizes a *type* of state-of-mind. Dasein has a state-of-mind essentially, entailing that Dasein is *always* in a mood. A state-of-mind, then, is meant to capture the way Dasein's comportment toward the world allows the world to present itself.

Moods—which are *particular* states-of-mind—also tell us something about individual Dasein: namely, they tell us how it is that Dasein is coping with its world. In this respect, moods are *cognitive*. They tell us something about the individual Dasein in the mood, as well as something about the ways in which Dasein can encounter the world generally.

Consider how you experience a meeting (or a class) when you're depressed. Things stand out in a way remarkably different from the way they appear when you're angry, excited, or irritable. In depression, things that normally appear significant cease to be so: there is a weight to one's Being-in-the-world that seems to attach to all actions, making them more difficult and less worthy of one's efforts. Likewise, when one is irritable, what might normally be considered innocent joking can seem to us a deep insult: the thing (in this case, a joke) presents itself as it does based on one's mood (irritation). All of our moods are like this: they allow us to see things in a particular way; they *disclose the world*.

Moods are not simply psychical additions to our Being-in-the-world. Indeed, it isn't possible to separate our mood from our encounter of the world. Heidegger puts this point succinctly and forcefully: "The mood has already disclosed, in every case, Being-in-the-world as a whole, and makes it possible first of all to direct oneself toward something" (*BT*, 176). Moods do not merely arise from our engagement with a neutral world. Rather, our moods disclose things within the world, enabling us to encounter them in particular ways. In this respect, moods are crucial to Dasein's understanding of things.

The word rendered as "mood" here is the German *Stimmung*. In some contexts, this term is better translated as "atmosphere," as in "this restaurant has a good *Stimmung*." It might sound silly to say, "The restaurant has a good mood," but it is perfectly natural to say (in English), "The restaurant has a good atmosphere." What we have in mind here is the feeling of the place. In German, this can be captured with *Stimmung*. (Note that in English we *can* claim that "The movie has a dark mood," and perhaps even that "The movie has a dark atmosphere." As in many cases, there is simply no single English term to adequately translate the German term Heidegger employs.)

Are moods really as basic as Heidegger understands them to be? Isn't it possible to isolate our mood when we engage in theoretical observation? While we might grant that moods disclose how Dasein is coping with the world, we might also maintain that there are *some* ways of perceiving the world that are devoid of *all* moods. Does Heidegger offer any compelling reason to reject this view?

Addressing this question involves returning to a claim that Heidegger makes repeatedly in the pages of *Being and Time*: there is no perception that does not involve Being-in-the-world. Even our most abstract speculations and theorizations concerning the world involve us *being* in a particular way. If Heidegger's hypothesis is correct, our Being always involves being in a mood—that is, it always involves things mattering to us in a particular way, things being revealed in a particular way. If this is right, then even theoretical observation must involve moods. As Heidegger claims, "even the purest θεωρία [theory] has not left all moods behind it; even when we look theoretically at what is just present-at-hand, it does not show itself purely as it looks unless θεωρία lets it come towards us in a tranquil tarrying alongside" (*BT*, 177). Thus even theoretical observation involves a mood—one of tranquil observation, one free of outside disturbances. When one observes with the aim of theoretical nuance, one does not allow anger, sadness, or irritability to get in the way. Rather, one aims at calm, detached *looking*. This allows the scientist to see things in a way that can be obscured by other moods, to be sure, but this detached "calmness" (to give it a name) is, Heidegger contends, as much a mood as anything else.

Of course, this doesn't *exclude* the possibility that Heidegger is incorrect in his assessment of moods. What it shows is that pointing out that humans sometimes view the world from a detached, spectatorial point of view is not, by itself, a counterexample to Heidegger's claim. Heidegger contends that this kind of viewing *is itself* a way of allowing the world to matter to us: we want to see how it presents itself to us at our most detached.[4]

What argument can be offered if someone insists that *true* scientific observation is devoid of moods? How can we decide between these two accounts of our attempt to theorize about the world? The best account of any given phenomenon will be the one that allows us best to understand that phenomenon—that allows us to see it most clearly and perspicuously. Moods are ways that things matter to us. The idea that we investigate things that *do not* matter to us at all faces a very pressing problem: if we are *not* concerned with the object we are investigating in *some way*, why would we be investigating it at all? To investigate something, Heidegger has argued, is to be concerned about it in a specific way. It is our concern—our engagement in a project—that *motivates* our investigation to begin with. The attempt to grasp a thing without allowing our emotions to interfere, then, is one way in which we can concern ourselves with things (recall that an emotion and a mood are not the same thing). What this view of theoretical observation manages to accomplish is that it explains why and how we might engage in theoretical observation to begin with.

Heidegger claims that moods don't arise from our encounter with the world but are *prior* to it: Dasein's "mood has already disclosed, in every case, Being-in-the-world as a whole, and makes it possible first of all to direct oneself toward something" (*BT*, 176; italics removed). This view, as we've seen, explains *why* Dasein is involved in its world the way it is. If a mood doesn't arise from our encountering of the world—if, as Heidegger claims, moods are a condition for the possibility of experiencing the world—then whence do they arise? Where do Dasein's moods come from if they do not come from the world?

We need to be careful about the position we're attributing to Heidegger. The claim is that Dasein always has a mood, and that, moreover, this mood is a condition for the possibility of experiencing the world. This means that moods are not the result of interaction between a Dasein *with no mood* and a world that is present-at-hand. This is *not* the same as claiming that moods cannot be altered by encountering things within the world. Heidegger doesn't deny that this happens. Indeed, the ability of various stimuli within the world to bring about new or modified moods enables particular types of Being-with. We can be cheered by jokes, saddened by movies, jolted by speech. This is possible (in the normal cases) precisely because there are *standard ways of having and creating moods*.

> Publicness, as the kind of Being which belongs to the "they", not only has in general its own way of having a mood, but needs moods and "makes" them for itself. It is into such a mood and out of such a mood that the orator speaks. He must understand the possibilities of moods in order to rouse them and guide them aright. (*BT*, 178)

So our moods are not caused by the sensory stimuli of a neutral external world—but this is *not* to say that our moods are random occurrences, nor that we have total control over them. Dasein's basic Being involves a mood that discloses things in a particular way. The way things are disclosed can be altered, but there's no way to remove moods altogether. To do so would be to remove oneself from the Being of Dasein. Given our common understanding of the world, we can be triggered to have moods by the proper prodding—a joke, a flower, a hug, a slap, the tone of a voice, and so on. The cues seem endless. But our changes in mood are just that: we go from one mood to another, and there is no way outside of *all* moods.

Heidegger remarks in passing in *Being and Time* that it is possible to have a "co-state-of-mind." This marks an important corrective to the way we normally think about moods and emotions. Our state-of-mind, it's natural to think, is something that is private—it belongs to us, and to us alone. The notion of a co-state-of-mind casts doubt on this, and so it is worth pausing over. Despite the connotations of state-of-mind mentioned above, we should not think of it as a radically individual disposition (*BT*, 182). On the contrary, even moods are, for the most part, public.

Restaurants have moods, as do novels and films. Time periods can also have moods. Think here of the nineteenth century's fin-de-siècle (end-of-the-century) blues or of the paranoia surrounding Y2K. We can characterize the end of the nineteenth century (in the West) as a time of misanthropy and pessimism. Obviously, this is not a description of every person living in that period—but it does seem to capture something about *the mood* of the time. Likewise, Y2K names a period of time characterized by a kind of faint unease that technology would ultimately have the better of us. Another example might be the *mood* of the United States during the Cuban missile crisis or the Vietnam conflict—or following the attacks of September 11, 2001. The point of all of these examples is to ensure that we don't take too restricted a view of moods. They do *not* apply merely to persons in particular time slices. They apply to epochs, to places, to events, as well as to persons. We should, as usual, be careful not to fall back into a way of conceiving moods that presupposes the present-at-hand ontology of traditional subject/object analysis.

Moods also tell us how Dasein deals with its *own* Being. For the most part, Heidegger claims, Dasein's moods involve a turning away from Dasein's Being—a fleeing from our own existence. The mood of elation, for example, shows Dasein being oblivious to the burdensome aspects of its Being. The mood of depression shows us, perhaps, Dasein grappling with its Being-in-the-world. In all cases, we see Dasein existing in the world and encountering that world and its relation to it in a particular manner. The manner in which Dasein finds itself in the world is Dasein's "throwness." Heidegger sums up this point as follows: "Ontologically, we thus obtain the *first* essential characteristic of states-of-mind that *they disclose Dasein in its throwness, and—proximally and for the most part—in the manner of an evasive turning away*" (*BT*, 175). In this respect, recognizing that Dasein is always in a mood is recognizing one way in which Dasein fails to understand itself. We will return to this below.

An Example: Fear

Heidegger distinguishes three aspects of fear:

1. that in the face of which we fear (the fearsome)
2. fearing (fearfulness)
3. that about which we fear

By analyzing these constituent elements of fear, we're in a position to enrich our understanding of fear itself—or, at any rate, the phenomenology of fear (and for Heidegger here there will be no difference).

1. **That in the face of which we fear: the fearsome (** *Furchtbare* **).** The fearsome is that which threatens. We perceive something as threatening in a context: it can take away things that are important to

us—in this sense it is disclosed as detrimental. But the fearsome isn't already here. It is disclosed as a "might"—it is what might happen, but has not happened yet. It is a threatening that draws close.

2. **Fearing.** Fearing, for Heidegger, is a mode of Dasein's *Befindlichkeit* (state-of-mind, attunement). It is a way of Being-in-the-world that characterizes the way things are disclosed to Dasein when the "fearsome" is revealed.

3. **That about which we fear.** Fearing, as an openness to the fearsome, has a subject: there is an "about" to fearing. In fear, the subject of our fear is Dasein itself. This is not to say that fear is in some way always selfish. It is to say, however, that fear is always subject-referring.[5] Fear is possible precisely because I am concerned about things in the world. My concern makes it possible for something to threaten that which is concerned. This implicates Dasein because, as Heidegger puts it, "Dasein *is* in terms of *what* it is concerned with" (*BT*, 181).[6]

This phenomenology of fear may well strike some as rather stipulative. Has Heidegger actually *argued* for these claims about fear? Can't we produce counterexamples?

Heidegger is spelling out the constitutive elements of a particular mood (fear). Whether or not he has done this adequately will not be decided by any argument alone. Rather, a phenomenology is correct *only if* it captures the experience it aims to describe. Arguments, on the other hand, are essentially *indirect* means of establishing the truth of a conclusion (we know the conclusion *through* the premises, and hence indirectly). Experiences cannot be reached in the same way. To articulate the structure of fear correctly requires that the articulation picks out something we recognize (even if this requires some reflection) about the experience in question. So does Heidegger get fear right? Consider the following claim:

> Only an entity for which in its Being this very Being is an issue, can be afraid. Fearing discloses this entity as endangered and abandoned to itself. Fear always reveals Dasein in the Being of its "there", even if it does so in varying degrees of explicitness. If we fear about our house and home, this cannot be cited as an instance contrary to the above definition of what we fear about; for as Being-in-the-world, Dasein is in every case concernful Being-alongside. Proximally and for the most part, Dasein is in terms of what it is concerned with. (*BT*, 180–81)

So we cannot argue against Heidegger here that we fear for many things (e.g., the bills we need to pay, whether or not we left the gas on, whether or not our relationships succeed, and so on), and precisely because these things are not to be distinguished from the individual Dasein, understood as partially constituted by the world in which that Dasein exists—the world with which Dasein is constantly concerned.[7]

When we fear—when this is our way of understanding our environs—we become aware of things in a new manner: the projects we have are made explicit, as well as the fact that we have these projects, because we are worried that our projects (whatever these may be) won't come off—that something will get in the way of a good grade, a happy marriage, the new promotion, or whatever.

Of course, Heidegger quickly acknowledges that we can also fear for other Dasein—and this fearing-for cannot simply be assimilated to fearing for those projects that constitute our lived experience. Dasein is not like other things (the project considered present-at-hand, for example). This fearing-for, Heidegger claims, is a way of having a co-state-of-mind (*BT*, 181). We are attuned to the world in the same way as another Dasein. This can be distinguished from several other types of fear involving other Dasein—for example, fearing-about[8] —as well as from other types of fear for one's own Dasein.[9]

Understanding

State-of-mind (or attunement) cannot be distinguished in principle from the understanding of Dasein: "A state-of-mind always has its understanding, even if it keeps it suppressed. Understanding always has its mood" (*BT*, 182). In our overall projects (which, as we've just seen, simply means "in being Dasein"), an entire world is disclosed—a world of significance in which we carry out our projects, in which we live our lives. The disclosedness—this existence in significance and as our projects—is understanding. It is what Heidegger calls an existentiale—an existential structure of Dasein.

One of the fundamental constituents of our understanding is *possibility*. As usual, Heidegger insists on a careful distinction between construing possibility as a category of the present-at-hand, on the one hand, and as an ontological characterization of Dasein's Being, on the other. Construed categorically, possibility is a "modal category of presence-at-hand, [it] signifies what is *not yet* actual and what is *not at any time* necessary. It characterizes the *merely* possible. Ontologically it is on a lower level than actuality and necessity" (*BT*, 183).

To discuss Dasein as characterized and constituted by its possibilities is *not* to think about Dasein as having particular nonactual properties (potential properties), nor is it to talk about the nonnecessary features of Dasein (Dasein's height and weight, for example). These have been the two dominant senses of the term *possibility* in the history of philosophy in the West. Dasein's possibility is fundamentally different in nature.

Possibility in the existential sense is "the most primordial and ultimate positive way in which Dasein is characterized ontologically" (*BT*,

183). Something is possible, in the traditional reading, if it could come into existence (e.g., a future vacation, a beard that you're trying to grow, and so on). In this respect, a possibility is something that does not yet exist—and hence is merely a potential attribute of an object. Dasein's possibilities, though, are to be construed as *positive* phenomena—and hence *not* as identifying things that *can* exist but don't yet.

Likewise, the contrastive sense of possible, understood as the opposite of "necessary," is not to be confused with Dasein's existential possibilities. Because Dasein is its possibilities, there is a sense in which possibilities are necessary for Dasein. In other words, the contrast between possible and necessary shouldn't be drawn when we're discussing Dasein's being its possibilities. In this respect, Dasein's possibilities are primordial—absolutely basic, and hence necessary for Dasein to be the kind of being that it is. As Heidegger points out, "in every case Dasein, as essentially having a state-of-mind, has already got itself into definite possibilities" (*BT*, 183). These types of possibility are captured in table 4.1. Dasein is its possibilities; it is that set of things it can be or do: "Dasein is Being-possible which has been delivered over to itself—thrown possibility through and through" (*BT*, 183). It's in this notion that we can begin to capture what's involved in Dasein's understanding. We're in a world that sets out particular possibilities. We understand ourselves in terms of those possibilities into which we're thrown. Heidegger's choice of the term *thrown* highlights the fact that the possibilities *from which* we choose are never ones that we decide to have. We simply find ourselves existing in a particular with-world, the possibilities of which are given prior to our being there (to our *Da-sein*). Our understanding is in terms of these potentialities-for-Being.

Consider the very act of reading this book. Reading this book is one of the possibilities that constitutes your current Being-in-the-world. Certainly there are other things you could be doing now—things that *also* consti-

Table 4.1.   Dasein and Possibility

	Type of Possibility	**Contrast Class**	**Example**
Ontic, concerning the present-at-hand	Possible: contingent	Necessary	A four-sided triangle isn't possible
	Possible: potential	Actual	Getting a new job, a promotion, or a good grade is still possible, even though you've had recent setbacks
Dasein's Being	Possible	Objects without understanding	See below

tute the set of possibilities that you *are*. You might be exercising, or watching television, or playing a musical instrument (among other things). To choose one possibility is necessarily to exclude others, at least for a while. The set of possibilities available to you at any time, however, is not completely open-ended. In this respect, Heidegger's analysis of Dasein's choice of possibilities departs from the analysis offered by Jean-Paul Sartre.[10] While Sartre maintains that humans are radically free to choose to be or do anything at all, Heidegger recognizes that we are bound by our thrownness. The contexts into which we are born provide the sets of possibilities *from which* we might choose, and this set of possibilities is constrained on a number of different fronts. You, reader, were born into circumstances that made it possible for you to be exposed to Heidegger, to read in English, and to exist in an economy where books can be mass produced and distributed around the world. Had you been born into a different society, or in a different time period, the set of possibilities in terms of which you understand yourself could be radically different. As it stands, we are thrown into a way of understanding things, a way of doing things, as well as a set of things that can be done. All we can do is to live out those possibilities that our thrownness has made available to us. "Why does understanding—whatever the essential dimensions of that which can be disclosed in it—always press forward into possibilities? It is because the understanding has in itself the existential structure which we call 'projection'" (*BT*, 185).

To be Dasein is thus to be characterized by *projection*. The word itself suggests its significance: we throw ourselves into the future, somewhat like a movie projector projects an image into the space in front of it. We do this largely without thought. While Dasein certainly does plan out its future, we also simply unreflectively live our lives directed toward and into the future—we live out our possibilities, whether or not we've made a conscious plan to do this. At this moment, for example, you're immersed in living out several projects. As you read this line, you anticipate its end. You anticipate, moreover, reading past this particular point (though you might stop, of course). Moreover, if we wanted to understand why you were reading an introduction to Heidegger at all, we'd need to fit this into your overall understanding of yourself and your possibilities. Your reading may well be intelligible because it's part of a desire to understand Heidegger, to earn college credit, to review what others think Heidegger is up to, or a number of other things. The point here is that your action (reading the book) is not to be understood in isolation. It is part of a projection into the future and from the past. If we were to describe everything about you as you are now—your weight, your height, your beliefs, and so on, we would still not capture your nature as Dasein. "Dasein is constantly 'more' than it factually is" (*BT*, 185). We *are* the possibilities that we are living out, and these possibilities throw us forever into the future. We are more than merely a set of characteristics present-at-hand *at this time*. To be Dasein is to live *into the future* and to be constituted in part by our thrownness *into the past*.

Interpretation

Understanding, much like state-of-mind, has modes. The mode of understanding is interpretation. As Heidegger puts it, "development of the understanding we call 'interpretation' [*Auslegung*]" (*BT*, 188). Interpretation is how understanding *is*. It is "the working-out of possibilities projected in understanding" (*BT*, 189). Importantly, interpretation in this sense (as a mode of understanding) is not *thematic*—that is, it is not an interpretation in the sense of a consciously worked-out understanding of the world. We should explicitly note that interpretation (*Auslegung*) should be distinguished from Interpretation (*Interpretation*). The latter is not to be confused with the former. Interpretation (with a capital *I*—*die Interpretation*) involves a conscious interpretation of some entity in light of our investigations of it. By contrast, interpretation (lowercase *i*—*die Auslegung*) is a way of *seeing* the world, not an explicit articulation of this seeing. It is the understanding that we have of the world with which we are concerned. Heidegger proposes to examine the interpretation (*Auslegung*) that develops out of inauthentic understanding, as he puts it, "in the mode of its genuineness" (*BT*, 189).

Heidegger discusses circumspection as a way of bringing out what our everyday understanding and interpretation involve. As we've seen, "circumspection" is a way of seeing the world that discloses the world in terms of our possibilities. This "sight" involves seeing *as*, that is, seeing something *as* something. As Heidegger contends, this is made possible only in a world that is already understood. When we begin to make assertions about the world, this is possible only given the fact that the world is *already* understood in a particular way. "This Articulation lies *before* our making any thematic assertion about it" (*BT*, 190). Articulation" is here to be understood as splitting into regions or parts. The world is disclosed as having joints, or hinges (to borrow a phrase from Hubert Dreyfus). Based on our ability to *see* these discriminations in the world, we're capable of saying anything about it. Importantly, "the mere seeing of the Things which are closest to us bears in itself the structure of interpretation" (*BT*, 190).

There are at least two issues that arise here. First, what exactly is the structure of interpretation that also happens to be the structure of *perception*? Second, is it possible to see something without seeing it *as* something else?

Seeing *as* is, as Heidegger has demonstrated, a basic way of Being-in-the-world. We don't simply experience raw sensory data, sorting it into various objects through acts of judgment. We experience things that matter to us. To perceive is to interpret, but not in the sense of "theorize."

Prior to any theorizing (what Heidegger calls "thematizing"), the world is laid out in a particular way in our experience.

This view of Dasein's understanding is *not* the familiar one in which humans experientially confront a "bare world" and then impose some structured interpretation onto it. This familiar way of thinking about Dasein's relation to the world, Heidegger contends, isn't true to our phenomenology—to the way the world is structured in our experience. Phenomenologically speaking, we don't impose an interpretation on the world; the world, rather, is always already interpreted for us.

> But if we never perceive equipment that is ready-to-hand without already understanding and interpreting it, and if such perception lets us circumspectively encounter something as something, does this not mean that in the first instance we have experienced something purely present-at-hand, and then taken it *as* a door, *as* a house? This would be a misunderstanding of the specific way in which interpretation functions as disclosure. In interpreting, we do not, so to speak, throw a "signification" over some naked thing which is present-at-hand, we do not stick a value on it; but when something within-the-world is encountered as such, the thing in question already has an involvement which is disclosed in our understanding of the world, and this involvement is one which gets laid out by the interpretation. (*BT*, 190–91)

A worry about the circularity of our understanding often emerges in thinking about this feature of interpretation. If we want to ground knowledge, one objection runs, we cannot take for granted the very things we are trying to establish—and it initially looks as though the fore-structure of understanding—that things are always already interpreted—is simply another way of describing taking a particular view as an assumption prior to beginning one's investigation of a thing.

Heidegger's response to this worry has the effect of calling into question the entire epistemological tradition. As Heidegger sees it, "if we see this circle as a vicious one and look out for ways of avoiding it . . . then the act of understanding has been misunderstood from the ground up" (*BT*, 194). Indeed, to insist on the absence of circularity here is simply to ignore the phenomenon that Heidegger hopes to elucidate. It is to impose a particular conception of what knowledge *ought* to be on an analysis of Dasein's *actual* Being. Moreover, as Heidegger brilliantly argues, "an ideal is itself only a subspecies of understanding—a subspecies which has strayed into the legitimate task of grasping the present-at-hand in its essential unintelligibility" (*BT*, 194).

In other words, the idea of "ideal knowledge" is itself a way of *seeing* knowledge that stems from a certain preexisting understanding of things. Thus the ideal in question cannot be seen as fundamental. If it *is* seen as fundamental, it cannot be justified on its own terms, and, indeed, it simply isn't clear what *could* justify any epistemology that aimed at having no presuppositions: if we call into question the nature of knowledge, any attempt to define knowledge in this skeptical vortex will undeniably fail, as we have no presuppositions about the nature of knowledge to work with. In other words, any proposed test for knowledge will not itself be *testable* and hence will fail to be justified. The solution to this pseudo-problem, in Heidegger's view, is to recognize our ideals *as ideals*, and then to take as our point of departure Dasein's actual Being-in-the-world.

> What is decisive is not to get out of the circle but to come into it in the right way. This circle of understanding is not an orbit in which any random kind of knowledge may move; it is the expression of the existential *fore-structure* of Dasein itself. It is not to be reduced to the level of a vicious circle, or even of a circle which is merely tolerated. In the circle is hidden a positive possibility of the most primordial kind of knowing. To be sure, we genuinely take hold of this possibility only when, in our interpretation, we have understood that our first, last, and constant task is never to allow our fore-having, fore-sight, and fore-conception to be presented to us by fancies and popular conceptions, but rather to make the scientific theme secure by working out these fore-structures in terms of the things themselves. (*BT*, 195)

There is no investigation without presuppositions; there is no getting outside of an understanding in order to *check* that understanding. But this doesn't mean that we can say or think anything we want. We must operate within our understanding, but it is an understanding that is revisable in light of our investigations.

DISCOURSE AND LANGUAGE

> The fact that language *now* becomes our theme *for the first time* will indicate that this phenomena has its roots in the existential constitution of Dasein's disclosedness. *The existential-ontological foundation of language is discourse or talk.* (*BT*, 203)

Dasein is that Being who is capable of finding things intelligible. This is so, as we have seen, precisely because Dasein is characterized by state-of-mind and understanding. Discourse is the way this understanding is expressed. "The intelligibility of Being-in-the-world—an intelligibility which goes with a state-of-mind—*expresses itself as discourse*. The totality of significations of intelligibility is *put into words*" (*BT*, 204).

In discoursing or talking, we share understanding. This does not mean that we *did not* share understanding beforehand and that language miraculously enables this to occur. What it means, rather, is that discourse enables us to *explicitly* share at least some understanding about *particular things*. Importantly, if we didn't already share an understanding, it would be impossible for language and talk to *create* this understanding. Any sentence you uttered would be incomprehensible to me, as I would not understand the meanings of the words you used; any definition you gave me of the words would be meaningless, as they would require more words; any pointing to objects in an attempt to teach me particular nouns would be futile, as I would not understand what your extended finger represented; and so on. The fact that language *enables* particular understanding does not mean that there was no shared understanding before we used language. Our ability to use language, rather, already presupposes that we share quite a bit by way of understanding.[11]

> Communication is never anything like a conveying of experiences, such as opinions or wishes, from the interior of one subject into the interior of another. Dasein-with is already essentially manifest in a co-state-of-mind and a co-understanding. In discourse Being-with becomes "explicitly" shared; that is to say, it *is* already, but it is unshared as something that has not been taken hold of and appropriated. (*BT*, 205)

We also see here in Heidegger's treatment of language a rejection of the classical view that language is merely a tool that allows us to bring "inner" thoughts to the "outer" world. The very contrast between inner and outer is something Heidegger would like to set aside. Language itself is *not* something private—language itself is a public means of understanding the world. If it were *not* so, communication among speakers would turn out to be impossible, as I could never be sure of the meanings of any terms you were using. If I were certain of your meaning on one occasion, I could not transfer that to later occasions.

For communication to be possible, in other words, language must be the sort of thing that embodies a public understanding of the world around us. This is precisely what Wittgenstein has in mind when he offers what has (somewhat infelicitously) become known as the "private language argument." Here, as elsewhere, Heidegger and Wittgenstein have a lot in common.

Once we've understood these points, we're in a better position to grasp an assertion. The term *assertion* has several senses:

1. pointing out
2. predication
3. communication

Something can be predicated, Heidegger notes, only after it has been "pointed out." This should not be taken literally. Our attention can be directed by uses of language. If I make a claim about a hammer, for example, the hammer becomes "close" to us phenomenologically (provided, of course, that you are actually listening to me!). This directing of our attention to an object is a condition for the possibility of predicating the thing in question. As Heidegger puts it, "the second signification of 'assertion' has its foundation in the first" (*BT*, 197). Attributing a predicate to a subject requires restricting our phenomenology. This is first made possible by our ability to *direct* our phenomenology to particular things.

The third sense of assertion is perhaps the most ontologically interesting. The German term is *Mitteilung*, and it is translated as "communication." Unfortunately, the etymological sense of the German term is virtually lost in this rendering. *Mit* means "with," and *teil* means "part." When one communicates something, one *imparts* what one sees to another; the other *takes part* in the perception. To assert is, in this third sense, to bring another into an experience. "It is letting someone see with us what we have pointed out by way of giving it a definite character" (*BT*, 197).

Assertion, to put it succinctly, is a way of Being-with. We can share our perceptions with others in language. Our assertions can unify our perceptions with the perceptions of another. We can do this in such a way that what we share can, in the future, be shared with others. Of course, this does not mean that an experience now can be re-had by another Dasein in three thousand years. As Heidegger reminds us, "what has been pointed out may become veiled again in this further retelling" (*BT*, 197).

Heidegger emphasizes that assertion is *about entities in the world*. We are not here dealing with the contents of judgments, or mental representations, or "valid meanings." Based on the three significations of assertion, Heidegger defines assertion as follows: "a pointing out which gives something a definite character and which communicates" (*BT*, 199). We are to construe this as a mode of interpretation, Heidegger contends, precisely because we see *in* assertion the basic structure of interpretation. (We see what Heidegger calls fore-having, fore-sight, and fore-conception—in brief, a background understanding that guides what we can inquire about, the kinds of answers we can expect to acquire, and so on.) This is not obvious, Heidegger contends, because "the language already hides in itself a developed way of conceiving" (*BT*, 199).

Heidegger (correctly) insists that interpretation does not require any *assertions*. When we are absorbed in projects, we have a way of understanding the world, and this way of understanding the world need not be put in nice, clean assertoric statements. Indeed, given this mode of encountering the world, one can even ask *why* making assertions is ever necessary. The answer to this, of course, is that the world consistently interrupts our projects; it defies our will. When this happens, we isolate entities in a new way (i.e., we regard them as present-at-hand), and this way of regarding them is a condition for the possibility of assertion.

This is not to say that language does not accompany our everyday action. Discursive activity is basic to Dasein. Indeed, we should regard *most* linguistic behavior as interwoven with our daily activities. This sort of linguistic activity, however, is a far cry from the theoretical assertions made about objects with properties. Language is a basic way of being in the world. It is, as Wittgenstein would say, part of our form of life. It is bound to our activities. This *is not* equivalent to saying that *assertion* is a basic way of being.

We have now seen the basic structure of the "there" (*Da*) of Dasein: Dasein is constituted by state-of-mind, understanding, and discourse. These structures all involve particular modes, or manifestations—that is, one always has some particular state-of-mind (a mood), some particular understanding (an interpretation), and some particular mode of expressing that understanding. Importantly, we should not understand these three things as existing apart from one another. As Heidegger reminds us, understanding always has its mood, and moods always involve a way of seeing the world.

Now that we have an overview of the structure of Dasein's Being—of the *way* Dasein is in-the-world—we can begin to explore this Being-in-the-world in its primary mode: the inauthentic.

INAUTHENTICITY AND THE "THEY"

Dasein's primary mode of existence is one of immersion in the "they." We understand ourselves over and against an "Other." This Other is not a definite entity. The Other is, as Heidegger puts it, *das Man* (the "they").

The German term is important here, as it gives crucial context for understanding what Heidegger is driving at. The term *man*, in German, is an impersonal pronoun. In English, we frequently use *one* or *they* in exactly the same fashion (in sentences like, "They say patience is a virtue," and "One never knows . . ."). The point of an impersonal pronoun is exactly what it sounds like: it doesn't pick out anyone in particular, nor does it pick out the set of all people. In a crucial way, it picks out a "general person," for lack of a better term. Like other elements in a language, the impersonal pronoun picks out an important ontological feature of Dasein: namely, the everyday understanding we bring to bear on the world around us. What we believe is what *one believes*. Our hopes and dreams are the hopes and dreams *one has*. For the most part, we are fundamentally like everyone else, and they are fundamentally like us. If we ask, as Heidegger does, who Dasein is, we will see that Dasein *is* an impersonal, generic "I" the vast majority of the time. We are, in other words, "everyone and no one."

The term *das Man* could be translated as "the one" or "the they"—or, indeed, in other ways. What is crucial is not the term we choose to translate this central concept; what matters is that we understand *das Man* for what it is: generic, everyday understanding, in the broadest sense of that term. "This everyday way in which things have been interpreted is one into which Dasein has grown in the first instance, with never a possibility of extrication. In it, out of it, and against it, all genuine understanding, interpreting, and communicating, all re-discovering and appropriating anew, are performed" (*BT*, 213).

Even when one calls into question the everyday understanding of things, one does so *with and through* that very understanding. It is, as it were, the foundation for our Being-in-the-world. It is this that leads Heidegger to say, in several places, that *authenticity* depends on inauthenticity. Without a general understanding of the world, we would have nothing to develop or to make our own. Inauthenticity, in other words, is absolutely necessary for Dasein. It cannot be overcome; it can only be shaped and appropriated (we will return to this in much more detail in chapter 6).

A common misunderstanding of the "they" is to think of it as simply the beliefs that all Dasein have in common. On this view, the "they" would be something like the cumulative, shared beliefs of all Dasein. This is emphatically *not* what Heidegger has in mind. Understanding why this is so will help us better understand the significance and content of the "they." In the following passage, Heidegger explicitly rejects the idea that one can somehow "escape" the "they."

> In no case is a Dasein, untouched and unseduced by this way in which things have been interpreted, set before the country of a "world-in-itself" so that it just beholds what it encounters. The dominance of the public way in which things have been interpreted has already been decisive even for the possibilities of having a mood—that is, for the basic ways in which the world "matters" to it. The "they" prescribes one's state-of-mind, and determines what and how one "sees". (*BT*, 213)

The dominance of the "they" applies even to those who have rejected society, by becoming reclusive for example. To be a Dasein is to have a general understanding of things that one has inherited and through which one is able to navigate the world. Without this general understanding, nothing would be intelligible, and hence no actions of any kind would be possible. In this respect, Dasein would not *be* itself, as it would not exist within the web of significance constitutive of Dasein's world.

But couldn't a Dasein be born and develop its *own* understanding of things? The answer to this is an emphatic no. As counterintuitive as this may initially seem, infants are *not* Dasein. They lack the understanding of things characteristic of Dasein. At some point in the normal development of human beings, however, we *become* Dasein. When this happens is an interesting and important question, but it is not one that Heidegger is interested in. Not being able to pinpoint the time at which we develop into beings for whom Being is an issue—into self-interpreting animals—is also no objection to Heidegger's analysis. We're in exactly the same position in relation to "adulthood." We cannot say with any certainty when one becomes an adult. Indeed, the time seems to differ across persons.

So human beings are not *born* as Dasein. We develop into Dasein as we are trained by a social community (usually our immediate family). We come to acquire an understanding of things that is commensurate with that understanding of those around us. And then, at some later point, we simply *find ourselves* with a perspective on the world. No one remembers constructing our general outlook on the world because *no one did*. We simply find ourselves with a certain perspective on things, in certain relationships, and already deeply concerned with what we are doing. Obviously, we can reject some of what we learn from our parents, but we will do this with the very understanding we have been trained to have. This is the essence of what Heidegger calls "thrownness." We are thrown into a world we did not choose, and find ourselves with a perspective and an understanding we did not ask to have.

There is no escaping our inauthenticity if this entails being entirely independent of our social background, and, in fact, we shouldn't *want* to escape it. Without the "they"—without inauthentic everyday understanding—we wouldn't be Dasein at all, and we'd have no means through which we might *become* Dasein. The most we can do is *respond* to our inauthenticity, either by simply accepting it thoughtlessly or by taking it up in a way that makes it truly our own.

In brief, inauthenticity is both absolutely basic to our existence and inescapable. To get a richer sense of this indispensable mode of Dasein's Being, we can now examine the specific modes of state-of-mind, understanding, and discourse characteristic of our normal inauthentic existence.

INAUTHENTIC MODES OF DASEIN (BEING-THERE)

Idle Talk: Inauthentic Discourse

As we've noted before, Heidegger maintains that language carries within itself an understanding of things—that language embodies an implicit ontology. Heidegger makes this point explicitly when he says, "in language, as a way things have been expressed or spoken out, there is a hidden way in which the understanding of Dasein has been interpreted" (*BT*, 210). This claim, as we will see, explains much of Heidegger's (sometimes perplexing) tendency to examine etymology as a means of understanding a deeper sense of the Being of things. In language, not only do we carry a particular understanding of things that is contemporary, but we also carry remnants of past languages and hence of past conceptions of Being. Thus one key to getting beyond our current understanding of things, as we will see, is to attempt to understand the crustations of former ontologies—ontologies we can access only by linguistic archaeology, by chipping away at the semantic fossils until we see things more perspicuously.

Recognizing this, however, we can also recognize one of the primary ways in which language operates: it operates by expressing (and embodying) our everyday understanding of things. This average understanding, as well as the language that articulates it, is absolutely essential to the shared understanding we maintain and that constitutes (at least partially) our Being-with.

> The way things have been expressed or spoken out is such that in the totality of contexts of signification into which it has been articulated, it preserves an understanding of the disclosed world and therewith, equiprimordially, an understanding of the Dasein-with of Others and of one's own Being-in. (*BT*, 211)

Importantly, the fact that things are always already understood in a particular way *does not* entail that the understanding of the "they" is entirely stagnant. Quite the contrary, even in the "they" there is room for innovation—and innovation on many levels. One thing that is possible (and rather obvious) is the capacity of any Dasein to endlessly formulate new sentences—sentences some of which have never been said before. This, of course, *does not* make a particular Dasein authentic or unique. What it demonstrates, rather, is that our Being-with is in a flexible with-world, where certain kinds of innovative sentences count as legitimate, while others do not. Innovation and "discovery" always occur against a background understanding in which only certain things *can be* discovered. Thus,

> The understanding which has thus already been "deposited" in the way things have been expressed, pertains just as much to any traditional discoveredness of entities which may have been reached, as it does to one's current understanding of Being and to whatever possibilities and horizons for fresh interpretations and conceptual Articulation may be possible. (*BT*, 211)

Every era has its own modes of invention and discovery—its own sense of what sorts of things will *count* as having been discovered and what sort of things will not. The latter category, unfortunately, isn't easily recognizable to us, precisely because we tend to be blinded by our understanding of what discovery entails. There are, of course, easy (albeit somewhat silly) examples: we could not discover that the moon was made of cheese, or that the earth was flat, or that everything was made out of animal intestines. Such "discoveries" would so violently contradict our sense of things that they're unavailable to us. If the moon were, in fact, made of cheese, it would so shake our cosmology that we would likely fall into insanity. Who made this cheese? From what sort of animal did it come? How do such animals exist in space? Where do they exist, and why do they leave floating cheese orbiting around other planets? If someone claimed to make such a discovery, he would be regarded either as a lunatic or as joking.[12]

The language that expresses our shared understanding of the world thus contains within itself possibilities for expansion, manipulation, and innovation—though, as we can now see, this hardly means that anything is possible. The limits on what can be said (and the ways in which something can be said) should not be understood as *mere* limitations. Quite the contrary, it is the "average intelligibility" of language that allows us to understand things we're not invested in.

> In the language which is spoken when one expresses oneself, there lies an average intelligibility; and in accordance with this intelligibility the discourse which is communicated can be understood to a considerable extent, even if the hearer does not bring himself into such a kind of Being towards what the discourse is about so as to have a primordial understanding. . . . We have *the same thing* in view, because it is in *the same* averageness that we have a common understanding of what is said. (*BT*, 212; translation very slightly altered)

What this entails, for Heidegger, is a recognition that everyday discourse is only peripherally related to the entities that are discussed. For the most part, discourse refers only to the *understanding of the "they."* In this respect, the talk is always about itself and not really about anything else. It is in this respect that the talk is empty. Heidegger calls this kind of discourse "idle talk," or "chatter" (*Gerede*).

Of course, the expression *idle talk* shouldn't mislead us into thinking that Dasein's modes of discourse are only vocal. The chatter of idle talk permeates the written word as well (Heidegger calls this "scribbling"). One need only pick up a magazine devoted to celebrity culture for an obvious example; for another, less obvious example, one can pick up *any* magazine with mass appeal and mass circulation. Newspapers are full of "scribbling," where ideas are recycled and viewpoints rehearsed. The editorial page displays those possibilities of understanding that are all always already there. This is why there's rarely ever something that's truly surprising in an editorial.

Idle talk even infiltrates the way we *read*. We conform what we read to what we already "know," becoming blind to anything new the text might reveal to us.[13] All of the possibilities of understanding are already given in advance by the "they"—one can be for or against a cause, but the reasons one has for one's position are the reasons *they have*. The causes on which one takes a stand are *their causes*. Again, this does not mean that every Dasein has identical beliefs to every other Dasein. It means, rather, that the very way we understand what issues are important, what counts as reasons for or against particular issues, and what stances one can take on those issues are already given in our everyday understanding. "Idle talk is something which anyone can rake up; it not only releases one from the task of genuinely understanding, but develops an undifferentiated kind of intelligibility, for which nothing is closed off any longer" (*BT*, 213).

It is the pervasiveness of idle talk—its capacity to subsume anything and everything within its fold—that makes it difficult to step outside of. "Idle talk discourages any new inquiry and any new disputation" (*BT*, 213). This is a point made brilliantly by Plato in *Meno*: one can begin to question only when one recognizes *something questionable*—only when one sees there's *something one doesn't know*.

Average understanding—the understanding of Dasein in its primary way of Being—does not court complexity. The differences between writing and "scribbling," reading superficially and reading with depth, investigating fundamental questions and merely incidental ones, are not differences that the "they" concern themselves with—at least not in a way that means anything. As Heidegger sarcastically remarks, "the average understanding . . . will not want any such distinction, and does not need it, because, of course, it understands everything" (*BT*, 212).

Curiosity

Curiosity is the mode of understanding that characterizes inauthenticity. The German word *Neugier*, which we translate as "curiosity," literally means "greed for the new."

> When curiosity has become free, however, it concerns itself with seeing, not in order to understand what is seen . . . but *just* in order to see. It seeks novelty only in order to leap from it anew to another novelty. . . . That which is an issue for care does not lie in grasping something and being knowingly in the truth; it lies rather in its abandoning itself to the world. (*BT*, 216)

Dasein, in "seeing" the world in average everydayness, sees it as a potpourri of novel stimuli that might allow Dasein to forget the burden of its Being: Dasein goes to movies, watches television, plays sports, and much more besides—all in order to lose itself in these activities through the continual pursuit of entertainment. One fills up one's time with the latest fads—the newest films and TV shows, for example—so that one can say one "saw it." Curiosity "concerns itself with a kind of knowing, but just in order to have known" (*BT*, 217).

A personal example might bring out this last point in more detail. When I was a child, I recall desperately wanting to see a particular movie (one that, in retrospect, wasn't worth watching). I also wanted to see this movie before my best friend at the time saw it. I was very pleased when my family took me to see the film. Ironically, though, I was unable to really lose myself in the movie. I was continuously thinking about how I would *describe* the movie to my friend when I saw him next. I was watching the movie *only to tell someone that I had watched the movie.*

This same sort of experience often overtakes tourists when they're on vacation. It is a well-known phenomenon: the tourist is trapped behind the camera—he is "in" Paris insofar as his body is spatially located in the city, but he is *existentially* located in his future photo album. He isn't really *being-in* Paris. He is, rather, floating about in an environment, trying to capture it in snapshots that prove that he actually experienced the things he photographs (although, in fact, he's experiencing only his construction of the future photo albums he will share with other "curious" Dasein). This sort of thing is a constitutive element of curiosity "which we call the character of 'never dwelling anywhere.' Curiosity is everywhere and nowhere. This mode of Being-in-the-world reveals a new kind of Being of everyday Dasein—a kind in which Dasein is constantly uprooting itself" (*BT*, 217).

Our uprootedness, however, is anchored in the with-world. The ways in which we are uprooted are already determined by our everyday understanding of things.

> Idle talk controls even the ways in which one may be curious. It says what one "must" have read and seen. In being everywhere and nowhere, curiosity is delivered over to idle talk . . . for which nothing is closed off, and idle talk, for which there is nothing that is not understood, provide themselves . . . with the guarantee of a "life" which, supposedly, is genuinely "lively". (*BT*, 217)

Ambiguity

Because everyday Being-in-the-world encounters "the sort of thing which is accessible to everyone, and about which anyone can say anything, it soon becomes impossible to decide what is disclosed in a genuine understanding, and what is not. This ambiguity extends not only to the world, but just as much to Being-with-one-another as such, and even to Dasein's Being towards itself" (*BT*, 217).

Ambiguity is, quite literally, "meaning two things." This is even more obvious in the German term *Zweideutigkeit—zwei* ("two") *deutigkeit* (roughly, "significances"). So the understanding that we have in the everyday mode of our existence is one where all things have two significances: first, we regard things as having a genuine meaning, which is expressed in the idle chatter we employ to talk about things. Second, however, things have a significance that goes far beyond this everyday understanding. The result, then, is that our understanding is such as to *think* it understands everything when in fact it does not. "Everything looks as if it were genuinely understood, genuinely taken hold of, genuinely spoken, though at bottom it is not; or else it does not look so, and yet at bottom it is" (*BT*, 217).

This last line presents the real core of Dasein's ambiguity: we simply do not recognize—and are incapable of recognizing, when immersed in the "they"—what constitutes a genuine understanding of a thing. Even the perception that we do *not* understand something might be incorrect (for example, we might think we do not understand how we walk, or speak, when in fact our understanding of such things is basic, or "primordial," as Heidegger would say).

DASEIN AS "FALLING"

The term *falling* is one Heidegger introduces to capture Dasein's relation to inauthenticity. Dasein is constantly *falling* into the "they," Heidegger claims. In one respect, this simply captures much of what we have thus far explored. To be Dasein is to *find the inauthentic constantly compelling*. There is no escape from this. We always already lean toward the everyday way of understanding things. Heidegger fleshes this out by claiming that falling is characterized by several essential elements: it is tempting, tranquilizing, alienating, entangling, and turbulent. These ideas are glossed in table 4.2.

Dasein, in understanding itself, finds the "normal" way of understanding itself "natural." It seems obvious and intuitive to understand ourselves as others understand us, both as individuals and as a species. Inauthenticity, in this respect, is very tempting. Likewise, there are plenty of resources among the "they" enabling us to believe that the everyday way of interpreting ourselves is the *best* and most *fulfilling* way. We're offered encouragement on many fronts: by self-help guides, family praise, awards and recognition ceremonies, and the back patting of those around us. It makes little difference whether or not we receive praise *ourselves*. The message is still the same: the good life is the one *you see in*

Table 4.2. Dasein as Falling

Constituent elements of Falling	Significance
Tempting	Constant pull into the "they"
Tranquilizing/complacent	View that Dasein, in the "they," is living a "full" and "genuine" life
Alienating	We are hidden from our own most-potentiality-for-Being
Entangled	Dasein gets entangled in itself—in the understanding of the "they" in regard to the Self
Turbulence	Dasein is yanked forcefully from each attempt at authenticity

the "they." The "they" knows what you need to be happy, and so on. In this way, the "they" encourages a tranquilizing complacency that encourages Dasein to *stay put*—to live as "one" lives. In so doing, Heidegger contends, we are alienated from the nature of our Being. We cease recognizing our thrownness and projection for what they are, and come to think of ourselves as "they" think of us. And in this way we are entangled in the "they" and in the understanding of things constitutive of it. Our attempts to think through our lives are always informed by this everyday understanding, and there's no way to *completely* escape from it. Indeed, any effort to get outside of the inauthentic is a *turbulent* one, as we're constantly pulled back into our normal way of understanding ourselves and the world.

Despite how bleak this sounds, Heidegger insists that "this term does not express any negative evaluation" (*BT*, 219). Moreover, we cannot "take the 'fallenness' of Dasein as a 'fall' from a purer and higher 'primal status'" (*BT*, 220). Finally, we would misunderstand this notion "if we were to ascribe to it the sense of a bad and deplorable ontical property of which, perhaps, more advanced stages of human culture might be able to rid themselves" (*BT*, 220). To reiterate: fallenness is not intended as a negative term, nor as something it is even possible to overcome.

One common reaction to these claims is to question why Heidegger would use a term as loaded as *fallenness* to describe Dasein's Being. If this isn't negative, it's natural to ask, why would Heidegger use this word—a word with obvious religious baggage? (The term *fallen*, in German and in English, is used in the Judeo-Christian Bible to describe the state of sinful humanity.) While it might well be the case that Heidegger is being disingenuous with the claim that fallenness is not evaluative, I think it's more plausible to read the notion of "falling" as attempting to *appropriate* the idea of fallenness that we're all familiar with. Recall that Heidegger thinks that all of Dasein's ways of understanding Being reveal *something*. If this is so, then powerful concepts like "the Fall of Man" should be based, in some way, in Dasein's ontology. The challenge is to see the ontological truth *within* such ideas without allowing them to further mislead us. In other words, the challenge is to see *why* our tradition has gone so wrong, and why it covers up so much. We can do this only by seeing what original insight our traditions begin with and then tracing how these insights have been covered up as we have moved along historically. The idea of humanity as fallen *does capture something about our condition* (and Heidegger thinks he's shown what it captures—namely, that inauthenticity is a fundamental mode of our Being). The problem with this concept is that it has been welded to an untenable conception of what it means to be a Dasein, as well as what it means for Dasein to exist in a world. Thus I want to suggest that the explanation of the "negative" connotation of the term likely has more to do with our own Judeo-Christian tradition (and our deep thrownness into it) than it does with Heidegger's use of the term. Heidegger is trying to *recover* the insight of fallenness from the very tradition we doggedly relate it to.

In table 4.3, much of what we have thus far explored in this chapter is summarized, as well as some hints at what we will explore in the remainder of the chapter. The table is meant to offer a summary guide of Dasein's Being-in-the-world in a way that distinguishes general existential structures (like state-of-mind), the modes of those structures (like moods, which are particular state-of-minds), and the way that these modes are filled out in everyday existence. I have also tried to summarize the core features of each structure, as spelled out by Heidegger, even when we have made only passing reference to them.

ANXIETY

Certain essential elements of Dasein have been brought to the fore. We have answered many questions one can raise about Dasein: what it means to be "there" in the way Dasein is, the types of entities disclosed to Dasein-in-the-world (as well as their ontological order), and questions concerning the "who" of Dasein. Heidegger is quick to remind us that we cannot simply add up all of the pieces and end up with a unified Dasein. The very presumption that we could would attempt to explore Dasein's Being in a present-at-hand fashion. Instead of proceeding in this manner—a manner that would essentially pass over what is unique about Dasein—Heidegger poses the following question: "Is there in Dasein an understanding state-of-mind in which Dasein has been disclosed to itself in some distinctive way?" (*BT*, 226). If the answer to this query is in the affirmative, perhaps we might use this mode of Dasein as a clue toward acquiring a unified conception of that being for whom Being is an issue.

> If the existential analytic of Dasein is to retain clarity in principle as to its function in fundamental ontology, then in order to master its provisional task of exhibiting Dasein's Being, it must seek for one of the most far-reaching and most primordial possibilities of disclosure—one that lies in Dasein itself. The way of disclosure in which Dasein brings itself before itself must be such that in it Dasein becomes accessible as simplified in a certain manner. With what is thus disclosed, the structural totality of the Being we seek must then come to light in an elemental way. (*BT*, 226)

The place to look for this kind of disclosure, Heidegger thinks, is in the experience of *Angst* (anxiety). Examining this state-of-mind (mood) will reveal the totality of Dasein—namely, it will reveal that care is what characterizes Dasein.

The importance of the notion of *Angst* in Heidegger is manifold. *Angst*, first of all, is a mode of Dasein in which Dasein comes to see its own Being. For this reason, *Angst* also plays a crucial role in the possibil-

Table 4.3. Dasein's Being-There

	State-of-mind [*Befindlichkeit*]	Understanding [*Verstehen*]	Discourse [*Rede*]
Mode (general)	Mood [*Stimmung*]	Interpretation [*Auslegung*]	Signification
Constituent structural features of modes	1) objects disclosed (e.g., the fearsome) 2) the mood itself (e.g., fearing) 3) that about which we have the mood (viz. Dasein) (*BT*, 179–180).	1) fore-having 2) fore-sight 3) fore-conception [*Vorgriff: anticipation*] (*BT*, 191) This is the structure of interpretation, which understands x "as" y. (*BT*, 201)	1) what the discourse is about 2) what is said-in-the-talk 3) the communication [*Mitteilung*] 4) making-known (*BT*, 206)
Levels of modality	The three constituent features of the "there" (of the "da" in Dasein) exist equiprimordially at many levels. When speaking generally about them, we might distinguish the following levels at which these features can be found. Moods, interpretations, and significations can be found in: (1) a historical epoch (e.g., the Middle Ages is characterized by certain interpretations, common moods, and a distinct way of sharing the world with other Dasein). (2) a culture (e.g., the United States has its own reservoir of common moods, interpretations, and ways of speaking). (3) a situation (e.g., a religious ritual has a "mood," and this is accompanied by a particular interpretation of the events in question, as well as a way of sharing these events with other Dasein). (4) a particular Dasein encountering a situation (e.g., being stressed-out by a Heidegger paper can infect the way you understand the world, the way you understand particular things, and the way you talk with other Dasein).		
What is disclosed through the existential structure	Thrownness	Projection	Fallenness
Inauthentic modes	Curiosity	Ambigu	
Temporal significance	Past	Future	

ity of an authentic existence: it is only through seeing ourselves for what we are—thrown projection, constantly falling—that it is possible to take up that mode of existence wherein we understand in an authentic manner *what we are.*

> Dasein's absorption in the "they" and its absorption in the "world" of its concern, make manifest something like a fleeing of Dasein in the face of itself—of itself as an authentic potentiality-for-Being-itself. (*BT*, 229)

> Only to the extent that Dasein has been brought before itself in an ontologically essential manner through whatever disclosedness belongs to it, can it flee *in the face of* that in the face of which it flees. (*BT*, 229)

This "fleeing" from oneself is, for Heidegger, that which characterizes anxiety (*Angst*). It is in this mode of Dasein, Heidegger thinks, that we have found an access point into what we will call the "care-structure"— and it is the care-structure that unites all of the elements of the existential analytic of Dasein we have thus far discussed. To begin to see how *Angst* might play this role, we must first see what it is that distinguishes fear (which we have already discussed) from it.

> The turning away of falling is not a fleeing that is founded upon a fear of entities within the world. Fleeing that is so grounded is still less a character of this turning-away, when what this turning away does is precisely to *turn thither* towards entities within the world by absorbing itself in them. *The turning away of falling is grounded rather in anxiety, which in turn is what makes fear possible.* (*BT*, 230)

One departing point for distinguishing fear from anxiety is to notice that what gets disclosed with and through these different modes of state-of-mind isn't equivalent. Fear is concerned with entities that can have a threatening character, that might break up one's concernful absorption in the world. Anxiety has a different character: one is not encountering the "fearsome" that threatens one's Dasein. Rather, *one is confronted with one's own ontology.* "That in the face of which one has anxiety is Being-in-the-world as such" (*BT*, 230).

In fear, the fearsome only presents itself because we are involved in a world—because our Being is a Being-in-the-world. It is in light of our particular (existentiell) world that something can be threatening at all. Anxiety has a different character: the very fact that we are Being-in-the-world is that which confronts us. What is revealed in this confrontation is the significance we attribute to things with which we are involved is that—that the meanings of those things with which we are en-given in advance of our acting with them in our concernful world has the character of completely lacking significance" menacing presence of the fearsome is intimately tied to spatiality (it comes toward one from somewhere), anxiety does not have this character. Anxiety comes from nowhere (*BT*, 231). It obtrudes, robbing the present-at-hand and ready-to-hand alike of significance, leaving only the bare fact of the worldhood of the world: "Being anxious discloses, primordially and directly, the world as world" (*BT*, 232). It is precisely this bare disclosure of our Being-in-the-world that forces itself upon us.

> That which anxiety is anxious about is Being-in-the-world itself. In anxiety what is environmentally ready-to-hand sinks away, and so, in general, do entities within the world. The "world" can offer nothing more, and neither can the Dasein-with of Others. Anxiety thus takes away from Dasein the possibility of understanding itself, as it falls, in terms of the "world" and the way things have been publicly inter- preted. Anxiety throws Dasein back upon that which it is anxious about—its authentic-potentiality-for-Being-in-the-world. Anxiety indi- vidualizes Dasein for its ownmost Being-in-the-world, which as some- thing that understands, projects itself essentially upon possibilities. Therefore, with that which it is anxious about, anxiety discloses Dasein *as Being-possible*, and indeed as the only kind of thing which it can be of its own accord as something individualized in individualization.
> Anxiety makes manifest in Dasein its *Being towards* its ownmost poten- tiality-for-Being—that is, its *Being-free for* the freedom of choosing itself and taking hold of itself. Anxiety brings Dasein face to face with its *Being-free for* (*propensio in . . .*) the authenticity of its Being, and for this authenticity as a possibility which it always is. (*BT*, 232)

As we can see in this passage, anxiety is an uncovering of Dasein's own existential condition. We come face-to-face with our own Being-in-the- world and must deal with it as such. But what Heidegger highlights in this passage, unlike earlier ones, is not that we always flee from our Being-in-the-world, but rather that anxiety is always in some sense avail- able to us—and this means that we always have the potential to face up to what we are, to face up to our thrown projection in a world of signifi- cance we did not create.

This constant potential should come as no surprise. We can only be characterized as "falling" and "fleeing" if it is always possible for us to recognize what we are. If this were unavailable to Dasein, it would make little sense to claim that Dasein is "fleeing" from itself, and that such fleeing was part of what it means to be Dasein. We can only flee from our Being-in-the-world if we are always, in some sense of the term, recogniz- ing this Being.

Anxiety, as Heidegger goes on to say, is characterized by the uncanny (*unheimlich*). We experience the world as uncanny—as not quite fitting who and what we are, as not quite making sense. Heidegger himself wants us to see that the term *unheimlich* conveys the etymological sense of "not-at-home" (*BT*, 233). When we are anxious about Being-in-the-world, we no longer feel "at home with" the world: it becomes a foreign thing, uncomfortable and unfamiliar.

For the most part, Dasein attempts to escape this "feeling." To do this, Dasein attempts to immerse itself in the "they" world once again—to cover up the question of its Being and its involvement with the world. Dasein does this precisely by grabbing hold of those possibilities that make so much sense within the public world of significance.

CARE

Where has all of this led us? We began with one question: What is the meaning of Being? We proceeded by asking about the meaning of Dasein's Being in order to find an access point into our original question. If we are to know the meaning of Being, we will examine that being for whom Being is an issue (Dasein) and who has an understanding of Being. At this point, Heidegger is ready to say what constitutes Dasein's Being-there in a fundamental way. He specifies this as "care" (*Sorge*).

In certain respects, the revelation that the underlying structure of Dasein's Being is "care" isn't a revelation at all. As Hubert Dreyfus contends, Heidegger is simply giving an additional name to all of the terrain he has already covered. What does come out, however, is the fundamentally *temporal nature* of Dasein's Being. Heidegger, in clarifying care, recasts much of what he has already done in terms that allow us to see much more transparently how time pervades Dasein's basic existence. The basic features of Dasein's existence are here shown to correspond to the basic moments of time: past, present, and future. The basic threefold structure of Dasein revealed by anxiety (facticity, existentiality, and Being-fallen[14]) corresponds to these moments. Taken collectively, these three things characterize the Being of Dasein as care—but they also reveal that underlying Dasein's Being is temporality as such.

Facticity: we are thrown into a web of significance wherein things have certain meanings.

Existentiality: we project ourselves onto those possibilities that have been handed over to us in our thrown Being-in-the-world.

Being-fallen: the possibilities and significance in which we have a world are not our own. We constantly flee toward the established meaning of things given by the public self (the "they").

As we can see, these terms are simply paraphrases of a great deal of the previous discussion (you'll also notice that I have included them in table 4.3). The paraphrases serve a twofold function: First, they insist once again that Dasein's Being is not simply *additive* in the way that, say, the Being of a heap is additive. If one piles up straw, one will eventually get a "heap" of straw. (The time at which this occurs, of course, is notoriously

difficult to discern!) The same cannot be said of Dasein. If we add together facticity and existentiality, we are *not* thereby closer to achieving the Being of Dasein. The reason for this is straightforward: Dasein does not consist in parts. To assert otherwise, as we have repeatedly seen, is to make Dasein into something merely present-at-hand—one more independent object with distinct properties.

The second function of Heidegger's paraphrases, as mentioned above, is to reveal the temporal structure of Dasein's Being. We are thrown into a set of possibilities we did not create. It is from these possibilities that we must choose and act. Hence, our existence is *always* drawing on what has come before (the past): "existing is always factical. Existentiality is essentially determined by facticity" (*BT*, 236). Our thrownness into the world determines the range of possibilities we can appropriate—it determines the way in which we can resolve the issue of our own existence.

Nevertheless, the issue of our own existence *does get resolved*. We throw (project) ourselves into the future, and it is in light of this throwing that we understand ourselves, as well as how we relate to the past. Thus our existence is fundamentally "ahead-of-itself" (*futural*).

Finally, the way that we discover our past and project ourselves into the future has a certain primary mode of being. The way I *am*, in the present, both thrown and projecting, is characterized by average everydayness. That is, *I am currently characterized as Being-fallen* (present).

Here we find, through the analysis of Dasein, a hint about the meaning of Being in general: at the core of Dasein's Being is care, which is made possible in existence as fundamentally *temporal*, or involving time. From this vantage point, we get a glimpse of Heidegger's projected answer to the question of the meaning of Being in general: the meaning of Being, Heidegger hopes to show, is *time*.

POETIC CONFIRMATION

Dasein's Being, then, is constituted by care. In section 42 of *Being and Time*, Heidegger claims "confirmation" of his results in a poem from antiquity—an "ancient fable." For anyone steeped in epistemology or natural science, this claim of confirmation will seem worse than weak—it will seem downright laughable. How can a document that involves mythological stories and figures possibly confirm Heidegger's thesis? What is the status of this "confirmation," and how seriously are we really to take it? Many commentators have become so frustrated with the section that they decline to even mention it in their commentaries.[15]

There is, however, much to be said by way of explanation here—and a lot of it quite nuanced and revelatory. The key to understanding how this "proof" is intended to work lies in reconceiving the nature of language along Heideggerian lines. It is also crucial to understand exactly what

Heidegger takes himself to be proving. We will deal with each of these in turn.

Heidegger takes himself to be demonstrating *not* that the basis of Dasein's Being really is care, but rather that this conception of Dasein's Being is a primordial, pre-scientific one. In other words, Heidegger does not claim any sort of novelty in his conception of Dasein as care. In our oldest literature, Dasein's Being is recognized as being constituted by care. All that Heidegger is doing in *Being and Time* is to thematize an ancient wisdom—to make explicit, in theoretical terms, something that lurked inchoate before—and for a long time. Given that this is Heidegger's aim, his appeal to this early piece of literature is in fact quite appropriate. There is little else one *could* appeal to in order to show that Dasein's self-understanding has for a long time involved the notion of care. A "scientific" confirmation would be entirely inappropriate, as it would make Dasein's Being equivalent to the being of entities present-at-hand, and would regard care as a mere property of Dasein's Being, rather than as the *ontological basis* for Dasein's existential condition.

But there is also a sense in which the poem is meant to show more than mere historical precedent. To see this, we must look in more detail at the way language carries with it an implicit ontology—as well as the ways in which language has a revelatory capacity that is missed when we regard it as merely a present-at-hand thing or, indeed, as merely a ready-to-hand instrument. Language, as Heidegger later says, is the house of Being. It has the ability to reveal a world. It is precisely this that the ancient poem does, in Heidegger's view. It presents Dasein's very nature by capturing Dasein in mythopoetic form. Through such a presentation, Dasein is able to see itself as itself.

Of course, one instance of such a "revealing" is insufficient to "prove," in the strictest sense, that Dasein is care. Heidegger is aware of this. The burden of demonstration thus does not lie in this poem but rather in the analysis that Heidegger has already given. The function of the ancient poem is to ground Heidegger's analytic of Dasein in a concrete expression of Dasein's Being—one that is not anchored to the modern world and that displays the conception of Dasein that Heidegger has been striving to articulate. Construed in this way, Heidegger's "confirmation" of the existential analytic—perhaps surprisingly—works well.

CONCLUSION

Dasein is Being-in-the-world. This has been cashed out in terms of involvement in a web of significance. This web of significance is given first by a *public* understanding of things in which we live and breathe. The implications of this are astonishing enough: the problem of other minds, as well as the problem of solipsism and subjectivism, are seen to be

pseudo-problems. Both of these are ultimately explained only in terms of their point of departure—they emerge only when one takes a present-at-hand point of view of Dasein, ignoring the Being of this being. The world in which we exist, firstly and mostly, is a public world. We are only "selves" (as individuated psychological beings) after we have been immersed in a common web of significance.

NOTES

1. It is a little misleading to say that the philosophical tradition has ignored this. One finds this view, to be sure, in Hegel's *Phenomenology of Spirit* as well as in Nietzsche. One could also plausibly make the case that some of the ancients had a similar notion of the self and its relation to society.

2. The difficulty of these questions, as well as Heidegger's persistence in asking the most basic kinds of questions, further reveals, I think, the exceptional depth of Heidegger's thinking.

3. I want to emphasize that Joan Stambaugh's translation has much to recommend it. It is truly an accomplishment (as is Macquarrie and Robinson's translation). Each translation has both its merits and its problems. I have been using the Macquarrie and Robinson translation for approaching twenty years, however, and old habits die hard.

4. There's more to it than this, of course. After all, scientists are often incredibly excited about their research. I am using the idea of "calmness" as a stand-in for whatever mood or moods characterize scientific observation.

5. For an interesting treatment of fear and other subject-referring emotions, see Charles Taylor's "The Concept of a Person." Taylor does not often explicitly invoke Heidegger in his treatment, but Heideggerian themes are omnipresent in his work.

6. Heidegger makes several further distinctions in moods that bear a family resemblance to fear. I do not think these taxonomic considerations are of much philosophical importance.

7. And this, of course, is the world of the "they."

8. Here Heidegger claims that we are in actuality in a different mode of fearing for our own Dasein, albeit in a special sense: we fear that the Other will be torn away from us.

9. For example, alarm: when what is fearful emerges suddenly into one's concernful Being-alongside objects disclosed as ready-to-hand. When what is fearful is unfamiliar, one experiences dread. When the dreadful is sudden, one experiences terror.

10. In his *Being and Nothingness* and *Existentialism Is a Humanism*, for example.

11. This is revealing about language acquisition, as well. We do not learn individual word after individual word. We learn languages in large chunks. To see this, try to imagine someone who only understood a single word. Such a state of affairs is impossible.

12. Wittgenstein makes a similar point when he says that if a lion could talk, we would not understand him. Our form of life is so fundamentally different from that of the lion that there is simply no crossover possible. We inhabit fundamentally different worlds. Thus, we might here extrapolate, it is *impossible* to discover that lions talk: we do not regard this as a possibility; we could never recognize it. Thus it cannot be the sort of thing that might ever be discovered.

13. This is a well-documented phenomenon. In psychology, it is called "confirmation bias."

14. Notice that Heidegger here moves from talking about "discourse" to talking about "Being-fallen." The reason, presumably, is that the locution *Being-fallen* more easily reveals a temporal dimension (namely, the present). The same cannot be said of "discourse."

15. It is explicitly discussed in Mulhall's commentary.

FIVE

Truth and Reality

Implications of an Appropriate Interpretation of Dasein

In this chapter, we'll explore the implications of Heidegger's analysis of Dasein for two traditional areas of philosophical reflection: the investigation of reality on the one hand, and truth on the other.

REALITY

As we've seen, Heidegger's ontology of Dasein has significant implications for the question of the relation of mind to world. He claims (rightly) that this problem has typified investigations into reality. These investigations have been, in large part, based on one question: Can the human mind know things that are independent of it? Once again, we see that this very question has already presupposed the Being of the entities in question—it has presupposed that the idea of "reality" is in some sense transparent, as well as that the "mind" is not ontologically problematic. Heidegger's existential analytic of Dasein[1] and worldhood, however, shows us that the question cannot even arise in any sensible fashion. "The question of whether there is a world at all and whether its Being can be proved, makes no sense if it is raised by Dasein as Being-in-the-world; and who else would raise it?" (*BT*, 247).

Consider Kant's attempts to demonstrate the existence of the external world. In the *Critique of Pure Reason*, Kant tries to show, via time, that there are other present-at-hand objects that must be presupposed in order to have experience as we know it.[2] This is fine, so far as it goes, but the problem according to Heidegger is that it doesn't go far enough: it never gets beyond the present-at-hand disclosed as such. Indeed, because Kant presupposes the present-at-hand as his primary ontology, one never gets a glimpse of anything else. It is this very mode of Being that both solves and gives rise to the problem in question. Kant famously claims that it is a scandal that philosophy has not yet effectively proven the existence of the external world. In reply, Heidegger writes:

> The "scandal of philosophy" is not that this proof has yet to be given, but that such proofs are expected and attempted again and again. Such expectations, aims, and demands arise from an ontologically inadequate way of starting with something of such a character that independently of it and outside of it a world is to be proved as present-at-hand. (*BT*, 249)

All epistemological stances on the existence of the external world make the same basic mistake: they presuppose that Dasein is worldless—that the world is something that must be discovered and proved. This error is at the basis of the entire epistemological tradition.

Of course, it is easy to say of a tradition that it has made some error, that we ought to move beyond it, and the like. Heidegger does not think simply waving a hand to dismiss an approach is an adequate response to those epistemological issues that have gripped so many great minds. Rather than simply dismissing his philosophical predecessors, Heidegger wants to show why the mistakes of the epistemological tradition are *understandable ones*.

> Our task is not to prove an external world is present-at-hand or to show how it is present-at-hand, but to point out why Dasein, as Being-in-the-world, has the tendency to bury the "external world" in nullity "epistemologically" before going on to prove it. (*BT*, 250)

The answer to this issue, Heidegger claims, is to be found in Dasein's state of Being—in Dasein's falling into the "they." The "they," under the substantial weight of tradition, views things (reality) as fundamentally present-at-hand.

The problem of reality, then, reflects a larger problem: the tendency to view things under one dominant rubric—that of objects and subjects coinciding in a world entirely independent of Dasein. The "entirely independent" should not mislead us. The point here is that viewing objects and subjects in this way presupposes a particular understanding of what it means to be an object. It is only within this understanding that we can think of objects as independent of us. Heidegger is not claiming that there are no objects independent of Dasein, but he is claiming that viewing objects in this way already presupposes the Being of an entity existing in-the-world. Both idealism (the view that the nature of the world is constituted by our cognition) and realism (the view that the world is mind-independent) presuppose the Being of Dasein—a being for whom Being is an issue.

Much turns on formulating the question appropriately. If we start with the wrong kind of question (e.g., Can we know the external world?), we will *inevitably* be led down the wrong path, regardless of whether we answer this question in the positive or the negative. The positions staked out in philosophy in relation to the question of "reality" and the "external world" have uniformly started with the wrong question. Thus the problem with a doctrine like realism *is not* that it is false. The problem, rather, is that the position is ungrounded and results from asking the wrong *type of question*. This explains Heidegger's response to realism: "In so far as this existential assertion does not deny that entities within-the-world are present-at-hand, it agrees . . . with the thesis of realism in its results. But it differs in principle from every kind of realism; for realism holds that the reality of the 'world' not only needs to be proved but also is capable of proof" (*BT*, 251).

To say that realism is false, then, is to understate what is wrong with realism. The very idea that realism could be *either* true or false presupposes that this position is a reasonable (and possible) response to an actual *problem* (namely, the problem of the external world). To presuppose that there is an issue here is to take for granted a view of Dasein as separated from its world, and hence it is to misunderstand the very being of Dasein, as well as the entities with which Dasein is concernfully absorbed.

A similar problem arises in the case of idealism, the traditional counterpart to realism. Interestingly, however, Heidegger claims that it—at least in certain forms—has a marginal advantage over realism in that it acknowledges that Being is only possible through the understanding of Dasein (*BT*, 251).

Having characterized Dasein's Being as one constituted by care, Heidegger has also shown the way in which "reality" emerges as a problem. It is here, above all other places perhaps, that we find a clue to some of Heidegger's rather strange remarks about entities existing apart from Dasein's understanding of them (even though Being does not). It is only in relation to Dasein as care, Heidegger notes, that "the character of the 'in-itself' becomes ontologically intelligible" (*BT*, 252).

This sentence is of immense importance in trying to understand Heidegger's thinking regarding the existence of objects apart from Dasein—an issue that has, in effect, divided the literature on Heidegger in a rather serious way. Some maintain that Heidegger embraces the thesis that there are objects apart from all human understanding, and these commentators produce passages that indeed seem to support this view. Others produce equally compelling passages that suggest that "objects" are only things that reveal themselves to Dasein—and that the conception of objects existing apart from Dasein is in fact only one more perspective that one might take on the present-at-hand; indeed, it seems to be part of the very *Being* of the present-at-hand that we regard such objects as having some kind of existence apart from our interaction with them. (In this respect, the present-at-hand can be understood fundamentally as that which disrupts our absorption in the world.)

This point comes out well, I think, in Heidegger's discussion of two roughly contemporary thinkers on the question of reality: Dilthey and Scheler. In both cases, Heidegger is flogging the same horse. "'Consciousness of Reality' is itself a way of Being-in-the-world. Every 'problematic of the external world' comes back necessarily to this basic existential phenomenon" (*BT*, 254). While one can, with some philosophical legwork, make this compatible with some version of "realism," I am not convinced this is a particularly useful way to expend one's intellectual energies. It's just not clear that the payoff is worth the price—nor that it even *fits* with Heidegger's overall conception of ontology. Indeed, in many respects, recent attempts to make Heidegger into a realist seem to obscure more than they clarify. While these efforts are important insofar as they help us see that Heidegger is not an *antirealist*, this intellectual labor is hardly worthwhile if it produces a similar error by taking realism in the wrong way.[3]

In brief, Heidegger rejects both realism and antirealism. He also rejects their sister epistemological concepts: skepticism and foundationalism. Claiming either that we cannot know the world or anything in it (skepticism) *or* that certain beliefs secure a foundation upon which knowledge can be secured (foundationalism) commits one and the same error: it misunderstands the relationship between Dasein and the world. When we begin with a proper understanding of Dasein as Being-in-the-world, knowledge of the world must be construed as basic to the kinds of beings we are—not as something we do not have access to, and not as something that requires particular beliefs that can then act as a foundation for other beliefs. To develop this point, we'll need to clarify Heidegger's account of the fundamental meaning of truth.

TRUTH

Heidegger argues that "truth," understood in its original Greek sense as *aletheia*, has a direct connection to *things*, and hence to Being (*BT*, 256). It is through this connection, Heidegger thinks, that "the phenomenon of truth comes within the range of the problematic of fundamental ontology" (*BT*, 256). This justifies a more fundamental inquiry into the nature of truth—one that takes into account the investigation already accomplished (albeit under guises other than the inquiry into "truth").

To tackle truth, Heidegger proposes a method that is by now familiar: he will begin with the traditional conception of truth and attempt "to lay bare the ontological foundations of that conception" (*BT*, 257). This, in turn, will reveal "the primordial phenomenon of truth" (*BT*, 257). Of course, it is not enough to claim that one conception of truth is more basic than another, nor can one simply claim that our current conception of truth is inadequate. As usual, Heidegger recognizes the need to *explain* why we have the current (inadequate) conception of truth. He needs to give an account of why we have passed over truth in its most fundamental form and replaced it with a pale imitation. Finally, Heidegger will investigate what our speaking about truth reveals about its nature, as well as the way it relates to our Being-in-the-world. As we will see, Heidegger thinks that we have a primordial relationship with truth—we are both "in" truth, as Heidegger will reveal, and "outside of it."

The traditional view of truth, Heidegger contends, involves the following elements: (1) that truth is linguistic (i.e., that assertions are those things that can be true or false); (2) that what makes an assertion true or false is the relation it bears to that which it is about—it either "agrees" with the world or fails to do so; and (3) that Aristotle managed to set us straight about truth.

The traditional picture would have us believe that agreement consists in "*adaequatio*": the assertion is adequate to what it represents. As Heidegger is quick to point out, this notion of agreement is but one possibility. Mathematical equations, for example, express one type of agreement (that of equality), and corresponding sentences another. Which type of agreement is appropriate when we think of truth?

In addressing this question, Heidegger considers the following case: Imagine someone with his back to a painting that is hanging on the wall. The person says, "The painting is crooked." What analysis are we to give of this claim if we hold that it is true? Assume that the man turns around to "verify" what has been said. The traditional notion of truth would have us say that he has demonstrated that the content of his assertion agrees with a state of affairs in the world. We might add that the assertion presented the man's representation of the spatial location of the picture, and this picture matched up with this representation.

Heidegger aims to unearth a more primordial notion of truth than the one captured here. There is little (traditional) argument for his alternative conception of truth—a situation that is, perhaps, unavoidable. The force of Heidegger's alternate notion of truth and logos (see chapter 1) lies in its ability to enable us to see more clairvoyantly the phenomenon under description—something no argument alone *could* accomplish. That Heidegger's alternate conception of truth *should* be vindicated in this way (if it is vindicated) stands to reason. Indeed, Heidegger's account is an *instance* of the very point he is attempting to make. Certain kinds of linguistic activity enable us to *understand*—to see perspicuously that which is talked about. In such instances, logos does not merely penetrate beneath the surface of things; it also makes the hidden manifest.

Rather than thinking that this capability is part of the mere orthography of a sentence (as some direct-reference theorists seem to suggest[4]),

Heidegger encourages us to see that the capacity to engage Being in this way is fundamentally a part of our Being-in-the-world (it is this mode of Being that leads Heidegger to speak of Dasein as a "clearing"). All language use must be understood against this background.

"Asserting," Heidegger says, "is a way of Being towards the thing itself that is" (*BT*, 260). The question we must pose concerns whether or not this type of Being uncovers the Being of the thing in question. "What is to be confirmed is that such Being uncovers the entity towards which it is. What gets demonstrated is the Being-uncovering of the assertion" (*BT*, 261). Whereas the philosophical tradition has claimed that true assertion reveals something about the way the world is, Heidegger here offers us a look at what this view of truth misses: our true assertions are self-referential. They reveal something about the mode of Being of an assertion itself—namely, that it can uncover something that, before the assertion was made, was hidden (covered). As Heidegger puts it,

> What is to be demonstrated is not an agreement of knowing with its object, still less of the psychical with the physical; but neither is it an agreement between "contents of consciousness" among themselves. What is to be demonstrated is solely the Being-uncovered of the entity itself—that entity in the how of its uncoveredness. This uncoveredness is confirmed when that which is put forward in the assertion (namely, the entity itself) shows itself *as that very same thing.* "Confirmation" signifies the entity's showing itself in its selfsameness. (*BT*, 261)

Logos (*Rede*) is the thing we use to uncover entities, allowing us to see them as they are. Heidegger claims that this conception of truth is to be found in the Greeks—in the notion of *aletheia.* We use logos to un-cover Being, and it is through logos that we can get a glimmer of the Being of things in-the-world.

> In citing such evidence we must avoid uninhibited word-mysticism. Nevertheless, the ultimate business of philosophy is to preserve the force of the most elemental words in which Dasein expresses itself, and to keep the common understanding from leveling them off to that unintelligibility which functions in turn as a source of pseudo-problems. (*BT,* 262)

This analysis of logos and *aletheia* (truth as un-covering), Heidegger claims, has not simply abandoned the philosophical tradition. Indeed, as he claims, "in proposing our 'definition' of 'truth' we have not shaken off the tradition, but we have appropriated it primordially" (*BT*, 262).

One can read Heidegger's own assertions here as revealing the Being of truth—as uncovering something from our collective history that has been covered up through philosophical exercises. Heidegger's use of logos has itself been an instance of *a-letheia* (un-covering or dis-closing—the hyphens are meant to draw attention to the root meanings of the terms).

The business of thinking, then, is not simply to reject what we have come to think of as the significance of language and truth. Rather, it is to unearth the origins of this conception—to show how it is that this conception has arisen out of a more fundamental understanding of language and its ability to disclose being. The business of thinking is to restore to language its power to house Being—to get us beyond the conceptualization of language as a mere instrument. This is a point that dominates much of the later Heidegger's thought, but it is already present in the pages of *Being and Time*: The conception of language as mere instrument leads to an inability to understand ourselves or, indeed, even the world around us. It leads us, as Heidegger says, to become forgetful of Being.

Language, on this view, when it is construed as a mere instrument, inhibits the very thinking it makes possible when it is understood in its fullness—as disclosive of what is, as that which lets things appear to us as they are. The emasculation of language when instrumentalized in this way is nicely articulated by Horkheimer in *Eclipse of Reason*:

> The more ideas have become automatic, instrumentalized, the less does anybody see in them thoughts with a meaning of their own. They are considered things, machines. Language has been reduced to just another tool in the gigantic apparatus of production in modern society. . . . Meaning is supplanted by function or effect in the world of things and events. In so far as words are not used obviously to calculate technically relevant probabilities or for other practical purposes, among which even relaxation is included, they are in danger of being suspect as sales talk of some kind, for truth is no end in itself. (15)

I do not mean to suggest, in quoting Horkheimer, that antirealists and realists are mere salesmen. I do mean to suggest that the persistent instrumentalization of language is a condition for the possibility of conceiving language as merely the froth atop Being, and hence it is a precondition for the type of arguments for realism and antirealism that are here of interest. It is when we view language as merely the thing employed in light of our purposes and interests—as one more tool to manipulate the world—that we no longer see the relation in which *logos* stands to *things*. In this precarious situation, we come to forget the disclosive power of language, its power (as Heidegger would say) to house Being.

It is in this notion that one can see what it means, fundamentally, to speak of truth. "The most primordial phenomenon of truth is first shown by the existential-ontological foundations of uncovering" (*BT*, 263). As Heidegger immediately goes on to say, this uncovering belongs to a type of Being, not merely to sentences and their relation to states of affairs. As Heidegger sums up this important point, "Dasein is 'in the truth'" (*BT*, 263) precisely because Dasein is the clearing through which there is truth at all. If there were no Dasein, there would be no being *to whom* things might be revealed.

This is elucidated in terms of the existential analytic we have thus far seen. Dasein is (a) disclosedness, (b) thrownness, (c) projection, and (d) falling. We are in the truth insofar as we have an understanding of the world (this is primordial, or basic) that uncovers things. However, we are thrown into this world of significance, and we must take up the possibilities available to us. We can do this inauthentically or authentically. For the most part, we do not project ourselves on our ownmost potentiality for Being. Rather, we succumb to the average publicness and leveling off of the "they." We are fallen, thrown Being-in-the-world, projecting upon possibilities disclosed to us. It is because of falling that Dasein is equiprimordially (equally basically) also in the untruth: we are led to cover up and pass over our very own Being, led to see all questions concerning the meaning of existence as pre-decided in the inauthentic realm of the "they."

> The upshot of our existential-ontological Interpretation for the phenomenon of truth is (1) that truth, in the most primordial sense, is Dasein's disclosedness, to which the uncoveredness of entities within-the-world belongs; and (2) that Dasein is equiprimordially both in the truth and in the untruth. (*BT*, 265)

For Heidegger, our notion of assertion legitimates a conception of truth as a mapping-out of objects present-at-hand maintaining a relation among other objects present-at-hand. The philosophical tradition has missed (passed over) the more fundamental, hermeneutic "as" involved in discourse. We end up, under the impress of the assertion, thinking that truth is fundamentally categorical or apophantical (i.e., that true sentences are ones that assert something about the world independent of Dasein). As Heidegger explains, "the primordial phenomenon of truth has been covered up by Dasein's very understanding of Being—that understanding which is proximally the one that prevails, and which even today has not been surmounted explicitly and in principle" (*BT*, 268). We think of truth as lurking in judgments, when the fundamental locus of truth lurks rather in the sort of Being that is capable of uncovering Being (or of covering it up). Dasein is thus the fundamental source of truth—it is part of our basic constitution that we can both cover and uncover. In this sense, Dasein "is the ontological condition for the possibility that assertions can be either true or false—that they may uncover or cover things up" (*BT*, 269).

Heidegger makes this point more bluntly as well: "'There is' truth only insofar as Dasein is and as long as Dasein is" (*BT*, 269). Likewise, there is falsity only in so far as Dasein exists. Dasein is the condition for the possibility of both truth and falsity.

Of course, Heidegger is quick to acknowledge that part of what it means to uncover an object is to uncover it such that it presents itself as having already existed. This is just the sort of Being, as Heidegger claims, that belongs to truth. This is entirely compatible with the claim that "all truth is relative to Dasein" (*BT*, 270). Things could not present themselves as existing before they were discovered if it were not for Dasein, the condition for the possibility of such a presentation. This does not mean, of course, that there is nothing apart from Dasein. Trees still fall in the woods even if Dasein is not there to hear the sound made. Nevertheless, without Dasein, there would be no being capable of understanding the significance of the falling of the tree (or whatever else) and to whom such things might be disclosed. Heidegger is extremely careful to distinguish his view from merely "subjective" views about truth. What presents itself is not the product of will, nor is it merely left to our discretion (*BT*, 270).

It is following this that Heidegger begins to discuss the notion of presupposing. In Heidegger's view, it is truth (in the existential-ontological sense) that makes presupposition possible. It is only because certain things are disclosed to us that we can take these things for granted (that we can presuppose). Moreover, "because this presupposing of itself belongs to Dasein's Being, 'we' must also presuppose 'ourselves' as having the attribute of disclosedness" (*BT*, 271). Given Dasein's mode of Being, as always ahead of itself in a field of possibilities, Dasein always presupposes the understanding that it has and the mode of Being that is its own. Indeed, to even explore the Being of Dasein involves presupposing having the sort of Being that might investigate other modes of Being. When we aim to uncover the fundamental Being of Dasein, we thus end up presupposing that we exist in a world that can be disclosed. Indeed, this presupposition lies at the basis of each and every question we can ask.

CONCLUSION

Skepticism and foundationalism, realism and antirealism, live by taking in each other's washing, to borrow on expression from J. L. Austin.[5] These "isms" only make sense against a common background that *assumes* our relation to the world and to knowledge is a problematic one. The skeptical worries of our philosophical tradition arise only when we misunderstand Dasein's existence as Being-in-the-world. Foundationalism only makes sense against the background of such skeptical worries. Once we begin on the right ontological foot, so to speak, neither position remains intelligible—except, we might concede, as a mistake stemming from an infatuation with the present-at-hand.

NOTES

1. Just as a reminder, the analysis of Dasein is an "existential analytic" because it is an analysis of that being whose essence is existence (hence the analysis is "existential").

2. For more on this issue, see my "The Case for Anti-Antirealism: Wittgenstein, Heidegger, and Aristotle on Language and Essence," *Philosophical Frontiers* 3.2, 2008.

3. For more on this issue, see my "The Case for Anti-Anti-realism," available at http://www.hartwick.edu/academics/majors-and-minors/arts-and-humanities/philos ophy-home/faculty/wisnewski/selected-published-and-in-progess-work. Some of this chapter draws from that article.

4. See Saul Kripke's *Naming and Necessity*, for example. Kripke criticizes Frege's view that terms refer to the world through their "sense" (*Sinn*). He argues, by contrast, that a term itself directly refers to what it signifies and is not mediated through a sense (or meaning). If Kripke's view is to contrast with the view he criticizes, then he needs to claim that terms themselves, independent of their meaning, can pick out objects in the world. This seems to suggest that a simple arrangement of letters, independent of any meaning a competent language user attaches to it (this is how Frege characterizes "sense" in a famous footnote), can refer.

5. See his *Sense and Sensibilia*.

SIX

Death and Authenticity

At the beginning of Division II of *Being and Time*, Heidegger is confronted with a potential problem with his analysis of Dasein as being-in-the-world, and as constituted by a care structure. What has been lacking, Heidegger claims, is a *complete* picture of Dasein *as a whole*. While we have managed to capture Dasein as it exists in its "there"—in a web of significance in which things are disclosed—we have not yet tried to conceptualize Dasein from beginning to end. We have seen Dasein, rather, only in particular slices of time. To round out this picture, we need to understand Dasein from beginning to end—from birth to death. We must understand Dasein as a whole, as more than simply an understanding that is constituted by care.

THE PROBLEM(S) WITH DEATH

The task of grasping Dasein as a whole is a problematic one. Indeed, Heidegger claims, "there are important reasons which seem to speak against the possibility of having [Dasein's being-a-whole] presented in the manner required" (*BT*, 279).

What exactly are these reasons? Why might it prove difficult to grasp Dasein's Being as a whole? Heidegger states the main problem explicitly in the following sentence: "the possibility [of Dasein] Being-a-whole is manifestly inconsistent with the ontological meaning of care, and care is that which forms the totality of Dasein's structural whole" (*BT*, 279). The reason care is antithetical to grasping the whole of Dasein is one we saw in chapter 4: care is the ahead-of-itself—it involves Dasein projecting itself into a future that does not yet exist. If Dasein is constituted by care, and is hence always ahead-of-itself (because it lives *into* the future), how could we ever see Dasein as a whole? The "ahead-of-itself," by definition, suggests that in any particular moment when considering Dasein there is still something left to say—some possibility that has not yet been captured—there is something, as Heidegger puts it, "still outstanding." "It is essential to the basic constitution of Dasein that there is *constantly something still to be settled*" (*BT*, 279).

If we imagine a Dasein that is, somehow, *complete*, Heidegger suggests, we have robbed the entity imagined of the Being of a Dasein. To imagine a Dasein without the ahead-of-itself is to imagine Dasein as *no longer itself*. "As long as Dasein *is* as an entity, it has never reached its 'wholeness'" (*BT*, 280).

The problem isn't that we lack the concepts, or the mental ability, to imagine Dasein as complete. The problem, rather, concerns the very Being of Dasein itself. On analogy with this problem, we might try to imagine a *square* circle: the instant we have transformed the square into a circle, it ceases to be a square. When we begin to make it circular again, it ceases to be a square. The Being of a square, to put it rather cryptically, disappears when it becomes a circle. Likewise, when we try to imagine Dasein as complete, we are imagining a Being that has a Being other than that of Dasein, as Dasein is constituted by a "Being-ahead-of-itself" that rules out the possibility of completeness.

Of course, the impossibility in question seems to lurk only when we are concerned with a particular (existentiell) Dasein: Dasein can never have itself as a whole (or so it would seem). This doesn't mean that *existentially* we're condemned to this same position. What is required is an existential interpretation of the notion of an "end," as well as that of "totality." Instead of giving up on the existential analytic, then, we must turn our attention to an ontological analysis of these things. Heidegger thinks that an existential conception of death will facilitate this.

Death robs a Dasein of its "there" (its *da*). In dying, we are not "there" to experience the transition from a Dasein to a Sein (Being) of a different sort. Dasein, in dying, becomes an object close to present-at-hand—an object that does not have the character of Dasein—a lifeless thing devoid of care. We don't experience a corpse as just an object; we experience it as an object that was once alive, but which no longer is. We experience it as "unalive" (*BT*, 282). More, we see an unalive Dasein that has been deprived of its world, that has been robbed of its Being-with and the solicitude constitutive of it. This deceased Dasein is one for which we still have concern—is one to which we still stand in a relation of solicitude. It is in our solicitude toward the no-longer-Dasein that loss is experienced.

The dead, as no longer there with us in a world of significance, do not experience the loss that the living do. What this suggests is that our experience of the death of others—the loss we feel—is in principle distinct from the phenomenological notion of death for the Dasein who has died. Witnessing the death of others does not provide us with access to dying itself. "The dying of Others is not something which we experience in a genuine sense; at most we are always just 'there alongside'" (*BT*, 282).

What this account suggests is that an attempt to capture death onto-logically that takes its point of departure from the way the living experi-ence the death of another Dasein will miss the point completely. This move is based on the notion that one Dasein can "stand in" for another. While this, in general, is an accurate picture of our Being-with, it cannot capture the ontology of death, if only because death is *unique* ontological-ly: "No one can take the Other's dying away from him" (*BT*, 284). Even self-sacrifice fails here, as we still die our own death. In this sense, dying defies the "substitutability" of one Dasein for another, despite the fact that "representability is not only quite possible but is even constitutive for our being with one another. Here [in representability] one Dasein can and must, within certain limits, '*be*' another Dasein" (*BT*, 283–84). Death marks the point where this is no longer possible—it constitutes one cru-cial limit for our ability to stand in for one another.

The account we need to give of death must be an ontological one—an account that captures the unique relationship between Dasein *qua* Being and death *qua* the end of that Being. To facilitate this, Heidegger intro-duces some terminological distinctions that might facilitate our keeping the ontological significance of death for Dasein distinct from the phenom-enon of death when it occurs in other entities. Heidegger stipulates that "perishing" will designate the cessation of life. This is not to be construed as the ontological role of death when we discuss Dasein's Being. Pheno-menologically understood, Dasein's death, in other words, is more than the cessation of life.

WHAT IS STILL OUT-STANDING

Heidegger considers the view that "to be still out-standing means that what belongs together is not yet altogether" (*BT*, 286). One must be care-ful, however, to avoid thinking of this in terms of the present-at-hand—in terms of something that is missing from a sum and will later be tacked on. For Heidegger, this would miss in its entirety Dasein's relation to death. Indeed, when in dying Dasein "acquires" that which is still out-standing (its death), there is no longer any Dasein there. To die is to cease to be Dasein.

Instead of viewing the still-outstanding in this manner, we should focus our attention once again on the unique sort of Being that Dasein is. As Heidegger (rather cryptically) puts is, "Dasein must, as itself, *become*— that is to say, *be*—what it is not yet" (*BT*, 287). We must here recall that Dasein's essence lies in existence, that what makes any individual Dasein who she is will be the product of a life lived out, not the product of an antecedent nature. What it means to be Dasein is precisely that the sort of life we live is, in some limited sense at least, up to us. This "becoming" is our essence. To grasp the significance of this in our analysis of death, we must focus our attention on this particular notion. What, exactly, is involved in the notion of becoming?

Heidegger employs the example of a ripening fruit to elucidate what he has in mind. When we speak of the unripe fruit, we do not imagine that ripeness is something that will merely be added on to the unripe fruit. Rather, our intuitive grasp of how an unripe fruit becomes a ripe fruit is that the fruit simply *becomes* ripe. In this respect, we don't view the eventual ripening of the fruit as something exterior to it: the fruit will become ripe; nothing needs to be added to the fruit. Dasein is in an analogous position in relation to its death. "The 'not-yet' has already been included in the very Being of the fruit, not as some random characteristic, but as something constitutive. Correspondingly, as long as any Dasein is, it too is already its 'not-yet'" (288). The fruit contains its eventual ripeness. This should not be read as an ontic claim about the fruit. We are discussing, rather, what sort of Being the unripe fruit has. The Being it has is such that it will eventually become ripe. Dasein stands in the same relation to its death, albeit with some crucial differences. Dasein does not reach its "ripeness" (maturity[1]) with death, as a fruit does with its ripeness. Indeed, as Heidegger explicitly points out, "Dasein may well have passed its maturity [*Reife*] before its end" (*BT*, 288; translation altered).

Heidegger distinguishes the notion of "ending" that characterizes Dasein's death from other sorts: the rain stopping, the road coming to an end, and so on. The important difference, Heidegger thinks, is that death is something with which Dasein always has a relation. "The 'ending' which we have in view when we speak of death, does not signify Dasein's Being-at-an-end, but a Being-towards-the-end" (*BT*, 289). This is exactly what we should expect of that Being for whom Being is an issue—that Being that is its possibilities. If Dasein were dead, there would be no Dasein: nothing would be disclosed to Dasein, no possibilities would be left to follow, no understanding would act as a "clearing" in the world. Because an exploration of Dasein's Being is existential (concerned with Dasein as that Being whose essence is existence), death cannot be ontologically construed as Dasein no longer Being Dasein. Such an analysis would fail to be an analysis of *Dasein*. To characterize death ontologically thus requires examining the role it plays for Dasein qua Dasein—for a Dasein that still is essentially Dasein, that still *exists*.

Heidegger helps himself to terminology, as usual, to distinguish the significance of death in regard to humans from the significance of death in regard to other entities who are not themselves Dasein. To this end, he distinguishes perishing, dying, and demise. "Perishing" is meant to pick out what happens to animals (the cessation of life). "Dying" is meant to designate the relation of Dasein to its death, while "demise" is meant to pick out what happens to Dasein when it dies (this is the human counterpart to "perishing").

The aim of these distinctions is to make terminologically manifest the difference between the death of an animal and the death of a human, as well as to demarcate Heidegger's own treatment of the phenomenon of death from other treatments of the subject as one finds them in psychology, biology, physiology, and so on. For Heidegger, all of these sorts of analysis fail to capture the ontological problem of death, as they all remain on the ontical level of analysis (that is, they presuppose that Dasein's kind of Being is adequately captured by the present-at-hand). Heidegger's task, as he sees it, is to provide an ontological account of death as that which provides Dasein's life with boundaries on both sides (and hence as that which can allow us to see Dasein as a whole), without falling prey to the popular conceptions of death that we employ in everyday social reality.

The analysis of death to be offered must coincide with those things we have already discussed in relation to Dasein's Being—namely, existentiality (projection), facticity (thrownness), and Being-fallen (fallenness). The view of death as "something still outstanding" is a misleading, if not outright false, conception of the role death plays in Dasein's existence. The problem with this view is that it makes death yet another thing present-at-hand that stands in a relation to Dasein, again construed as present-at-hand. For Heidegger, "death is something that stands before us—something impending" (*BT*, 294).

The character of the impending, of course, is not unique to Dasein. As Heidegger is quick to remind us, all of those things that make up the field of expectations in which we live are in fact impending, though death is not the same as any of them. What is unique about death, it turns out, is that it is Dasein's uttermost, ownmost nonrelational possibility (*BT*, 294). Death is *not* nonrelational in the sense that it stands apart from Dasein (as we've seen, Dasein is partially constituted by its relation to death). Rather, death is nonrelational precisely because it is the one thing that every Dasein must do *on its own*. We can characterize, in summary form, those things that make death the unique ontological feature of Dasein that it is.

1. Death is not to be outstripped: death is something that cannot be avoided. There is no cheating death.
2. Death is nonrelational: Dasein must die alone. One cannot "step in" for another Dasein to die his death for him. (Note: sacrificing oneself for another Dasein amounts to dying alone in his place, not dying his death—something only he can do.)
3. Death is impending, but impending as one's ownmost possibility. Death is possible at any moment (and must be), making death the only possibility that is a necessity.

Death is thus constitutive of Dasein's very Being. It is not merely some-thing we occasionally face and from which we might ultimately escape. "On the contrary, if Dasein exists, it has already been thrown into this possibility" (*BT*, 295). This does not mean, of course, that we have any theoretical knowledge of death. Indeed, for the most part we flee from our inevitable impossibility, falling back into the "they" world. It is through anxiety, however, that we can come to recognize this peculiar feature of our Being—namely, that at some point we will *no longer be.*

Robert Pogue Harrison has offered an interesting objection to the claim that death is nonrelational in Heidegger's sense. Harrison claims, rather, that death is *necessarily* linked to other Dasein. As Harrison puts it, in his typically lyrical way, "the idea of death must proceed from the dead. Indeed, it must proceed from the corpse" (92). This, Harrison con-tends, is thus the source of a serious error on Heidegger's part.

> Heidegger makes a serious blunder in *Being and Time* when he states that the corpse is a mere "thing" which, in its presence-at-hand, gives Dasein no access to its own death as such (pp. 281–2). A corpse is the site of something that has disappeared, that has forsaken the sphere of presence, that has passed from the body into . . . what? (92)

The significance of this is greater than we might initially think. To see the issue Harrison is raising here, I'll quote more fully the critique Harrison offers.

> Before it became the ultimate, unrepresentable possibility of my own impossibility of being—indeed, before it became exclusively *mine*—death wore the mask of the dead. Heidegger insists that Dasein cannot relate to its own death by way of the death of others (he calls this "non-relational"), yet this is as philosophically inadequate as his reduction of the corpse to mere presence-at-hand. On this score we should listen rather to Freud . . . only the shock of the loved one's death persuades us—against our deeper instinctual convictions—that we will or even *can* die. . . . All of which confirms that it is essentially the death of others—institutionalized and ritualized in funerals, burial, lamentation practices, and protocols of commemoration—which provokes the erup-tion of being-toward-death in human existence. (93–94)

Harrison may well be right in these passages—that is, he may be right about how we come to recognize mortality. But he's got Heidegger wrong—or at least his criticism of Heidegger is misplaced. It is no "blunder" to say that death is nonrelational. In fact, death being nonrela-tional is entirely compatible with the claim that we learn about death through the dead. Yes, Heidegger might respond to Harrison, we learn of death through the loss of those we love—but the thing we learn *about* is fundamentally nonrelational. We learn *from the dead* that there is at least one thing regarding which we are fundamentally alone—namely, our own death. We learn of the isolation of our death through an encounter with the dead.[2]

BEING-TOWARD-DEATH AND THE EVERYDAYNESS OF DASEIN

If death, as grounded in care, is a part of Dasein's Being, it must also be apparent in everyday, inauthentic Dasein. As we should at this point expect, the "they" swallows the phenomenon of death, making it palatable and digestible to everyday Dasein.

> In the publicness with which we are with one another in our everyday manner, death is "known" as a mishap which is constantly occuring — as a "case of death." Someone or other "dies," be he neighbor or stranger. People who are no acquaintances of ours are "dying" daily and hourly. "Death" is encountered as a well-known event occurring within the world. As such it remains in the inconspicuousness characteristic of what is encountered in an everyday fashion. The "they" has already secured an interpretation for this event. It talks of it in a "fugitive" manner, either expressly or else in a way which is mostly inhibited, as if to say, "one of these days one will die too, in the end; but right now it has nothing to do with us."
>
> The analysis of the phrase "one dies" reveals unambiguously the kind of Being which belongs to everyday Being-towards-death. In such a way of talking, death is understood as an indefinite something which, above all, must duly arrive from somewhere or other. . . . "Dying" is leveled off to an occurrence which reaches Dasein, to be sure, but belongs to nobody in particular. (*BT*, 296–97)

Once again, we see that the average understanding of something levels it down to a phenomenon we can all easily understand and deal with. The most frightening aspect of human existence — that it ends, irreparably — is understood by the anonymous "they" in a way that dumbs down death. Indeed, "death" is understood as removed from us — as something that occurs always outside of us, in the distance. As such, the average understanding of death effectively hides its very nature (as well as our own) from us. "'Dying' is levelled off to an occurrence which reaches Dasein, to be sure, but belongs to nobody in particular. . . . Dying, which is essentially mine in such a way that no one can be my representative, is perverted into an event of public occurrence which the 'they' encounters" (*BT*, 297). To put the tranquilizing effect of the "they" succinctly: "The 'they' does not permit us the courage for anxiety in the face of death" (*BT*, 298). This amounts to fleeing from death, and hence to a fleeing in the face of our own Being.

According to Heidegger, we must get past this everyday manner of understanding death. To recognize it existentially is to recognize that death is part and parcel of Dasein's Being. "Factically one's own Dasein is always dying already; that is to say, it is in a Being-towards-its-end" (*BT*, 298).

Even though our everyday understanding of death is one that covers up part of its essential nature (for example, its nonrelational, not-to-be-outstripped character), the "they" nonetheless understands particular features of this phenomenon, albeit in a perfunctory manner.

> Everydayness concedes something like a certainty of death. Nobody doubts that one dies. . . . [But] everydayness confines itself to conceding the "certainty" of death in this ambiguous manner just in order to weaken that certainty by covering up dying still more and to alleviate its thrownness into death. (*BT*, 299–300)

The sort of certainty the "they" maintains, Heidegger suggests, might be seen as an empirical certainty (we have seen Dasein die again and again). But this empirical certainty passes over the role that death plays in Dasein's ontology. Indeed, the average understanding of death acknowledges that death will happen but refuses to see it as possible in any particular moment. "The 'they' covers up what is peculiar in death's certainty—that it is possible at any moment. Along with the certainty of death goes the indefiniteness of its 'when'" (*BT*, 302).

Given this character of Dasein in everydayness, Heidegger is led to the obvious question: Is it possible for Dasein to grasp its end (its death) in a way that is not inauthentic? That is, can we have an authentic understanding of death (*BT*, 304)? As part of our ontology, Heidegger acknowledges that such an understanding of death must be possible. He now turns his attention to the conditions of its possibility.

AUTHENTICITY AND DEATH

By the time a reader reaches the end of the section on death in Division II of *Being and Time*, the prospects for authenticity seem dim indeed. Heidegger acknowledges this in a rhetorical question: "Is it not a fanciful undertaking, to project the existential possibility of so questionable an existentiell potentiality-for-Being?" (*BT*, 304). That is, given Dasein's state of fallenness, how is it even *existentially possible* for a particular Dasein to become authentic?

To begin to see how an authentic understanding of death might be possible, we must first ensure that we understand our relation to death as a Being toward a possibility—a possibility that is "a distinctive possibility of Dasein itself" (*BT*, 305). It is a distinctive possibility, as Heidegger goes on to explain, precisely because we don't comport ourselves toward this possibility as we do toward those things we encounter ready-to-hand in-the-world. Death is not something we strive to actualize. The key to this possibility is that, in a certain sense, it can never be actualized by a

Dasein. If a Dasein brings about his own death, he is no longer Dasein. We must recognize death, Heidegger thinks, as a sort of pure possibility inherent in being the sorts of beings that we are.

Possibilities, by and large, can be expected by a Dasein. If one is in college, it is possible to graduate. One "expects" to graduate while existing in this possibility. Heidegger wants to distinguish our relation to death from this sort of expecting. He chooses the word *anticipation* to draw this distinction. The reason for making this distinction lies in the unique character of death: we're not constantly expecting its approach—anxiously awaiting it as we do, say, a tax return or upcoming vacation time. The character of death is wholly removed from this sort of expectation.

> The more unveiledly this possibility [death] gets understood, the more purely does the understanding penetrate into it as the possibility of the impossibility of any existence at all. Death, as possibility, gives Dasein nothing to be "actualized," nothing which Dasein, as actual, could itself be. It is the possibility of the impossibility of comporting oneself to anything, of every way of existing. (*BT*, 307)

Death, then, is essential to Dasein *owning itself*—that is, to being *authentic*, and hence to separating in some way from the "they."

> The "they" has always kept Dasein from taking hold of these possibilities of Being. The "they" even hides the manner in which it has tacitly relieved Dasein of the burden of explicitly *choosing* these possibilities. It remains indefinite who has "really" done the choosing. So Dasein makes no choices, gets carried along by the nobody, and thus ensnares itself in inauthenticity. (*BT*, 312)

Recall that an "existentiell" possibility is here the possibility of a particular Dasein. The question Heidegger is raising is how any *individual* Dasein can free itself from lostness in the "they" and come into an authentic existence. If we are constituted, at least for the most part, by our social understanding of things, how are we to free ourselves from this understanding? Is it even possible?

The issue here is in fact quite complex. As Heidegger has noted on numerous occasions, one cannot have authenticity without also having inauthenticity. This suggests that, in a certain respect, *there is no* getting beyond the inauthentic. We are always and already the "nobody"—the Self that we are living out in particular social roles made available and foisted upon us by our culture. The challenge—and it is a significant one—is to see how we can break away from this immersion in pregiven roles—roles that we didn't choose—and somehow find a Self that is in some significant way our own.

The projection of an answer to this question is found in the notion of the "call of conscience." Importantly, Heidegger *does not* claim that we get beyond the social understanding of things (and of our own existence) that is constitutive of average, everyday, inauthentic Dasein.

> When Dasein thus brings itself back from the "they", the they-self is modified in an existentiell manner so that it becomes *authentic* Being-one's-Self. . . . In choosing to make this choice, Dasein makes possible, first and foremost, its authentic potentiality-for-Being. (*BT*, 313)

So authenticity does not require an *elimination* of the they-self. Rather, it requires a *modification*, on the part of a particular Dasein, of this average, everyday, inauthentic understanding that has so far constituted it. Authenticity *is not* a casting off of the "they" and could never be such a thing. The reason for this is quite plain: Dasein *is inauthentic fundamentally, and inauthenticity actually makes authenticity possible.* (More on this below.)

To pull one's Self free from the "they" requires "finding one's self" (as Heidegger puts it). This involves seeing the possibility that "one" can be an "I"—that there is something *beyond* the "they." This is made possible by the "call of conscience." Dasein must be prepared to hear "the call," and in this respect must also "want to have a conscience." As with other terms Heidegger employs, however, the meaning of such claims isn't to be understood with reference to the way we might normally understand terms like *conscience*. As usual, we should understand Heidegger here as taking very normal ways of speaking and revealing what lies beneath them. It is common for persons to speak of "finding themselves" and to speak of something called "conscience." As with other things Heidegger has subjected to analysis, we should understand him here as revealing that normal, inauthentic notions actually cover some deep truths about Dasein. The task of a phenomenological analysis is to *uncover*—to allow the thing to reveal itself as it is in itself. Allowing this to happen is precisely what Heidegger has in mind when he grabs hold of particular everyday locutions: fallen, "one," conscience, and so on.

CONSCIENCE AND GUILT

Conscience plays an interesting and pivotal role in *Being and Time*. Heidegger begins, as all phenomenologists should, with the phenomenon: we all experience what we sometimes call "the voice of conscience." Heidegger contends this "voice" must be understood as "within the range of those existential phenomena which constitute the *Being of the 'there'* as disclosedness" (*BT*, 315). In other words, conscience does disclose something *about us*, though what it discloses, Heidegger thinks, has been covered over by the traditions in which we find ourselves. We must start with everyday Dasein, despite the fact that this will miss the essence of the thing sought. Nevertheless, "whenever we see something wrongly, some injunction as to the primordial 'idea' of the phenomenon is revealed along with it" (*BT*, 326).

The common understanding of conscience is that it pronounces guilt. This is correct, Heidegger thinks, although we typically misunderstand the significance of the pronouncement. For the "they," guilt is understood as a debt—as something that one owes to another. Heidegger, however, thinks that guilt in fact captures something much more basic—it in effect represents Dasein's ontological condition. Before exploring this in more detail, we'll need to explore the idea that conscience "calls" us to recognize this guilt.

Conscience discloses, first of all, that Dasein has the capacity to *listen*. As we would expect given our analysis so far, *what* we hear is, by and large, inauthentic. As Heidegger puts this point, "losing itself in the publicness and the idle talk of the 'they', it fails to hear [*überhört*] its own Self in listening to the they-self" (*BT*, 315). What most interests Heidegger, however, is an *alternative* form of "hearing the call" of conscience. Heidegger emphasizes *hearing* in a way that few philosophers do. The dominant metaphors regarding acquiring knowledge tend to be ocular (the figure of Socrates, hearing his *daimon*, is a notable exception). In the context of the conscience, Heidegger abandons sight for audition. We are lost in the "they" primarily because we do not *listen* to the call of conscience—because the chatter of the "they" covers up what we might hear: namely, that we are more than we are pretending to be.

Heidegger claims that "that which, by calling in this manner, gives us to understand, is the conscience" (*BT*, 316). So conscience gives us something to understand—namely, *conscience itself*. While this initially sounds rather unelucidating, Heidegger in fact wants us to examine *the voice of conscience itself*. Where does this call come from? What does it "say"?

Ultimately, the call of conscience provides Dasein with the opportunity to see itself. It is through the call of conscience that we get a glimpse into our own basic ontology: we recognize ourselves as capable of authenticity and inauthenticity. The call of conscience, Heidegger contends, pronounces us "guilty." The *caller*, Heidegger further contends, is *Dasein itself*.

What does it mean to call Dasein "guilty"? How are we to understand Heidegger's claim that Dasein *calls itself*? As everyone will by now expect, the answer to these questions can't simply be read off of the normal meaning of the terms Heidegger employs. These terms, rather, capture the everyday notions, the ontological foundations of which Heidegger aims to uncover. In Heidegger's view, "guilt," as it is commonly understood, involves a *lack*. Interestingly, Heidegger thinks this is correct, though the type of lack has been misinterpreted by inauthentic Dasein. Dasein's Being involves a lack *essentially*. Inauthentic Dasein understands this lack as a present-at-hand *thing*—one owes a debt to society, or an amount of money, or has moral "debts" incurred through immoral actions. According to Heidegger, Dasein's guilt is much more basic—indeed, it is a part of Dasein's very *Being*. This leads him to a classic Heideggerian move: our notion of indebtedness is based on Dasein's Being-guilty, and not the reverse of this. (In other words, Dasein is guilty *prior to* owing anything; Dasein's ontological guilt makes possible individual instances of ontic guilt.)

What is this ontological lack that characterizes Dasein's Being? Put bluntly, to be Dasein is to have an existence based essentially on what one is *not*. Dasein is essentially *un*-self-sufficient. As thrown, we find ourselves immersed in projects (and *constituted* by these projects) that we did not and that we *cannot* choose. Although we ourselves are the *basis* of this lack (because we exist), we can't get back behind this "nullity" (or "not-ness" (*Nichtheit*)—this lack that is constitutive of the kinds of beings we are). We want to be our own foundations—to build ourselves from the ground up, but this would mean becoming beings fundamentally unlike the beings that we are. Being the basis of a "not"—being essentially constituted by "not-ness"—"means never having power over one's ownmost Being from the ground up" (*BT*, 330).

As projection, Dasein is *also* constituted by a nullity (by a negation or not-ness). As you'll recall, every choice we make in living out our possibilities closes off other possibilities. This means that in *simply choosing* to act, Dasein is, essentially, *not* some of the possibilities that currently constitute it. Nullity, in other words, pervades every choice—Dasein "always stands in one possibility or another: it constantly is *not* other possibilities, and it has waived these in its existentiell projection" (*BT*, 331). Finally, as fallen into inauthenticity, Dasein is what it *is not*. Being inauthentic means, essentially, that Dasein is not itself, and hence, once again, we see negation at the very core of Dasein's Being.

This provides us with a better sense of what the pronouncement of guilt involves. When Dasein hears the call of conscience, Dasein is brought face-to-face with its nullity—with all the ways it is not itself and all the ways in which it cannot be so.

This still leaves the question of *who* does the calling. Heidegger is explicit in his response: "In conscience Dasein calls itself" (*BT*, 320). The call is "against our expectations and even against our will. On the other hand, the call undoubtedly does not come from someone else who is with me in the world. The call comes *from me* and yet *from beyond* me" (*BT*, 320). It is easy to read these remarks as reinstating a kind of inner dualism in Dasein: the "authentic" self calls to the "inauthentic" self to be what it is. Heidegger even says, explicitly, that "the caller is Dasein in its uncanniness" (*BT*, 321)—that is, the caller is Dasein recognizing that it does not quite fit into the world of the "they." "The caller is unfamiliar to the everyday they-self; it is something like an *alien* voice" (*BT*, 321).

It's easy to get carried away with this kind of language. We might think of one "part" of Dasein calling to another "part." To see how deeply implausible this reading is, we need only remember that Dasein does not have parts in any present-at-hand sense. Dasein *is its possibilities.* Moreover, as Heidegger repeatedly insists, Dasein is a *unitary phenomenon,* albeit one that can be explored with different emphases. I thus want to suggest a deflationary reading of the call of conscience, though one that I think is more plausible than any nondeflationary one: the call merely signifies one recognizing oneself by managing to listen to something other than the chatter of the "they" — that is, by trying to understand things in a way that hasn't automatically been leveled off. The call, after all, is "silent," as Heidegger says (*BT*, 322).

It is this *quiet* that allows Dasein to catch a glimpse of itself. Moreover, as Heidegger argues, this is a constant possibility for Dasein, albeit one we ignore most of the time and for the most part. A certain stillness, however, sometimes settles over us, and in this stillness we call into question the way we are currently living our lives — the significance of what we have chosen, its potential emptiness, and the myriad ways we have been prodded into the life we now live. Even if one does not care for Heidegger's language, seeing in it a danger of inner dualism, he has certainly diagnosed an experience that many of us have had: the uncanny recognition, thrust upon us suddenly, that our lives might just be meaningless and our decisions not our own.

Obviously, this kind of experience is *not* the same as the one we refer to in talking about "conscience" in everyday life. Heidegger recognizes this (in section 59 of *Being and Time*). His analysis of conscience does *not* in fact map nicely onto the everyday conception of conscience. Initially, this must seem like a rather significant problem, as Heidegger insists that he must be able to make sense of everyday conceptions of phenomena if his own analysis is to have any grounding at all. Nevertheless, Heidegger asks, "*must* the ontological Interpretation agree with ordinary interpretation at all? Should not the latter be, in principle, ontologically suspect?" (*BT*, 335).

In response to this question, Heidegger reaffirms his methodological principle: while an analysis of some particular phenomenon (death, conscience, observation) need not be *identical* to our normal understanding of that phenomenon, it better be able to account for said phenomenon. As Heidegger puts this point:

> On the one hand, the everyday way of interpreting conscience cannot be accepted as the final criterion for the "Objectivity" of an ontological analysis. On the other hand, such an analysis has no right to disregard the everyday understanding of conscience to pass over the anthropological, psychological, and theological theories of conscience which have been based upon it. *If* existential analysis has laid bare the phenomenon of conscience in its ontological roots, then precisely in terms of this analysis the ordinary interpretations must become intelligible. (*BT*, 336)

Heidegger's insistence here is instructive. We can be assured that our phenomenological analysis is correct only if it can accommodate, and make sense of, the everyday understanding of things. The underlying assumption that Heidegger is making here is that the average conception of things is not entirely ungrounded. It, too, reveals things, though only in a partial and incomplete way. The task of the phenomenologist is to understand *what* everyday interpretation captures, and then to uncover the rest of the phenomenon that has been leveled-down by the "they." As Heidegger insists, "even the ordinary experience of conscience must somehow—pre-ontologically—reach this phenomenon" (*BT*, 348). Dasein is indeed in the truth.

Curiously, this insistence is one that Heidegger shares with Wittgenstein, J. L. Austin, G. E. Moore, and to a lesser degree and in a more tenuous way, Donald Davidson (among others!). The mistake many philosophers have made is to simply reject the common conception of a thing in favor of what the philosopher's argument and analysis reveals. Thus we're familiar with Plato's jettisoning of the empirical world in favor of the realm of forms; or with Hegel's infamous claim that, if his work conflicted with experience, then so much the worse for experience. Perhaps strangely, there is a kind of trust in our perceptual capacities—a trust that Heidegger inherits from Aristotle on the one hand and Husserl on the other. Although our common understanding may mislead us, it is nevertheless in the path through our common understanding that we can uncover ontological truths.

Heidegger contends that the notion of a "bad conscience" (a "guilty conscience") fails to capture the phenomenon of conscience in its fundamental aspects. The everyday interpretation involves what Heidegger calls a "reckoning up"—essentially an economic understanding of guilt and absolution, where one stands with a balance of guilt that is to be "paid off" through good deeds or forgiveness. This, Heidegger contends, makes guilt into a kind of "lack" that fails to understand it in its positivity.

The everyday notion of conscience interprets it as something that *gives concrete possibilities to us*. As Heidegger claims, this is "a way of interpreting which forces Dasein's existence to be subsumed under the idea of a business procedure that can be regulated" (*BT*, 340). This explains, in a certain respect, why much traditional ethics goes wrong: we want rules to control our behavior, to guarantee certain kinds of outcomes, but this is utterly impossible adequately to complete.[3]

By contrast, Heidegger's account emphasizes that nullity (not-ness) pervades Dasein's Being. "Guilt" thus captures, ontologically, Dasein as thrown projected Being-toward-death.

WANTING TO HAVE A CONSCIENCE

We have noted that authenticity and inauthenticity are both basic modes of Dasein's Being-in-the-world. In attempting to explain how authenticity might be possible in the face of inevitable fallenness into the "they," Heidegger has explored a particular experience of Dasein: namely, when we experience ourselves as *more than* what the "they" says we are. Guilt and conscience, construed ontologically, capture core elements of this experience. We can recognize our not-ness (guilt) through the "call of conscience"—through those moments when we are not absorbed in the idle chatter of the "they." Those Dasein who have resolved to be authentic, Heidegger contends, are not *immune* to fallenness—a state of affairs that would involve ceasing to be Dasein. Rather, Heidegger contends, fallen Dasein, once it has seen what it is (and seen the possibility of authenticity) *wants* to have a conscience. That is, Dasein wants to have experiences in which it recognizes its own ontological predicament.

"Wanting to have a conscience," Heidegger points out, is yet another way in which Dasein is disclosed to itself (*BT*, 342). As such, we can expect a particular state-of-mind, understanding, and discourse to correspond to this particular mode of Dasein's being "there." In this section, we'll aim to spell this out precisely, and to thereby get a sense of what sort of life hearing the call might lead to.

One's mood in hearing the call of conscience is one we have seen before: it is anxiety. One's understanding of things is constituted by the uncanniness that we've also already discussed. This means that "wanting-to-have-a-conscience becomes a readiness for anxiety" (*BT*, 342). The *call itself* is the kind of discourse that characterizes Dasein's Being-there. This mode of discourse, however, also has an articulated mode, in Heidegger's view. This mode he calls "reticence" (*BT*, 342). It is the remaining silent of the Dasein who has heard the call of conscience—a silence that involves *having something to say* but not saying it. Once one has seen one's own being, there is a recognition that any articulation that follows might well *falsify* what one has heard in the call. The language we normally speak to one another is the language of the "they," and it is something that perhaps intrinsically levels-down our meanings to those that are regarded as adequate by average understanding. Thus, in a significant sense, to speak of hearing the call is *to stop listening*. It is to recast the uniqueness of the call into the language of the "they." It is for this reason that Heidegger remarks that "the call comes from the soundlessness of uncanniness" (*BT*, 343).

This perhaps enables us to move away from some of the worries we initially had about a kind of dualism present in Heidegger. If the call in fact comes from *the silence of uncanniness*, and it is Dasein calling to itself, we would be wrong to think of the call as from some *other part* of a Dasein. In fact, we would do better to understand the call as a *listening*.

To hear the call is to listen to oneself—it need not be understood as splitting oneself into two parts, one of which calls to the other. Rather, we can understand the call as that which occurs when the chitchat of the everyday has died away and one listens to the uncanniness of one's thrownness. To listen, here, might mean simply to *pay attention* to this thrownness, rather than to immediately flee back into the "they."

So the "silence" of the call is to be understood *not* as the silent calling of a caller, on the one hand, and the reticence of a listening Dasein, on the other. This would be to bifurcate Dasein—to make it essentially a present-at-hand structure with parts that must be put back together. In revealing the mood of Dasein as uncanniness and anxiety, Heidegger also reveals that the call doesn't *come from anywhere*. It is there, all along, with us. To hear the call authentically is to pay attention to what one is and to be reticent about trying to articulate this in the language of the everyday. This "silent discourse" "takes the words away from the common-sense idle talk of the 'they'" (*BT*, 343).

Heidegger characterizes the state of a Dasein who hears the call authentically as shown in table 6.1. Collectively, Heidegger refers to a Dasein in this state as "resolute" (*BT*, 343). This, as should be obvious to us at this point, "is a distinctive mode of Dasein's disclosedness" (*BT*, 343)—a distinctive way in which things are revealed to us. Heidegger claims that "in resoluteness we have now arrived at that truth of Dasein which is most primordial because it is *authentic*" (*BT*, 343). This should give all of us pause. In this passage, we're faced once again with a difficult problem: Why is the authentic truth of Dasein the most primordial? Isn't Dasein as it is inauthentically just as important—perhaps even *more* important—to understanding the truth of Dasein? Consider: "Whenever a 'there' is disclosed, its whole Being-in-the-world—that is it say, the world, Being-in, and the Self which, as an 'I am', this entity is—is disclosed with equal primordiality" (*BT*, 344). As this passage reminds us, *all* manners of Being reveal Dasein. How, then, can Dasein's truth be revealed *most primordially* by authenticity? In what respect can this be "most primordial" if authenticity and inauthenticity are equiprimordial (equally basic)?

One suggestion runs as follows. Dasein is disclosed *in its Being* when it is authentically hearing the call. In this state, Dasein is such that it discloses what it is to itself in as fundamental a way as possible. Hence, the truth of this mode of being is "most primordial."

Table 6.1.   Authentically Hearing the Call

State-of-Mind	Anxiety
Understanding	Projection upon Being-Guilty
Discourse	Reticent silence

As I hope is clear, this cannot be what Heide... ...
were what Heidegger had in mind, it would follow...
access to Dasein through authenticity than through inauth...
however, seems to conflict with the claim that what Dasein is, ...
mostly (or "proximally and for the most part"), is the "they." Obvio...
we see Dasein as inauthentic in all states other than resoluteness. Hence,
it would seem peculiar to say that Dasein's truth is *more* revealed in
resoluteness, since Dasein is *equiprimordially inauthentic*.

There are a couple other possibilities here: (1) Heidegger is talking
about an individual Dasein's awareness of itself. In such a case, *the individual Dasein* sees itself as it is in a way that is not possible in that
Dasein's normal absorption in the "they." In other words, Heidegger is
not making a claim about what reveals Dasein's ontology most primordially to *someone investigating Dasein*. His claim, rather, is about how a
Dasein can see itself in its own Being. While this reading has the advantage of being plausible, it does not seem to mesh with the sentence already quoted: "in resoluteness we have now arrived at that truth of
Dasein which is most primordial because it is *authentic*" (*BT*, 343). The
"we" here is obviously those Dasein engaged in the existential analysis
that Heidegger is presenting. This leads us to a second possibility: (2)
This truth is most primordial because, in seeing ourselves in authentically answering the call, we are able *also* to see what we are for the most
part—namely, fallen, inauthentic Dasein. On this reading of the passage,
this truth is most primordial because it *reveals* the equiprimordiality of
authenticity and inauthenticity to those investigating Dasein's Being. We
recognize, in one particular instance, that Dasein *is both*, and that it can be
either authentic or inauthentic existentially. In other words, this particular state is most primordial only because it is the most complete picture of
Dasein's being that we have yet been able to see.

Let's grant that what we claimed above was correct: we *can* in fact see
Dasein at its most complete in its authenticity. But there's more to it than
this, as we will see. One of the things that we will come to see in Dasein's
authentic moment is *Dasein as a whole*, and beneath this whole—or, better,
pervading every aspect of this whole—we can get temporality into focus.
It is in this respect that the truth of Dasein is revealed in its most primordial sense. As Heidegger goes on to say, we "get a conception of the
entire phenomenal content of Dasein's basic existential constitution in the
ultimate foundations of its own ontological intelligibility" (*BT*, 351). This
foundation is temporality, and it is revealed most thoroughly in resoluteness.[4]

Dasein's resoluteness affects absolutely every aspect of Dasein's Being.
As Heidegger notes, resolute Dasein understands "both the way in which
the 'world' is discovered . . . and the way in which the Dasein-with of
Others is disclosed" in a modified way (*BT*, 344). We should thus not

, Dasein into a new world, nor allow-
stence. Authenticity accomplishes nei-
soluteness brings the Self right into its
side what is ready-to-hand, and pushes it
ers" (*BT*, 344).

y might involve becoming someone like Ras-
y's *Crime and Punishment*) seems here to be
s on to claim some astounding things about the
ers when it is resolute.

Dasein. ess towards itself is what makes it possible to let the Others wh. with it "be" in their ownmost potentiality-for-Being, and to co-disclose this potentiality in the solicitude which leaps forth and liberates. When Dasein is resolute, it can become the "conscience" of Others. Only by authentically Being-their-selves in resoluteness can people authentically be with one another—not by ambiguous and jealous stipulations and talkative fraternizing in the "they" and in what "they" want to undertake. (*BT*, 344–45)

Here, perhaps as nowhere else, Heidegger gives us some hints about what kind of life, and what kind of Being-with-Others, the authentic life might involve. Unfortunately, Heidegger doesn't develop this suggestion.[5]

ANTICIPATORY RESOLUTENESS

Heidegger has demonstrated that authenticity is an *existential* possibility for Dasein. This demonstration, however, is not sufficient to reveal that authenticity is more than a *bare* possibility for Dasein—one that perhaps no individual Dasein has every actually attained. To capture this point in Heidegger's succinct jargon, we might say that Heidegger has revealed that authenticity is an existential possibility, but not an existentiell possibility. It is now time, however, to do just that.

Resoluteness, Heidegger reminds us, has been characterized "as a way of reticently projecting oneself upon one's ownmost Being-guilty, and exacting anxiety on oneself" (*BT*, 353). As Heidegger insists, our guilt is essentially connected with our thrownness. Because thrownness is constitutive of Being-in-the-world, we must regard guilt as an essential existential structure. "Dasein is essentially guilty" (*BT*, 353). In our resoluteness, we actually *see* our guilt—we become *transparent* to ourselves.

The issue, of course, is how this kind of transparent self-recognition is possible, not in the existential sense (that is, not in terms of Dasein's existential structures), but rather in terms of a particular acting Dasein. In resoluteness, Heidegger contends, we recognize our guilt, the nullity that constitutes us, and our inevitably impending death. Hence, the anticipation of our impending death is co-constitutive of resoluteness: "Resoluteness does not just 'have' a connection with anticipation, as with something other than itself. *It harbors in itself authentic Being-towards-death, as a possible existentiell modality of its own authenticity"* (*BT*, 352).

Importantly, Heidegger does not here claim that Dasein *as authentic*, is always authentic Being-toward-death. Rather, the claim is that the existentiell possibility of this is one that a resolute Dasein always has. This is an important point, I think, in understanding authenticity generally. As we will see, to be authentic might not mean to *constantly recognize* death. In fact, it might well mean that we do not recognize it in many instances. We will return to this issue below.

Our response to guilt is the crucial factor in authenticity, as we now see, and this response, when authentic, involves the existentiell possibility of anticipation as a mode of one's resoluteness. Being-guilty, in Heidegger's view, constitutes "the *existentiell* possibility of *being* authentically or inauthentically guilty" (*BT*, 353). The move from existential to existentiell is absolutely crucial. Being-guilty provides us with something to grab on to—indeed, something that must be taken hold of either authentically or inauthentically. When we are resolute, we understand ourselves *in* our guilt. When we are inauthentic, we do not.

Of course, this hardly demonstrates existentiell possibility in any robust sense. It only shows that there is a feature of our Being that can be taken hold of in myriad ways. We might well say the same thing about other parts of Dasein's existential constitution. How then do we get from the existential to the existentiell? Why should we even think of authenticity as more than an existential structure? (That is, why think a particular Dasein can actually be authentic?)

The phenomenological answer is plain: there must be some kind of experience in average everydayness from which we take a clue. If it is possible to answer the question of Being by taking hold of one's thrownness—by anticipating death and resolving to recognize the nullity of one's Being (in short, to recognize one's own ontology and act in a way that represents this recognition)—if this is a possibility we can recognize at the level of average everydayness, then there is something to the notion of the authentic. Importantly, this does not entail that we know what the authentic actually is. Far from it. Indeed, the fact that there is (or might be) some everyday conception of authenticity *reveals* that we most likely do not understand it, that understanding it requires that we uncover the more primordial basis inauthenticity has covered up.

So is there some reason to think that average everydayness has, in itself, some conception of authenticity? I think there is. For one, we are currently having a conversation about authenticity (insofar as reading involves a conversation between writer and reader). To have such a conversation requires that, minimally, we share a basic understanding—one that is inadequate, to be sure—of the concepts we're employing. So there *is* some notion of authenticity that we're playing with. A second piece of evidence is found in normal conversations about Heidegger, both in classrooms and elsewhere. The notion of authenticity seems to capture the imagination of readers of *Being and Time* from the start. It has also captured the imagination of others for a rather long time: Kierkegaard and Sartre, with perhaps equal passion, have allowed us to explore authenticity in detail. A condition for the possibility of this sort of reflection and conversation is that there is some (undoubtedly inauthentic) conception of authenticity that we have in our possession.

Of course, in one respect, this doesn't show as much as it needs to. After all, one might suggest that we've only demonstrated that authenticity, as something that we talk about, is an existential possibility. We haven't yet demonstrated that it's a possibility *for me*. This raises a rather more particular question: Do we have a notion of authenticity as an existentiell possibility? In one respect, I think the answer is obvious. We *do* have a notion of individuality—and, more importantly, the notion of an individual existence. We speak regularly of being a "true" individual. Also obviously, we have no idea what we're talking about: we view individuality as granted by product consumption or by filling roles that are socially given. One is a "rebel" by adopting socially constituted identities: gay, goth, radical intellectual, and so on. These examples show, I think, that the notion of authenticity has some grounding in the self-understanding of (at least Western) Dasein. Heidegger is thus not merely inventing a concept. He is, rather, attempting to describe the ontological foundations of this concept.

THE RELATIONSHIP BETWEEN AUTHENTICITY AND INAUTHENTICITY

Inauthenticity Depends on Authenticity

Heidegger claims that "inauthenticity is based on the possibility of authenticity" (*BT*, 303).[6] Admittedly, the significance of this claim is not entirely clear. There are several problems here that need to be addressed to understand what the exact relation between the authentic and the inauthentic is meant to be. The claim that one thing (the inauthentic) is based on the possibility of another (the authentic) might be one of several different kinds of claims. To grapple with the status of this claim is important, as it grounds much of what Heidegger is attempting to do in the remainder of *Being and Time*. Below are several ways of interpreting Heidegger's remark.

1. Semantic: one could not determine the meaning of "inauthentic" unless one had a contrast term in virtue of which one could understand the idea of the "authentic." Much as *blue* has meaning only in relation to other color terms, so too can *inauthentic* be understood

only in terms of a contrast. To call x blue is also to say that it is not yellow, not red, and so on. Likewise, to call someone inauthentic only makes sense if one is denying authenticity—but this requires that there *be* some concept of the authentic.

2. Metaphysical: on this reading, there is something like a metaphysical category, or mode of being, called "authenticity," that acts as a condition for the possibility of another metaphysical mode, called "inauthenticity," to exist. The idea of possibility here is quite concrete: one thing's actual metaphysical reality *allows* another thing's actual metaphysical reality.

3. Existentiell-ontic: The existentiell, as the reader will recall, is the particular mode of Being of a given Dasein. On this view, a particular Dasein actually *being* authentic would be a condition for the possibility of that very Dasein becoming inauthentic.

4. Existential-ontological: this regards authenticity as always a potential mode of Dasein's Being—one that is structurally equiprimordial with inauthenticity. Importantly, to say that authenticity *makes possible* inauthenticity need not entail that authenticity is more basic. It might well be the case that inauthenticity *also* makes possible authenticity. It is this view that allows us to claim (with earlier remarks that Heidegger makes) both that authenticity and inauthenticity are equiprimordial *and* that authenticity makes inauthenticity possible.

Of the above possibilities, (1) and (4) are the most promising. The metaphysical view, as I hope is clear to everyone, reduces the authentic and the inauthentic to mere present-at-hand properties. This obviously cannot be what Heidegger has in mind when talking about the fundamental modes of Dasein, understood as decidedly *not* identical to the merely present-at-hand. Likewise, the view that the above claim is to be understood as an existentiell-ontic one seems to forget much of what Heidegger has earlier said. In almost all that we have thus far covered, Heidegger has made the claim that our existence is fundamentally with and among those objects with which we are concernfully absorbed. Hence, first and foremost Dasein is Being-alongside-things in the mode of the ready-to-hand—and this is exactly the state that Heidegger identifies as "fallen," that is, as inauthentic. So it can't be the case that one is inauthentic *only after* being authentic.

This leaves the semantic reading and the existential-ontological reading. As I hope is clear, there is actually no need to decide between these two interpretations, as they are entirely compatible. It might well be the case that understanding the meaning of our ontologico-existential structures depends on these structures being understood contrastively. The same structures might well be understood as equiprimordial possibilities of Dasein: Dasein can decide the question of its Being by being either authentic or inauthentic. Notice too that if Dasein did not have *two* existential possibilities, it would be meaningless to speak of possibilities in the literal sense here at all: if one cannot in any case be other than x, then x is not a genuine existential possibility for that kind of Being. This example, I think, is a perfect instance of the union of semantic and ontological concerns. The authentic makes the inauthentic possible in two senses: it is that in virtue of which we can understand the significance of these things as ontological structures, but also that in virtue of which these can be understood as equally basic structures of Dasein.

Given that Heidegger thinks of the authentic as making possible the inauthentic, he must now turn his attention to the conditions for the possibility of authenticity as such. If he cannot spell out, with adequate rigor and precision, what authenticity *is*, then his entire analysis prior to this point will seemingly rest on nothing but a rather unwieldy question mark.

Authenticity Depends on Inauthenticity

Inauthenticity depends on authenticity, as we've seen. Heidegger also claims, however, that authenticity depends on inauthenticity.

> *Authentic Being-one's-Self* does not rest on an exceptional condition of the subject, a condition that has been detached from the "they"; *it is rather an existentiell modification of the "they"—of the "they" as an essential existential. (BT, 168)*

Dasein is constitutionally inauthentic. There's no escaping this. What authenticity consists in, then, is not *transcending* the inauthentic but taking hold of it. Heidegger makes this claim explicitly: "*authentic* existence is not something which floats above falling everydayness; existentially, it is only a modified way in which such everydayness is seized upon" (BT, 224).

To be resolute, Heidegger claims, is to "appropriate untruth authentically" (BT, 345). In other words, the authentic person takes up inauthentic understanding in a way that makes the possibilities inherent in this understanding, and which Dasein lives out, its *own* understanding. What matters to authenticity then *isn't* believing things that are *different* from everyday Dasein. What matters, rather, is *how one comes to have* the beliefs one has.

In Dasein's resoluteness, Dasein seizes its own possibilities. These possibilities are made possible by the "they," it is true, but the "they" doesn't do the choosing in a moment of resolution. Moreover, Dasein, in seizing its own possibilities, sees itself for what it is: thrown Being-toward-death. "When Dasein is resolute, it takes over authentically in its existence the fact that it is the null basis of its own nullity" (BT, 354). In seeing ourselves for what we are in our resolution, we see how dependent we are on the "they." Indeed, we see that we *are* the "they" through and through. As Heidegger explicitly claims, "even resolutions remain dependent upon the 'they' and its world" (*BT*, 346).

Resolute Dasein knows that it is falling and anticipates future instances of falling back into the "they." Thus "only in a resolution is resoluteness sure of itself" (*BT*, 345). This occurs in what Heidegger calls a "moment of vision"—the moment where we see ourselves for what we are and recognize that our momentary authenticity will not prevent us from falling back into the "they." Even in resoluteness, Heidegger claims, "Dasein is already in irresoluteness, and soon, perhaps, will be in it again" (*BT*, 345). In other words: to see our own guilt—that we are based on thrownness—is also to see that we will *misunderstand ourselves* again in the future (that we will "fall"). Thus authentic Dasein anticipates its future fallenness and resolves "to keep repeating itself." Thus "resoluteness gains its authenticity as *anticipatory* resoluteness" (*BT*, 434).

As Heidegger insists, we cannot say exactly what any particular authentic person resolves (*BT*, 434). This stands to reason. If we *could*, then authenticity would be formulaic. We could provide a rule for *becoming* authentic. This means, however, that there would be a *public* understanding of how to become authentic. As public, though, this understanding would be *by definition* inauthentic. Obviously, then, there can be no formula for becoming authentic. To offer a formula is simply to be inauthentic. There's no way to say what someone "must" resolve.

We can, however, say something about the *structure* of any resolution. A resolution will recognize Dasein as thrown, projecting, and fallen. It will further recognize that fallenness cannot be escaped, and that one's resolution must be to *repeat resolutions in the future*.

Despite the fact that fallenness is inevitable, even after resolution, we shouldn't assume that one's inauthenticity is *identical* to inauthenticity *prior* to the "moment of vision." Authenticity "modifies . . . both the ways in which the world is discovered . . . and the way in which the Dasein-with of Others is disclosed" (*BT*, 344). One of the primary ways Dasein's inauthenticity is modified is that Dasein is *prepared* to hear the call of conscience—it *wants to have a conscience* (in the sense discussed above). So even after future moments of fallenness, Dasein's resolution brings a kind of unity to its life: it resolves to pull itself out of the inauthentic again and again, being open to hearing the call—to seeing itself as it is. It is in this sense that (1) "irresoluteness is co-certain" with resoluteness (*BT*, 356) and that (2) resoluteness "by no means lets us fall back into irresoluteness" (*BT*, 355). These two claims are consistent because authentic resoluteness "resolves to keep repeating itself" (*BT*, 355).

THE AUTHENTIC LIFE

Authenticity is not a state one attains once and for all. If this were possible, we would be wrong to think of fallenness as a basic feature of Dasein's Being. As we have emphasized, there is no escaping from fallenness and inauthenticity. To be authentic is thus not to abandon inauthenticity entirely but to change one's relationship to it.

What, then, is an authentic life like? Obviously, we cannot provide a formula for such a life, specifying what a particular Dasein will believe or how that Dasein will act. If we could do this, the authentic life wouldn't be authentic at all, as there would be a way "one" becomes authentic. Nevertheless, we can specify some of the structural features of an authentic life given what Heidegger has so far claimed about what it means to be Dasein.

Figure 6.1 attempts to capture visually what we have thus far been claiming. Authentic Dasein will have what Heidegger calls "moments of vision" in which it sees itself for what it is. These moments, in an authentic life, will involve Dasein resolving to have *further* moments of vision in the future despite its inherent propensity to fall into inauthenticity. Put otherwise: in an authentic life, Dasein will still fall into the "they" (into inauthenticity) but will have *anticipated* such falling in those moments when it recognizes its own condition as Being-in-the-world. In these authentic moments, moreover, Dasein will resolve to react to future inauthenticity by having future moments of vision. The authentic life will thus involve a pattern in which one consistently recognizes fallenness and responds to it through resolving to have future moments of authenticity. The authentic life is not being authentic in each particular second. It is rather living in a resolution to continually see that one is more than the "they."

In thinking of authenticity as such a pattern, we are able to understand some peculiar remarks Heidegger makes early on in the discussion of the authentic and the inauthentic. In one such remark, Heidegger claims that "authentic understanding, no less than that which is inauthentic, *can* be either genuine or not genuine" (*BT*, 186). This remark produces an interesting set of possibilities: there are different ways of being authentic and inauthentic. Not every kind of inauthenticity is equal; not every moment of authenticity is equivalent. The possibilities are captured in table 6.2. Heidegger never spells out what he has in mind with this contrast. Why isn't "non-genuine authenticity" just inauthenticity, for example? Our discussion so far, however, allows us to hazard a guess as to what Heidegger has in mind in making these distinctions.

Dasein exists as thrown projection. When a Dasein confronts its own finitude—sees itself for what it is—it can either flee into inauthenticity or resolve to repeat such moments of authenticity. Genuine authenticity, I would like to suggest, involves genuine resolution. Non-genuine authen-

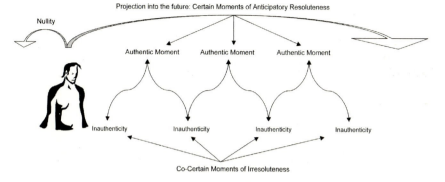

Cautionary Note: Anticipatory Resoluteness unifies Dasein's life. Each moment is what it is in relation to other moments. One should not understand this diagram as indicating that the authentic life is simply an accumulation of authentic moments. Anticipatory resoluteness changes even the way we exist as inauthentic, as we'll see.

Figure 6.1. The Authentic Life

ticity, by contrast, involves not having such a genuine resolution. What allows us to determine whether or not one's resolution is genuine, of course, is *the future*: if a Dasein does in fact hear the call of conscience in the future, then that Dasein's earlier resolution proves to be genuine.

This way of thinking about resolution also allows us to recognize that, although one will inevitably fall back into inauthenticity, one will not necessarily be inauthentic *in the same way* after one has such a genuine resolution. Anticipatory resoluteness, I am suggesting, changes the very manner in which Dasein lives through its inauthenticity. If this is correct, we have a way of understanding what non-genuine inauthenticity might involve: one is non-genuinely inauthentic when one has resolved to repeat moments of authenticity; one is genuinely inauthentic when one has not made such a resolution.

Table 6.2. Genuine and Non-Genuine Authenticity and Inauthenticity

	Genuine	Non-genuine
Authentic	Genuinely authentic	Non-genuinely authentic
Inauthentic	Genuinely inauthentic	Non-genuinely inauthentic

Admittedly, this is only one reading of Heidegger's perplexing remark that one can be genuinely or not genuinely authentic and inauthentic. We do not have much textual evidence to go on. Nevertheless, the above way of interpreting the distinction fits well with what Heidegger says about the authentic life in general.

Heidegger also indicates, early on, that authentic Dasein is capable of a different kind of Being-with. He claims that authentic Dasein can be the conscience of the Other

> There is also a possibility of a kind of solicitude which does not so much leap in for the Other as *leap ahead* of him [*ihm vorausspring*] in his existentiell potentiality-for-being, not in order to take away his "care," but rather to give it back to him authentically as such for the first time. The kind of solicitude pertains essentially to authentic care—that is, to the existence of the Other, not to a "what" with which he is concerned; it helps the other to become transparent to himself *in* his care and to become *free for* it. (*BT*, 158–59)

The suggestion here is an intriguing one. Heidegger claims that one Dasein can be concerned about another Dasein in a way that allows him to "become transparent to himself"—that is, in a way that enables a Dasein to see himself for what he actually is: an inauthentic being that has become swept up in the average everyday. This suggests that we can facilitate the authenticity of others. In our caring for others *authentically*, we can somehow make authenticity *possible* for the person for whom we care.

The fact that one Dasein can enable another to become "transparent to himself" also suggests a way in which two Dasein might be with one another. As Heidegger characterizes this relationship, the two Dasein "become *authentically* bound together, and this makes possible the right kind of objectivity [*die rechte Sachlichkeit*], which frees the Other in his freedom for himself" (*BT*, 159). This passage suggests that authenticity— normally regarded as fundamentally individualistic—might well involve special kinds of social relationships, relationships in which two persons facilitate one another in continuously recognizing their own possibilities for Being in a way that is both honest and free. (This claim about Being- with bears a striking resemblance to Aristotle's claims about true friendship in the *Nicomachean Ethics*[7]—a point that shouldn't surprise us, given that Heidegger worked out many of the central claims in *Being and Time* through a creative reading of Aristotle.)[8]

Later in *Being and Time*, Heidegger raises this issue again. In discussing the "call of conscience" in section 60, Heidegger remarks:

> When Dasein is resolute, it can become the "conscience" of Others. Only by authentically Being-their-Selves in resoluteness can people authentically be with one another—not by ambiguous and jealous stipulations and talkative fraternization in the "they" and in what "they" want to understand. (*BT*, 344–45).

One thing this passage brings out is that, whatever else Heidegger thinks about the possibilities one Dasein can open up for another, Dasein must have an *independent* access point to self-understanding. As Heidegger claims, only an *authentic* Dasein can act as the conscience of another. This seems to entail that a Dasein must already be authentic if she is to help another Dasein attain self-transparency. Thus authenticity is not a joint effort in every case, even if the maintenance of authenticity might eventually *become* the mutual engagement of two persons persistently allowing each other to maintain self-understanding.

Our remarks on the authentic life also provide a way of understanding Heidegger's claim that Dasein can be "undifferentiated"—something he mentions only very rarely in the pages of *Being and Time*. Dasein is neither authentic nor inauthentic precisely in those moments when Dasein sees itself for what it is and must then decide to *either* flee back into the "they" and the comfort of the inauthentic *or* to resolve to have future moments of authenticity. Only here, in the confrontation with finitude that robs one of the ready-made understanding of inauthenticity, and prior to any resolution to repeat the confrontation, can Dasein be said to be neither authentic nor inauthentic. Deprived of inauthentic understanding for a moment and not fully resolved, Dasein is "modally undifferentiated."

An alternative suggestion (made by Hubert Dreyfus) is that Heidegger has children in mind when he talks of modally undifferentiated Dasein. On this view, children are not yet developed enough to be either authentic or inauthentic, and hence can be understood as those Dasein who are *neither*. As is obvious, I do not find this suggestion persuasive. Dasein *is* its possibilities, and these possibilities are given as authentic, inauthentic, and, of course, undifferentiated. If it is not possible for a being to be authentic or inauthentic, then that being simply *is not a Dasein*. If a child is not yet capable of inauthenticity and authenticity, then *by definition* the child is not yet even a candidate for modally undifferentiated *Dasein*.

The problem with Dreyfus's suggestion, I think, is that it borders on making Dasein equivalent in scope with the concept "human"—something Heidegger explicitly warns us not to do. My objection is by no means to be understood as a disparaging remark about children. Nor should my objection be understood as claiming that we all automatically become Dasein when we reach the age of eighteen. The claim, rather, is that Dasein *is not the same as* "biological human," and, moreover, there will be some biological humans who are Dasein and some who are not. What will decide the issue are the possibilities that constitute a being, *not* its genetic makeup. In other words, if any particular child is a Dasein (and certainly, at some point in childhood, many are!), it will be exactly as capable of authenticity and inauthenticity as any other Dasein. Hence, we should *not* understand the category of "undifferentiated" as one that applies to children. As I've suggested, Dasein is undifferentiated in the moment when it must decide either to resolve to be authentic or to flee back into the inauthentic.

CONCLUSION

There is one additional aspect of authenticity that we have not yet adequately explored. Heidegger claims that anticipatory resoluteness involves "choosing a hero" from the past. This "hero," Heidegger suggests, enables one to see oneself in a way that differs from the standard interpretation of the "they." To make sense of what this involves, we'll need to say more about the nature of temporality and its relation to history, as Heidegger understands these things. This is our task in the following chapter.

NOTES

1. The German term *Reife* means both maturity and ripeness, hence the alteration of the following quotation.
2. Harrison also isn't correct about Heidegger's account of the corpse. As we've already seen, the corpse is "unalive" and "no longer Dasein," not a mere present-at-hand thing.
3. For more on this point, see my "Heidegger's Aristotelian Ethics," in *Ethics and Phenomenology*, ed. Mark Sanders and J. Jeremy Wisnewski, 57–74 (Lanham, MD: Lexington Books, 2012).
4. As we have seen (in chapter 4), temporality is *also* hinted at in the analysis of inauthenticity.
5. Others, however, have attempted to develop it. See, for example, the work of Frederick Olafson, Lawrence Hatab, Lawrence Vogel, and others. The bibliography contains a list of sources relevant to this issue.
6. As we will see, Heidegger also maintains that authenticity is based on inauthenticity.
7. In Aristotle's view, virtue requires having someone with whom one can be virtuous. Two persons (e.g., friends) can mutually enable each other to maintain the highest standards of action and character.
8. See, in particular, his *Plato's Sophist* and *Basic Concepts of Aristotelian Philosophy*.

SEVEN
Temporality and History

We began exploring Dasein with another aim in mind: to find an access point for answering the question of the meaning of Being. We have examined Dasein in its two primary modes: as authentic and as inauthentic. We have been led, through this exploration, to the claim that Dasein is constituted by care and that the ground of care is temporality. As we'll see, this insight provides a suggestive clue for the meaning of Being in general—namely, that time itself constitutes this meaning.

TEMPORALITY AS THE ONTOLOGICAL MEANING OF CARE

In the previous chapter, we explored Dasein in the mode of its authenticity. We're now in a position to explore temporality as the meaning of Dasein's Being. This is made apparent, first of all, by the *way* Dasein understands itself in its authenticity. "In the *state-of-mind in which it finds itself*, Dasein is assailed by itself as the entity which it still is and already was—that is to say, which it constantly *is* as having-been" (*BT*, 376). Here, quite explicitly, we see the connection with guilt and recognizing one's own ontological condition. We *are* this past self that is the "they," and we continue to be. To see ourselves is to see precisely this. We see that we are thrown into the future, toward death, and that this future also constantly *is us*. Finally, we see our inevitable falling, which constitutes the constant temptation of the present. In the moments of authentic resolution, Dasein sees itself stretched throughout time and sees that time is at the core of its very existence. As Heidegger explicitly says, "temporality makes possible the unity of existence, facticity, and falling, and in this way constitutes primordially the totality of the structure of care" (*BT*, 376).

In understanding that temporality is the ground of care, we must as usual avoid engaging in present-at-hand analysis. Our temptation is to read the care-structure in terms of the moments of past, present, and future, understood as distinct "things" that exist always apart from one another. When we view time this way, we see "time" as "composed" of different moments. It's this conception of time that Heidegger would like us to get beyond. His way of capturing this is in terms of the idea that temporality "temporalizes."

This, of course, is far from transparent. To say that temporality temporalizes must seem like the height of philosophical nonsense. Some reference to the German here helps, though. The term translated as "temporalizes" is *zeitigen*, which means "bring about" in ordinary German. Heidegger is drawing attention to the root word, *Zeit*, which of course is "time." Translations are forced to decide between the more readable "temporality brings about itself" and the more etymologically revealing "temporality temporalizes." The decision is indeed a difficult one, as there is no good choice to be made. As elsewhere, Heidegger wants to draw attention to the way that some central ontological wisdom is contained in our everyday speech. "Time" is essentially connected with "bringing about," which is essentially connected with *Being* (more on this below).

For our purposes, I will talk about temporality "bringing about" or "bringing itself about," depending on what the context demands. Let us now consider Heidegger's remarks about temporality with the altered translation: "Temporality brings about, and indeed it brings about possible ways of itself. These make possible the multiplicity of Dasein's modes of Being, and especially the basic possibility of authentic or inauthentic existence" (*BT*, 377). In one respect, what we recognize in temporality is that *stasis* is interrupted. If Dasein could only be what it currently *is*, there could be no sense to the idea of Dasein breaking away from the "they," nor would we be able to make sense of the very idea of "modification." A world of the present-at-hand is a static world, pure and simple. When time is added to this static world, we wind up with a static world that has *just one more property*—namely, that it exists in three different states (past, present, future).

What characterizes temporality, then, is *ec-stasis*—the fundamentally outside-of-itself—that which is not to be self-contained (this is the literal meaning of the term, based on its ancient Greek roots). The unity of the "things" that are not self-contained *is* temporality. The past, present, and future are *not* independent "things" or "events" that can be isolated from one another. They *are* one another, coming out of one another. This is the fundamental notion of ec-stasis and of temporality in general.

What we see in Heidegger's analysis, then, is a series of challenges to the way we have understood time and time's relation to our existence. The dominant understanding of time has been that captured in clock time: we view time as discrete units, measurable and organizable, that exist in a series progressing from the past into the future. Our ordinary conception of time tends to see time as *infinite*—as extending infinitely into the future, as well as infinitely into the past.

Heidegger's central claims regarding temporality are as follows:

- Temporality makes possible the structure of care.
- Temporality is "ecstatical" (outside of itself).
- "Temporality brings about itself primordially out of the future" (*BT*, 380).
- "Primordial time is finite" (*BT*, 380).

We've already discussed (albeit briefly) the first two claims. In what follows, we'll try to clarify the last two claims.

Heidegger sees that certain features of Dasein's existence now come to light in a way that they couldn't prior to our recognition of the "temporalization-structure" of Dasein. One thing that we're now able to see is that Dasein is a historical being *essentially*. Examining this, Heidegger claims, will reveal that the "everyday experience of time [is] both possible and necessary" (*BT*, 381)—that is, it will reveal how our inauthentic understanding of time is based on, and derives from, authentic temporality.

Heidegger aims to reconceive what we think of as the nature of temporality. The future is *not* to be construed as later than the present; the past is not *earlier* than the present. Rather, all of these ecstases emanate from one another in the constitution of temporality.

Dasein as "clearing" is made possible only by temporality. This is a significant claim, as it indicates that Dasein's "letting Being be"—its capacity to allow Being to present itself in itself—is made possible by virtue of Dasein's temporal structure. In one respect, this should not be surprising. Temporality "is what primarily regulates the possible unity of all Dasein's existential structures" (*BT*, 402). What does it mean to "be the basis" of a thing? Temporality is *not* the basis of Dasein in the sense of a deduction or an inference. Heidegger seems rather to mean that temporality *makes Dasein intelligible*. That is, without temporality, we would not have attained the ground of intelligibility that allows us to fully grasp Dasein's existential structures. The ideas of thrownness, projection, and fallenness only make sense in light of temporality. The idea of anticipatory resoluteness, likewise, is unintelligible without it. Thus the dominant possibilities of Dasein—the inauthentic (fallenness) and the authentic (anticipatory resoluteness) require temporality if we are to make sense of them at all.

It is Heidegger's aim to further demonstrate this. We can understand him as offering additional argument for the claim that temporality is the meaning of Dasein's Being. After all, if one *cannot* articulate the temporal underpinnings of Dasein's existential structures, then temporality is inadequate as the meaning of Dasein's Being. In other words, temporality must be able to *clarify and ground* Dasein's existential structures if we are to be justified in the view that temporality is the meaning of Dasein's Being.

THE TEMPORALITY OF CIRCUMSPECTIVE CONCERN

As mentioned above, Heidegger wants to explore the temporal foundation of all of those structures he has so far excavated phenomenologically. An initial clue that temporality will be discovered beneath the structures of circumspective concern is found in the general trajectory that *Being and Time* has so far followed: we have seen that circumspective concern is based on care, and we have seen that care is based on temporality. Given that care has been shown to rest on temporality, and circumspective concern on care, why doesn't Heidegger regard this as sufficient for demonstrating that circumspective concern is *itself* based on temporality?

This question is surprisingly difficult to answer, but addressing it reveals something about Heidegger's notion of "foundations" as well as his thinking about the significance of his achievements in *Being and Time*. Our temptation is to think of foundations spatially, in a more-or-less present-at-hand manner. We tend to think that one thing is the foundation for another if and only if certain conditions are met: (1) there are two separate things, and (2) the separate things stand in some particular relation such that one "rests" on the other. This notion of foundation, I think, is familiar from Descartes's *Meditations on First Philosophy*. The basis of all knowledge, for Descartes, is the "thinking thing." It is through uncovering the existence and necessity of the thinking thing that Descartes believes he is able, eventually, to deduce the existence of the external world as well as the trustworthiness of our clear and distinct ideas. What seems crucial in this type of explanation is that what is deduced is *not identical* to that from which it is deduced. There is supposed to be genuine epistemic gain in Descartes, where we understand "epistemic gain" to mean that our knowledge of things in the world is increased.

As this description of classic foundationalism makes clear, there is something fundamentally inauthentic about this kind of enterprise. First, the parts of a given deduction are construed as present-at-hand. Second, the very language of deduction here is fundamentally *spatial*. One thing "rests on" another. Propositions *reach* a conclusion. Although this is not surprising, especially given Dasein's own primordial spatiality, neither is it particularly elucidating. The ground of something, in Heidegger's view, is more like that *in which and out of which* something grows. The thing itself is intimately intertwined with its ground, so much so that any distinctions we make between ground and what grows there will be only heuristic. Insofar as we take these distinctions too seriously, we will mis-understand the phenomenon.

With this in mind, we can now see why showing that care is based on temporality, and circumspective concern on care, is insufficient for dem-onstrating that temporality is the basis of circumspective concern. This view of "grounding" regards these things as though they were some type of building, with temporality standing at the base. This spatial concep-tion of present-at-hand concepts supporting one another misses Heideg-ger's sense of grounding completely. If we have shown that circumspec-tive concern is based on care, this means that these things are *the same* phenomena, so intimately intertwined that one thing cannot be pulled apart from the other without fundamentally distorting the thing in ques-tion. The same applies to care and temporality: these things are so inter-twined that all distinctions must be regarded as falsifications aimed at elucidation, and no more.

To claim that temporality is the basis of Dasein's Being, which is care, is thus not *excluded* from anything that has thus far been said—but nei-ther is it demonstrated. To demonstrate this, we must revisit circumspec-tive concern, examining how it grows through and out of temporality, if we are to justify the claim that temporality is the meaning of Dasein's Being. We must do this because the previous analysis of circumspective concern was *not* obviously temporal (though, as we've seen, temporality was implicit in the earlier analysis—which, if Heidegger is correct, is exactly what we should expect). If temporality is the soil that sustains circumspective concern, this must now be demonstrated. By demonstrat-ing this, moreover, we will secure the thesis that temporality is indeed the ground of Dasein's Being.

Heidegger remarks that we can see temporality in the very structure of the ready-to-hand: "the understanding of the 'towards-which'—that is, the understanding of what the equipment is involved in—has the tempo-ral structure of awaiting" (*BT*, 404). As we should remember, this has nothing to do with a theoretical understanding of the equipment. Indeed, one's absorption in a project involves the disappearance of the theoretical analysis of what one is concernfully absorbed with (although scientific practice constitutes an interesting exception, as we will see). Moreover, the Self of a Dasein *forgets itself* in its work. This is *constitutive* of Dasein's absorption in its work.

> When one is wholly devoted to something and "really" busies oneself
> with it, one does not do so just alongside the work itself, or alongside
> the tool, or alongside both of them "together". The unity of the rela-
> tions in which concern circumspectively "operates", has been estab-
> lished already by letting-things-be-involved—which is based upon
> temporality. (*BT*, 405)

The ready-to-hand is "made-present" in our concernful absorption with it. As should come as no surprise, any particular entity can be "made-present" in several ways, all of which imply temporality (these are conspicuousness, obtrusiveness, and obstinacy). What Heidegger wants to bring out here is that "missing" a piece of equipment, or "finding" it, or even a piece of equipment snapping in half—all of these things involve temporality fundamentally. For something to be missing means that one was involved with it before, and that it is no longer available. To find something means that one has engaged in a particular seeking. Seeking is ecstatical: one seeks after what is not present-at-hand—what goes beyond one's current factual state. Interestingly, we see here something that Heidegger will later make much of: terms that initially seem spatial (one finds something in space) ultimately have their basis and sense in temporality.

TEMPORALITY AND THEORETICAL OBSERVATION

As before, Heidegger turns to an examination of the alteration of our circumspective concern to our detached theoretical observations. Once again, his aim is to show how this particular mundane piece of our phenomenology can be explicated in temporality and how such explication grounds the thing we are examining.

Heidegger turns his attention to what he calls an "existential conception of science" (*BT*, 408). This is to be distinguished from the "logical" reconstruction of science in much the same way that we distinguished logical "grounding" from ontological-existential grounding: we are not talking about setting fundamentally distinct present-at-hand entities in relations such that we can deduce new entities. Rather, "the existential conception understands science as a way of existence and thus as a mode of Being-in-the-world, which discovers or discloses either entities or Being" (*BT*, 408).

When we approach science in this way, we become aware of the artificiality of the distinction between theory and praxis (practice). The view that theory involves the absence of praxis, Heidegger contends, rests on a mistaken understanding of Dasein's existence in the world. Examining the world "scientifically" is *not* simply detaching ourselves from all circumspective concern. Rather, scientific experimentation and manipulation "can take on the character of a more precise kind of circumspection, such as 'inspecting,' checking up on what has been attained, or looking over the 'operations' which are now 'at a standstill'" (*BT*, 409). This way of recognizing theoretical investigation links it immediately and inextricably with temporality.

Science itself, as a way of looking at things, is not to be construed as the antithesis of praxis. Likewise, praxis should not be understood as anathema to theoretical viewing. As Heidegger insightfully notes, "'practical' dealings have their *own* ways of tarrying. And just as *praxis* has its own specific kind of sight ('theory'), theoretical research is not without a *praxis* of its own" (*BT*, 409).

These considerations lead Heidegger to explore another type of practice involved in our theoretical speculations—one that he dubs "deliberation." Deliberation concerns the thinking-through of particular hypotheticals ("If . . . then . . ."). Dasein is a master of the counterfactual, and we should understand such activity as a way of seeing the world as well as our place in it. What we deliberate about, of course, must be seen as made possible by a world that is already disclosed. "That which is considered with an 'if' must already be understood *as something or other*" (*BT*, 411). This serves to show that deliberation, like other modes of present-at-hand (and theoretical) observation, requires antecedent disclosure. One can discover something about "what will happen if x" only because "x" is something disclosed to us and that we can manipulate in our ongoing deliberations.

This mode of present-at-hand circumspection reveals temporality in a way that links it inevitably to deliberation. The very notion of a counterfactual involves throwing oneself into a future that may or may not eventually exist, and to understand the events in that future in light of actions that will be what has been (that is, future pasts).

The fundamental function of knowledge, Heidegger argues, is to decontextualize a thing. It is arguably for this reason that so many philosophers have thought that knowledge requires grasping that which stands outside of time (Aristotle makes this claim explicitly in discussing the function of science). In this decontextualizing, we are in danger of missing the Being of the things we were formerly concernfully absorbed with.

> In the "physical" assertion that "the hammer is heavy" we *overlook* not only the tool-character of the entity we encounter, but also something that belongs to any ready-to-hand equipment: its place. Its place becomes a matter of indifference. This does not mean that what is present-at-hand loses its "location" altogether. But its place becomes a spatio-temporal position, a "world-point", which is in no way distinguished from any other. This implies not only that the multiplicity of places of equipment ready-to-hand within the confines of the environment becomes modified to a pure multiplicity of positions, but that the entities of the environment are altogether *released from such confinement*. The aggregate of the present-at-hand becomes the theme. (*BT*, 413)

The radical decontextualization of entities that constitutes a scientific description moves us from the ready-to-hand to the present-at-hand. This kind of movement, however, is a movement from *everyday* seeing of individual entities to a much more specialized way of seeing and understanding things. Hence, in encountering things in terms of physics, we encounter a world that has been "mathematicized." Consider what Heidegger has to say about the rise of mathematical physics:

> What is decisive for its development does not lie in its rather high esteem for the observation of "facts", nor in its "application" of mathematics in determining the character of natural processes; it lies rather in *the way in which Nature herself is mathematically projected*. In this projection something constantly present-at-hand (matter) is uncovered beforehand, and the horizon is opened so that one may be guided by looking at those constitutive items in it which are quantitatively determinable (motion, force, location, and time). Only "in the light" of a Nature which has been projected in this fashion can anything like a "fact" be found and set up for an experiment regulated and delimited in terms of this projection. The "grounding" of "factual science" was possible only because the researchers understood in principle there are no "bare facts". In the mathematical projection of Nature, moreover, what is decisive is not primarily the mathematical as such; what is decisive is that this projection *discloses something that is a priori*. Thus the paradigmatic character of mathematical natural science does not lie in its exactitude or in the fact that it is binding for "Everyman"; it consists rather in the fact that the entities which it takes as its theme are discovered in it in the only way in which entities can be discovered—by the prior projection of their state of Being. (*BT*, 413–14)[1]

The "observations" of science are by no means "pure observations." Indeed, there are no such things. Rather, one encounters entities that are a priori projected onto the world through the presupposition of ontology. Thus even seemingly "timeless" observations of mathematical facts wind up being grounded in temporality, as one can only "observe" mathematical facts insofar as an ontology has been presupposed and projected— and "projection" and "presupposition" are intelligible only in and through temporality. What is "projected" entails a futural mode of Being-in-the-world; what is "presupposed" is essentially a "having-been" that is pulled along with one into the present.

This raises an essential problem for Dasein: in order to articulate a world as only present-at-hand, Dasein must be able to see the world in a way that is essentially beyond Dasein's own being. This is at the core of what Heidegger calls "the problem of transcendence."

Dasein, as we know, is its world. But Dasein is also more than it is— and the world that constitutes Dasein is constantly stretching beyond our current concernful absorption. This is at the heart of the idea of transcendence. Heidegger is interested in making sense of how this is possible: How can the world that we *are* be something that is also, in some sense, *beyond us*? The answer to this question, it will come as no surprise, is temporality: "*The existential-temporal condition for the possibility of the world lies in the fact that temporality, as an ecstatical unity, has something like a horizon.* . . . There belongs to each ecstasis a "whither" to which one is carried away" (416).

When we speak of temporality as ecstatic, we do not mean merely that it is randomly outside of itself. Temporality is *directional*—it has a "*whither*" that provides intelligibility to each of the three ecstasies (ecstasies presupposed by our ordinary notions of past, present, and future). If there were no such structure to the ecstatic moments of temporality, it is by no means clear that these moments would be distinct at all. After all, if there were no *direction* of ecstasis—if there were nothing toward which temporality was directed—then such ecstases might well be identical. That is, if past, present, and future had the same structure, there would be no way to tell these things apart—and hence, there might well be no reason to say that they were in fact *distinct* ecstases.

As it happens, though, these ecstases *do* have distinct structures, and these structures correspond to aspects of the world that Dasein factically *is*. The world is temporally constituted. In one sense, the significance of this is not adequately captured in table 7.1, as it suggests a rather rigid separation of the ecstases and a self-contained significance that Heidegger would reject. As we've seen, part of the very essence of time is that it is outside-of-itself. It is not *static*. It moves out of itself into the past and the future, and as it reaches back and throws itself forward, it pulls the present out of itself. The image of temporality that we have must be of a throbbing, dynamic *being* (not thing) that is neither self-contained nor self-sufficient, but which is constantly beyond and outside of itself.

> Just as the Present arises in the unity of the temporalizing [or: bringing about] of temporality out of the future and having been, the horizon of the Present temporalizes itself [or: brings itself about] equiprimordially with those of the future and of having been. In so far as Dasein temporalizes itself [or: brings itself about], a world is *too*. In temporalizing itself [or: bringing itself about] with regard to its Being as temporality, Dasein *is* essentially "in a world," by reason of the ecstatic-horizontal constitution of that temporality. The world is neither present-at-hand nor ready-to-hand, but temporalizes itself [or: brings itself about] in temporality. It "is", with the "outside-of-itself" of the ecstases, "there." If no *Dasein* exists, no world is "there" either. (*BT*, 417)

This provides an insight into how we should understand the world in its relation to Dasein—one which, admittedly, should be rather familiar at

Table 7.1.   The Ec-Stases within the Ready-to-Hand

Horizontal Schemas	
Future	For-the-sake-of-which
Past/Having-Been	In-the-face-of-which
Present	In-order-to

this point. The world and Dasein are co-constitutive. The world is *not* "a network of forms which a wordless subject has laid over some kind of material" (*BT*, 417). Indeed, the very idea of "material" stems from a kind of decontextualization that is itself grounded in Dasein's being as care—and hence as temporal. Dasein can come to view the world as composed of "matter" only by projecting a particular ontology that allows the world to reveal itself in a particular, present-at-hand way.

TEMPORALITY AND HISTORY

History is used in several different senses in ordinary language. As Heidegger notes, it is fundamentally ambiguous: it can mean both (1) what happens and (2) the study of what happens (historiology, or *Historie* in German).

In addition to this fundamental ambiguity, "history" can also signify what is in the past both generally and specifically. Generally, "history" can mean "no longer present-at-hand" (*BT*, 430). It can also mean two *opposing things*—what has *no bearing* on our current situation as well as what will inevitably have bearing. One can talk of something being "lost to history" with as much ease as talking of "what history shows." This dual signification of history represents our confused attempts to understand ourselves in terms of history.

But our confusion about the past is by no means surprising: the "past" is that which is *no more* but which also endures into the present. "Thus 'the past' has a remarkable double meaning; the past belongs irretrievably to an earlier time; it belonged to the events of that time; and in spite of that, it can still be present-at-hand 'now'—for instance, the remains of a Greek temple. With the temple, a 'bit of the past' is still 'in the present'" (*BT*, 430). And this—the existence of the past as past but also as present—is only *one of many* ways in which the past is understood by everyday Dasein. Indeed, Heidegger outlines four such significations of "history."

1. The past as both past and present.
2. The past as involving the future—the past is the beginning of the trajectory we are on, which points toward the future. It directs us through our current state to our eventual goal.
3. History is the collection of artifacts and relics that can be studied—it is a domain of entities.
4. History is simply what has been "handed down" from the past to us—it is that which survives in tradition and practice into the present, and presumably into the future as well.

Taken together, these notions of history allow Heidegger to formulate the following definition:

History is that specific historizing [or "happening," *Geshehen,*] of exis-
tent Dasein which comes to pass in time, so that the historizing which
is "past" in our Being-with-one-another, and which at the same time
has been "handed down to us" and is continuingly effective, is regarded as "history" in the sense that gets emphasized. (*BT*, 431)

Heidegger aims to understand how history, so construed, is related to
Dasein's Being as temporality. The general strategy is to examine Dasein's obsession with the past as a means of getting clear about
Dasein's historical nature. Why is it, exactly, that Dasein is infatuated
with its past and the past of those Dasein who are no longer with us?
How does this connect to Dasein's existing as a stretching between birth
and death? The essential answer to this question is that "the Interpretation of Dasein's historicality will prove to be, at bottom, just a more
concrete working out of temporality" (*BT*, 434). It is because Dasein is
constituted by temporality—both what it is thrown into (a history) and
what it will be (a future)—that Dasein is that being that *studies* history.

AUTHENTICITY AND TEMPORALITY

Having explored the notion of temporality as the meaning of Dasein's
Being, we can now return to the issue of Dasein's authenticity.

What is the source of an authentic Dasein's existentiell possibilities? If
inauthenticity is pervasive, and Dasein is constituted in average everydayness, there must be some *source* from which Dasein can draw alternative possibilities for itself. It is not enough, after all, that Dasein is drawn
out of the "they" in its recognition of death. This is necessary, but not
sufficient for authenticity. Dasein must also resolve upon a particular
path, and if this path is not simply to be given by average everydayness,
it must come from elsewhere. The question Heidegger is here posing, of
course, is where such possibilities might come from. The answer, in brief,
is that these possibilities come from the past.

The resoluteness in which Dasein comes back to itself, discloses them *in
terms of the heritage* which that resoluteness, as thrown, *takes over*. In
one's coming back resolutely to one's thrownness, there is hidden a
handing down to oneself of the possibilities that have come down to one,
but not necessarily *as* having thus come down. (*BT*, 435)

One pulls possibilities from the past and utilizes these possibilities for
one's future projection. This does *not* mean that Dasein simply acts out
the actions of another, no longer present, Dasein. Indeed, Dasein could
not do this, as every Dasein is constituted in part by its thrownness,
which is of course located in a particular historical context. To be a
Dasein, as should now be obvious, is to exist in a particular temporal
horizon. It is thus simply *not possible* to relive that which is past. One

must live the past possibility, "not necessarily as having come down," but as *one's own* current existentiell possibility.

> Once one has grasped the finitude of one's existence, it snatches one back from the endless multiplicity of possibilities which offer them-selves as closest to one—those of comfortableness, shirking, and taking things lightly—and brings Dasein into the simplicity of its *fate* [*Schick-sals*]. This is how we designate Dasein's primordial historizing [or: hap-pening], which lies in authentic resoluteness and in which Dasein *hands* itself *down* to itself, free for death, in a possibility which it has inherited and yet has chosen. (*BT*, 435)

Dasein's authentic historizing involves taking over the past as one's own. As constituted by our thrown projection, which itself determines our conception of the historical, we thus in one respect hand ourselves to ourselves in the appropriation of history. We hand ourselves (the past possibilities that constitute us and from which we have appropriated a possibility) to ourselves (the thrown self lost in the leveled-down under-standing of average everydayness).

When Dasein does this—hands down itself to itself—it is authentic. As such, Heidegger claims, Dasein is in *fate*. Once again, I read Heideg-ger's use of terms like *destiny* and *fate* in a deflationary way: Heidegger is attempting to reclaim those terms of our tradition that lead us to mis-understand ourselves—he wants to reveal the ontological foundation of this misunderstanding. The notion of "fate" has its ontological roots in Dasein's ability to *make itself what it is* by taking over its past.

> Only an entity which, in its Being, is essentially **futural** so that it is free for its death and can let itself be thrown back upon its factical there by shattering itself against death—that is to say, only an entity which, as futural, is equipri-mordial in the process of **having-been**, can, by handing down to itself the possibility it has inherited, take over its own thrownness and be **in the mo-ment of vision** for "its time." Only authentic temporality which is at the same time finite, makes possible something like fate—that is to say, authentic historicality. (*BT*, 437; italics and bold in original)

As we saw in the previous chapter, resolute Dasein takes hold of its past. It "chooses a hero" as a means of seeing the present differently. It then resolves to see itself for what it is, and to take over possibilities from the past that authentic Dasein *also* makes its own.

> The resoluteness which comes back to itself and hands itself down, then becomes the *repetition* of a possibility of existence that has come down to us. *Repeating is handing down explicitly*—that is to say, going back into the possibilities of the Dasein that has-been-there. The au-thentic repetition of a possibility of existence that has been—the pos-sibility that Dasein may choose its hero—is grounded existentially in anticipatory resoluteness; for it is in resoluteness that one first chooses

the choice which makes one free for the struggle of loyally following in the footsteps of that which can be repeated. (*BT*, 437)

We should not think, in examining this passage, that Dasein simply repeats possibilities exactly as they've existed in the past. Obviously, this reading of repetition is untenable. First, it presupposes that the past (and what happens) admits of one "correct" reading. As is hopefully obvious, history is an ongoing interpretive endeavor, where different things will present themselves depending on the background understanding one brings to the events in question. Second, if authentic Dasein aimed simply to repeat the past, such a repetition would amount to inauthenticity, as Dasein would be choosing those possibilities of *another* Dasein, rather than its own possibilities.

> Repetition does not let itself be persuaded of something by what is "past", just in order that this, something which was formerly actual, may recur. Rather, the repetition makes a *reciprocative rejoinder* to the possibility of that existence which has-been-there. But when such a rejoinder is made to this possibility in a resolution, it is made *in a moment of vision; and as such* it is at the same time a *disavowal* of that which in the "today" is working itself out as the "past". Repetition does not abandon itself to that which is past, nor does it aim at progress. In the moment of vision authentic existence is indifferent to both these alternatives. (*BT*, 437–38)

So while resoluteness does *repeat* past possibilities, it does this in a way that offers a "reciprocative rejoinder" to the "they" and the present more generally. In acting out past possibilities, we appropriate them—we make them our own. In thus repeating past possibilities, we offer *alternative* ways of understanding the past, and we thereby call into question the inauthentic understanding of things that we've inherited. This occurs in what Heidegger calls a "moment of vision." The resoluteness of Dasein, however, should not be understood as *merely* momentary.

> Resoluteness would be misunderstood ontologically if one were to suppose that it would be actual as "Experience" only as long as the "act" of resolving "lasts". In resoluteness lies the existentiell constancy which, by its very essence, has already anticipated every possible moment of vision that may arise from it. As fate, resoluteness is freedom to *give up* some definite resolution, and to give it up in accordance with the demands of some possible Situation or other. The steadiness of existence is not interrupted thereby but confirmed in the moment of vision. (*BT*, 443)

One thing we see here is a corrective to a tempting reading of repetition: that it constitutes a series of moments, understood sequentially, that occur over and over again, and in which Dasein reaffirms its authenticity. On this view, authenticity would be something brought about cumulatively as the past presses forward into the present.[2]

At this point, it's useful to remember Heidegger's prescient warning: "the ontology of Dasein is always falling back upon the allurements of the way in which Being is ordinarily understood" (*BT*, 439). This is precisely what's going on when we think of authenticity as cumulative and repetition as simply additive moments of experience. The steadiness of existence in authentic Dasein, Heidegger points out, "is not first formed either through or by the adjoining of 'moments' one to another" (*BT*, 443). Rather, the temporality of repetition "has already been stretched along" (*BT*, 443). Dasein, as authentic, *unifies its life*. Its resolution to repeat moments of vision provides a "constancy" that inauthentic Dasein does not have. "Resoluteness constitutes the *loyalty* of existence to its own Self" (*BT*, 443). As we saw in the previous chapter, once one resolves to live an authentic life, *inauthenticity itself* changes.

INAUTHENTIC TEMPORALITY

Contrasting authentic historicality and inauthentic historicality can further elucidate what an authentic life involves. Consider Heidegger's characterization of inauthentic temporality:

> With the inconstancy of the they-self Dasein makes present its "today". In awaiting the next new thing, it has already forgotten the old one. The "they" evades choice. Blind for possibilities, it cannot repeat what has been, but only retains and receives the "actual" that is left over, the world-historical that has been, the leavings, and the information about them that is present-at-hand. Lost in the making present of the "today", it understands the "past" in terms of the "Present" . . . one's existence is inauthentically historical, it is loaded down with the legacy of a "past" which has become unrecognizable, and it seeks the modern. (*BT*, 443–44)

Every previous moment is reduced to a previous "present." Rather than understanding the distinct nature of future (as projection) and past (as having-been), the everyday understanding reduces temporality to mere present. The past is merely past presents; the future is merely future presents. Each aspect of time is thus reduced to one aspect, and all essential differences are lost. There is nothing unique in the future (after all, it's just a present that isn't "here" yet) or in the past (it's just a present that is no longer "here").

In taking this view of time, the present is made paramount—and it is made paramount in a way that blinds us to the nature of time and temporality. Indeed, we are also blinded to the very nature of our own existence as Dasein (constituted by temporality). This notion of temporality as merely different cases of the present also blinds us to a proper understanding of time as such.

The ordinary understanding of time is captured in the mechanical clock. Ironically, the clock was originally developed for religious purposes—to help monks keep track of their religious obligations and to devote themselves for the appropriate amounts of time to these tasks.[3] The clock now has vastly different purposes. It organizes and runs our lives. The clock is, in its very essence, *totalitarian*. The clock quantifies time. It translates (and ultimately transforms) time into discrete quantities that can be measured, added, multiplied, and examined. With the advent of the clock, time comes to be seen in a fundamentally different way.

Seeing time correctly is required to see what it might mean to say that *time* is the meaning of Being. This is what Heidegger hoped to do in the remainder of *Being and Time*. Seeing appropriately the nature of time, Heidegger argued, was made possible by Dasein authentically seeing the nature of its own temporality.

> The temporality of authentic historicality, as the moment of vision of anticipatory repetition, *deprives* the "today" of its character *as present*, and weans one from the conventionalities of the "they" . . . when historicality is authentic, it understands history as the "recurrence" of the possible, and knows that a possibility will recur only if existence is open for it fatefully, in a moment of vision, in resolute repetition. (*BT*, 443–44)

To see time appropriately requires an exploration of the ways in which time has been misunderstood. It also requires a recognition of the ways in which *Being itself* has been misunderstood historically. These are the very issues Heidegger intended to take up in the remaining two-thirds of *Being and Time*.

CONCLUSION

Unfortunately, *Being and Time* remains unfinished. We will never see the finished form of Heidegger's working out of the rest of these problems. Readers can take solace, however, in the existence of substantial texts that take up these themes, even if they do not do so in the exact form that Heidegger initially planned. One can read Heidegger's *Kant and the Problem of Metaphyiscs* as well as his *Basic Problems of Phenomenology* (a lecture course given in the period when *Being and Time* came to print) to see him work through those topics planned for the remainder of *Being and Time*.

NOTES

1. The issue of mathematical science is explored in more detail in chapter 8.
2. There is a striking similarity between Heidegger's account of our relation to history and the one offered by Nietzsche in "On the Uses and Disadvantages of Histo-

ry for Life," from *Untimely Meditations,* in which Nietzsche likewise suggests drawing on the "monumental" figures of the past in our attempt to break out of our everyday complacency. Heidegger was undoubtedly familiar with this text.

3. See Lewis Mumford's *Technics and Civilization.*

EIGHT

The Later Heidegger

Technology, Thinking, and Dwelling

After the publication of *Being and Time* in 1927, Heidegger's fame soared. Despite its success, Heidegger became dissatisfied with the work and ultimately came to think of its project as misdirected. Heidegger's dissatisfaction, it can be argued, stemmed more from the emphasis of *Being and Time* than from its subject matter. The focus on Dasein, Heidegger came to think, covered up the very thing Heidegger wanted to investigate—namely, Being itself. By approaching Being through the understanding of Dasein, Heidegger had inadvertently overemphasized the idea of a *subject*, which he ultimately wanted to set aside. Likewise, the very language of *Being and Time* seemed to betray Heidegger's project: it attempted a systematic analysis of Dasein that tried to reach Being, but it did so in a way that suggested the ontology of the present-at-hand (despite Heidegger's explicit warning to his readers regarding the present-at-hand). Thus, in the beginning of the 1930s, Heidegger "turned" away from approaching Being through Dasein, along with the idea that one might capture Being in the traditional expository language of philosophy. Heidegger's work after "the turn" (*die Kehre*) is decidedly more poetic, focusing more on Being and truth than on Dasein and meaning.

THE TURN

Heidegger's turning was away from an emphasis on Dasein and toward an emphasis on Being itself, on the way Being presents itself. The modern world has become blinded to the many ways Being presents itself (or "presences" as Heidegger sometimes says). In Heidegger's view, this is

147

largely due to the dominance of the technological understanding of things that has emerged with (but not from) modern science. We've come to see Being as a set of manipulable items, set aside and counted, that are designed to serve whatever interests we happen to have. Being, however, is more than a set of resources. When we understand Being only as standing-reserve (or "resources"), we are blinded to what *is*. This poses what Heidegger calls "the greatest danger"—that we will become so subsumed by technological understanding that we will never be able to escape from the "oblivion of Being" in which we find ourselves. This will entail that we lose the ability to know the sense and significance of the world around us at its most fundamental. We will find a world without art and poetry, from which we are fundamentally alienated and toward which we no longer know how to act.

Heidegger's later philosophy is as difficult as it is expansive. Our aim in what follows will be to provide a path through some of the themes that permeate this work. There is perhaps no better place to begin than technology.

THE ESSENCE OF TECHNOLOGY

Heidegger's questioning of technology is, he points out several times, a questioning that is after the *essence* of technology rather than its manifestation. "Technology is not equivalent to the essence of technology" (QCT, 311). Heidegger is not claiming that any particular technology is problematic—though, of course, there might be Heideggerian reasons for making such claims.

> Everywhere we remain unfree and chained to technology, whether we passionately affirm or deny it. But we are delivered over to it in the worst possible way when we regard it as something neutral; for this conception of it, to which today we particularly like to pay homage, makes us utterly blind to the essence of technology. (QCT, 311–12)

We tend to think of technology as simply a way of more efficiently reaching those goals that we have. In this respect, we think of technology as a means to an end—and to this extent, Heidegger thinks, we're correct. But "the merely correct is not yet the true" (QCT, 313). To *see* what technology involves is to *see* what the instrumentality of technology means for us, and for the world we inhabit.

To understand technology, then, we must understand instrumentality. This leads Heidegger to a discussion of cause. True to form, Heidegger searches for the essence of "cause" in its etymological origins in ancient Greek. He begins by reviewing Aristotle's classic notion of the "four causes"; although, as we have seen, Heidegger thinks that truly understanding a tradition (like the tradition of ancient Greek thought) requires *more* than simply restating the standard interpretations of those things we think we know. To understand Aristotle's analysis of the four causes, we must try to think like the ancient Greeks—an impossible task, in many ways—and we must disrupt the normal patterns of thinking that dominate us.

The essence of technology has colonized the very way we understand the world—the meaning of things around, the way we see the world, the way we experience value, and more besides. As Heidegger claims, technology *enframes* us. It constitutes the window through which we experience everything. Our ordinary notions of causation—including our ordinary understanding of Aristotle's account of causation—are already hostage to technology's essence. Our standards for determining whether or not we understand a thing are themselves structured by the technological framework through which we see things (we see the worth of a piece of writing in terms of grades, or where it is published, or how many people read it or cite it). Thus it is not enough to simply begin with our standard interpretations of *anything*—and perhaps especially Aristotle—as these standard interpretations have already fallen prey to the very thing Heidegger wants to call into question: the relentless instrumentalizing of technological understanding.

Techne, from which the German *Technik* derives, is a term from ancient Greece that involves a way of *revealing* things.

> What has the essence of technology to do with revealing? The answer: everything. For every bringing-forth is grounded in revealing. . . . *Technikon* means that which belongs to *techne*. We must observe two things about this word. One is that *techne* is the name not only for activities and skills of the craftsman but also for the arts of the mind and the fine arts. *Techne* belongs to bringing-forth, to *poiesis*; it is something poetic. (QCT, 318)

The second thing that Heidegger wants us to consider about the term *techne* is that it was connected with *episteme* (roughly, "knowledge") in earliest Greek thinking. "Both words are terms for knowing in the widest sense. They mean to be entirely at home in something; to understand and be expert in it" (QCT, 319). Aristotle points out that *techne* and *episteme* are both ways of revealing, though they differ in the manner in which they reveal, as well as in what they reveal. "*Techne* is a mode of *aletheuein*. It reveals whatever does not bring itself forth and does not yet lie here before us, whatever can look one way and now another" (QCT, 319). Again: "Technology is a mode of revealing. Technology comes to presence in the realm where revealing and unconcealment take place, where *aletheia*, truth, happens" (QCT, 319). The primary problem with the essence of technology is an *ontological* one. Technological understanding views the world and all of its inhabitants as of a single kind—what Heidegger calls "standing-reserve" (or "resources"). Technological understanding is thus reductionist and monistic. The world is *just* a reservoir of resources that can be counted up, divided, bought, sold, processed, and so on.

Different kinds of Being are ruled out in principle in this way of thinking. Those things that do not fit the model of technological understanding are simply excluded from our ontological inventories—they are either misunderstood, and are really just resources in disguise, or they are entirely illusory. Education, for example, becomes simply the number of quantifiable qualifications that can be exchanged for a salary and a number of measurable benefits.

> The revealing that rules in modern technology is a challenging [*Herausfordern*], which puts to nature the unreasonable demand that it supply energy which can be extracted and stored as such. But does this not hold true for the windmill as well? No. Its sails do indeed turn in the wind; they are left entirely to the wind's blowing. But the windmill does not unlock energy from the air currents in order to store it.
> In contrast, a tract of land is challenged in the hauling out of coal and ore. The earth now reveals itself as a coal mining district, the soil as a mineral deposit. The field that the peasant formerly cultivated and set in order appears differently than it did when to set in order still meant to take care of and maintain. The work of the peasant does not challenge the soil of the field. In sowing grain it places seed in the keeping of the forces of growth and watches over its increase. But meanwhile even the cultivation of the field has come under the grip of another kind of setting-in-order, which *sets upon* nature. It sets upon it in the sense of challenging it. Agriculture is now mechanized food industry. Air is now set upon to yield nitrogen, the earth to yield ore, ore to yield uranium, for example; uranium is set upon to yield atomic energy, which can be unleashed either for destructive or for peaceful purposes. (QCT, 320)

Heidegger's descriptions of the ways we experience nature in an age of technological understanding constitute some of his most powerful writing.

> The hydroelectric plant is set into the current of the Rhine. It sets the Rhine to supplying its hydraulic pressure, which then sets the turbine turning. This turning sets those machines in motion whose thrust sets going the electric current for which the long-distance power station and its network of cables are set up to dispatch electricity. In the context of the interlocking processes pertaining to the orderly disposition of electrical energy, even the Rhine itself appears to be something at our command. The hydroelectric plant is not built into the Rhine River as was the old wooden bridge that joined bank with bank for hundreds of years. What the river is now, namely, a water-power supplier, derives from the essence of the power station. In order that we may even remotely consider the monstrousness that reigns here, let us ponder for a moment the contrast that is spoken by the two titles: "The Rhine," as

dammed up into the *power* works, and "The Rhine," as uttered by the *art*work, in Hölderlin's hymn by that name. But, it will be replied, the Rhine is still a river in the landscape, is it not? Perhaps. But how? In no other way than as an object on call for inspection by a tour group ordered there by the vacation industry. (QCT, 321)

Even our need to break away from the workaday world, where everything is quantified, measured, and assessed, provides no real release from technological rationality. Our vacations themselves are carefully calculated according to a rigid calendar; employers offer paid vacations according to a system that is designed to promote future productivity, employee loyalty, and other, equally measurable benefits.

The experiences we have while on vacation in "nature" are no less colonized by technological understanding: paths are placed in ideal places to allow an efficient "consumption" of the natural world—now a set number of acres regulated by a governmental agency for your enjoyment. Signs indicate the route you will travel, the distance of any particular hike, as well as the quantified skill level required to make a specific hike in a specific amount of time. Even where no such paths are present, one is already in an area *set aside* as "undeveloped"—a place where nature can be "discovered" and hence set aside as a quantifiable resource that will generate a specific number of leisure hours per vacationing person.

Following any such excursion—be it to a natural "reserve" or to an urban area—one can immediately purchase a concretion of one's experience. Postcards offer ideal pictures, made for all in mass quantities, and designed as a kind of "description" of what you saw (or didn't see—it really doesn't matter) that can be sent to others (or kept) to demonstrate the kinds of things one has seen. Statuettes—of, for example, a Greek figure or of the Parthenon—can be purchased to take what one has consumed back to one's home. The museum itself is a collection of artifacts to be consumed. One goes to the museum to see the artwork outside of any context—save a context where one is simply supposed to see art. The museum itself is simply the place where one consumes highbrow culture. Even the avant-garde have their museums—the irony of which can hardly escape anyone. One goes to an establishment specifically designed to house work that is outside of the establishment. One can thus consume one's portion of "radical work," buy postcards and take pictures, and carry back one's recreational revolutionizing with one.

Technological understanding dominates everything. In writing this book, my contract states that I am not to exceed a specific number of words. Heidegger is thus a commodity to be presented, and then consumed, within a set quantity of terms. You will pay a set price for these words (and their packaging), and some percentage of this (a very small one!) will come to me. The effectiveness of the book will be assessed in terms of the number of reviews that praise it, as well as the number of persons who buy it.

An education is no different. A college education is measured by the number of credits one has acquired. Credits themselves are given in units of time spent in instruction. One can earn three credits by spending three hours a week for fifteen weeks, completing a quantity of assignments, which in turn are quantified as to their quality: points above a certain threshold will be given an alphabetic equivalent that manifests the numerical "quality" of the education you have received (ninety points will be an A-, eighty-five points will be a B, and so on). The sum total of one's educational endeavors will then be quantified into a single number—the GPA, or grade point average, which is meant to offer a "summing up" (in a quite literal way) of one's education. If one continues on past high school or college, one can then add additional degrees to one's resumé, which in turn can be counted by prospective employers. The higher the number of degrees, the "more" education one has. Technological enframing, then, has colonized everything about daily life. In Heidegger's view, this enframing constitutes the greatest danger of modernity.

Heidegger's concerns about technology remained with him until his death in 1976. In his continued correspondence with Hannah Arendt, for example, Heidegger remarks (in 1974, two years before his death):

> Unlike you, I am only slightly interested in politics. For the most part, the state of the world is clear, after all. The power inherent in the essence of technology is scarcely recognized. Everything moves along at a superficial level. The individual can no longer do anything to oppose the arrogance of the "mass media" and the institutions—nothing at all when it comes to uncovering the origins of thinking in ancient Greek thought. (Arendt and Heidegger, *Letters, 1925–1975*, 208)

THE HISTORY OF BEING: FROM THE PRE-SOCRATICS TO US

How did we arrive at this point? How did we come to be so *thoroughly* enframed by technology?

In "The Origin of the Work of Art," Heidegger provides a brief history of ontology, marking what he regards as the foundation of our current predicament in ancient Greece.

> This foundation happened in the West for the first time in Greece. What was in the future to be called Being was set into work, setting the standard. The realm of beings thus opened up was then transformed into a being in the sense of God's creation. This happened in the Middle Ages. This kind of being was again transformed at the beginning and during the course of the modern age. Beings became objects that could be controlled and penetrated by calculation. At each time a new and essential world irrupted. At each time the openness of beings had

to be established in beings themselves by the fixing in place of truth in figure. At each time there happened unconcealment of beings. Unconcealment sets itself into work, a setting which is accomplished by art. (OWA, 201)

Heidegger recognizes the way in which Dasein is affected by its place in history. Different periods of history involve Dasein experiencing itself and the world around it in remarkably different ways. History is, in effect, the series of divergent ways in which Being presents itself—in which Being is disclosed to Dasein. Our current epoch is one in which the essence of technology reigns. As Heidegger argues, the birth of modern science is *not* the source of our absorption in technological thinking. Rather, technological thinking is the source of modern science.

On Heidegger's view, the differences between ancient science and modern science have been misidentified. Ancient science concentrated on facts just as much as modern science does; it also engaged in experimentation as a means of improving knowledge of the world (although this occurred mostly in the realm of handicrafts and other skills, such as blacksmithing and building). Experimentation was thus already prevalent in ancient times—in crafts and in the use of tools. What changes in modern science are the preconceptions one has about the things tested. Likewise, while it is correct to say that modern science "is a calculating and measuring investigation" (OWA, 273), it is incorrect to claim that ancient science did not involve the same techniques. Calculation and measurement, after all, were crucial in designing and building temples standing to this day.

What distinguishes modern science, Heidegger claims, is that it is *mathematical*. The significance of this claim, of course, is not transparent. Heidegger points out that the etymology of "mathematics" traces back to the practice of *teaching*. "The *mathemata* are things insofar as we take cognizance of them as what we have already known them to be in advance, the body as the bodily, the plant-like of the plant, etc" (OWA, 275). Thus "the mathematical is that evident aspect of things within which we are always already moving and according to which we experience them as things at all, and as such things" (OWA, 277). Numbers are an *instance* of this, not its essence—but it is this instance of revealing that dominates modern science.

The history Heidegger presents is a fascinating one, and it is in many ways plausible. The point to take from the history, however, is *practical*. Our current enframing in technology is a *contingent* one. We do not *have to be* so enframed. Much as the Greeks paved the path to our current submission to instrumental and technological thinking, they also present us with a way *beyond* our current predicament—a way that we must choose to follow ourselves if we are ever to recover from our forgetfulness of Being. This saving power, Heidegger claims, is an alternative way of comporting ourselves to Being—a way that is to be found in art and poetry, and in what Heidegger comes to call "thinking."

ART AND UNCONCEALMENT

In one of his most celebrated essays, Heidegger raises the question of the origin of the work of art. As readers of Heidegger have come to expect, the obvious answers are ruled out. One might initially think that an *artist* is the origin of the work. It is the artist, after all, that puts brush to canvas, chisel to stone. But we must proceed carefully here. Not everyone who uses a brush on canvas (or elsewhere) is an artist—the child, the student, the house painter might all paint without ever appropriately being called "artists." Likewise, not everyone who intentionally alters the shape of marble, stone, or wood deserves the name "artist," or more specifically "sculptor." The construction worker, the lumberjack, and the whittler all utilize material—altering its form through intentional action—and may or may not be artists.

What we recognize here is that, in a certain respect, it is *art* that makes someone into an artist—it is what comes into being as a result of one's labor that turns the amateur into the actual artist. Without her works, the artist is undeserving of the name. The origin, Heidegger ultimately says, is art itself: "The origin of the work of art—that is, the origin of both creators and the preservers, which is to say of a people's historical existence—is art. This is so because art is in its essence an origin: a distinctive way in which truth comes into being, that is, becomes historical" (OWA, 202).

Perhaps unsurprisingly, the force of Heidegger's analysis lies not so much in the answer he gives but in the route he takes to get there (ways, Heidegger's motto runs, not works). The route to Heidegger's analysis of the origin of the work of art is through the thing. "All works have a thingly character" (OWA, 145). Heidegger aims to show us that we do not understand what it means to call something a "thing." We have allowed Being to slip into oblivion. All of our attempts to characterize this essentially fall back into the technological framework that currently dominates our phenomenology. We have come to think of all being as, for example, "that around which properties have assembled" (OWA, 148), or as what is delivered by "sense-data," or even simply as "formed matter." None of the traditional definitions, however, actually capture the "thingly" character of a thing.

Artwork, Heidegger claims, can allow us to rethink what it means to be a "thing." When we see Van Gogh's painting of a pair of shoes, we do not merely see the colors used. Likewise, we do not merely see some "representation" of actual shoes. We might see both things, of course, but that is not *all* we see. We also see the *truth* of the shoes, as bizarre as that might initially sound.

> The artwork lets us know what shoes are in truth. . . . The equipmental-ity of equipment first expressly comes to the fore through work and only through work. . . . [T]he work, therefore, is not the reproduction of some particular entity that happens to be at hand at any given time; it is, on the contrary, the reproduction of things' general essence. (OWA, 162)

Artworks all display thingly character, but in a unique way. They display this thingly character in a way that subtly defies our current enframing. This is seen even more easily in the artwork that is a Greek temple. When we see the temple, we see *a world*—a site that gathers the past and dis-plays it to us. This also allows us to see the earth surrounding the temple in a fundamentally different way—we see it as "that whence the arising brings back and shelters everything that arises as such" (OWA, 168). The temple itself, Heidegger provocatively suggests, "is the god himself" (OWA, 168). Artwork sets up a world, but also displays this world as arising out of (and returning to) the earth (OWA, 170–71).

The Earth, as it is presented when we see the artwork appropriately, is something unanalyzable: "Earth thus shatters every attempt to penetrate it. It causes every merely calculating importunity upon it to turn into destruction" (OWA, 172). Over and against the earth we have the world of the work (the shoes, or the temple, which springs from the earth). Heidegger characterizes the relation between earth and world as one of "strife," thus recasting Heraclitus's famous claim that strife is the center of all things.

Rather than lingering longer on this point, let me suggest that this "strife" is a poetic way of understanding the constant play between what is revealed and what is concealed in our experience of things. The prob-lem of modern humanity is that we think we understand everything when we understand it in terms of manipulable resources. The temple becomes a revenue source for the government; fences are erected, along with a gate, to ensure tourists pay the appropriate amount to consume their "history." The "world" of technological understanding dominates the thing entirely, preventing us from seeing it as it is. When we break free—even if only momentarily—from such enframing, we see that near-incomprehensible source from which such "worlds" emerge—we see that Being presents itself, that truth *is*. Truth, for Heidegger, is a "happening" of unconcealment (OWA, 179). This "happening" is precisely what we can encounter in the work of art, or in the poem, or even in the thinking of the thinker. When art allows truth to happen, Heidegger suggests, art is able to *found a world*. Art "lets truth originate" (OWA, 202). It "founds history." To escape from our enframing, then, we need the saving power of art.

Truth is the unconcealment of beings as beings. Truth is the truth of Being. Beauty does not occur apart from this truth. When truth sets itself into the work, it appears. Appearance—as this being of truth in the work and as the work—is beauty. Thus the beautiful belongs to truth's propriative event. (OWA, 206)

It is difficult not to be reminded of Keats's famous lines, also reflecting on the works of ancient Greece: "'Beauty is truth, truth beauty,'—that is all / Ye know on earth, and all ye need to know." What Heidegger refers to as "art," as is perhaps already obvious, is much broader than the set of objects we call "art" currently. In fact, Heidegger claims explicitly that poetry and art are essentially the same. In both cases, we have a way of comporting ourselves to things that allows them to speak for themselves. "Poetry is the saying of the unconcealment of beings" (OWA, 198).

DWELLING AND HOMELESSNESS

As we've seen, technological enframing leads us to a certain disconnectedness from the world—a disconnectedness from all forms of unconcealment other than the technological. This, in turn, is the source of a certain homelessness. We are adrift among beings we do not understand, and we are oblivious to our plight.

The way in which you are and I am, the manner in which we humans are on the earth, is *buan*, dwelling. To be a human being means to be on the earth as a mortal. It means to dwell. The old word *bauen*, which says that man *is* insofar as he dwells, this word *bauen*, however, *also* means at the same time to cherish and protect, to preserve and care for, specifically to till the soil, to cultivate the vine. (BDT, 349)

In the throes of technological enframing, we have lost this sense of dwelling—"dwelling is not experienced as man's Being; dwelling is never thought of as the basic character of human being" (BDT, 350). This is the consequence of our enframing.

One of the most striking aspects of Heidegger's discussion of dwelling is what he calls "the fourfold." Consider the following passage from his essay "Building Dwelling Thinking":

Human being consists in dwelling and, indeed, dwelling in the sense of the stay of mortals on the earth.

But "on the earth" already means "under the sky." Both of these *also* mean "remaining before the divinities" and include a "belonging to men's being with one another." By a *primal* oneness the four—earth and sky, divinities and mortals—belong together in one.

Earth is the serving bearer, blossoming and fruiting, spreading out in rock and water, rising up into plant and animal. When we say earth, we are already thinking of the other three along with it, but we give no thought to the simple oneness of the four. (BDT, 352)

In the paragraphs that follow, Heidegger makes a refrain of the line "but we give no thought to the simple oneness of the fourfold." In fact, he follows this paragraph with four paragraphs all ending with this line, each devoted to one element of the fourfold: earth, sky, divinities, and mortals. To dwell, Heidegger explains in these passages, means to "save the earth," "receive the sky," "await the divinities," "initiate their own essential being." Dwelling, moreover, "is always a staying with things" (BDT, 353).

The significance of these passages is by no means obvious. It isn't intended to be, at least not after only one reading. In one respect, Heidegger's writing is meant to provide us with something that itself requires dwelling. We must linger over these passages; we cannot assume their significance is clear, nor that we can easily fit them into our current understanding of things. It is this kind of relation, in fact, that Heidegger implores us to have to *things themselves*. Rather than simply assuming we understand the Being of those things around us, skimming over their surface, Heidegger asks us to *dwell among things* — to allow them to be what they are, in their unity. The refrain itself is a call to us — a call to *think of the unity of the fourfold*, to give the fourfold the attention that we no longer give it, and hence to prevent the fourfold from falling into oblivion.

But what does any of this even *mean*? Why are we talking of divinities and mortals? Of earth and of sky? There's no simple answer to this. One thing that is clear, however, is that Heidegger is rejecting the standard ways we present various views in academic discourse. He is making explicit references to mythological, poetic thinking. Recall, for example, that "earth" and "sky" are the point of origin of the Titans (and later both gods and mortals) in traditional Greek mythology. All things come from Gaia, from Earth, which is itself deeply mysterious. In some way, "earth" is simply that point at which thought gives itself over to wonder — it is what is no longer explainable in terms of the canon of scientific method (we saw this above in our discussion of the Greek temple).

We have already seen the multiple ways in which we misunderstand our mortality. Technological thinking continues to contribute to this as humanity attempts to find a "cure" for death and combats every other limit to our faculties. Can we design humans who are smarter, faster, stronger than we are now? Even in Heidegger's time, these questions were of deep concern — and the possibilities of such "advances" have only become more pressing. The thought that only our technological capabilities prevent us from making ourselves into gods has occurred to more than one contemporary scientist. In light of such speculations, might it not be useful to wonder about "the gods"? That is, to again offer a deflationary reading of Heidegger's remarks here, might we not spend some time thinking about our essential limitations? Our finitude? In one respect, talk of divinity has *always* been talk at the edge of human capacities. What we are unable to do we attribute to the gods. The "divine" need not represent some strange metaphysical speculation. It can, as easily, simply represent those things that are somehow *more than merely human*—the majesty of the mountain range, the terror of the storm. Again, it might be useful to think of Greek mythopoetics: in earliest thinking, the forces of nature did not *represent* the gods. The forces of nature—those things beyond us—*were* the gods.[1]

My aim in offering this gloss is *not* to be definitive. In fact, any attempt to be definitive, it seems to me, would miss the spirit of Heidegger's reflections. I am merely offering one way of understanding the fourfold—that unity of things that Heidegger wants us to recognize, but whose recognition is constantly thwarted by technological enframing.

THINKING AND DWELLING

In the lectures "Was heißt Denken?" Heidegger aims to explore *both* what calls for thinking and what is called thinking (the German might be translated in either way, in fact). In Heidegger's view, we have misunderstood both the nature and the function of thinking: "it could be that prevailing man has for centuries now acted too much and thought too little" (WCT, 370). Moreover, our ways of understanding what is involved in thinking have led us to believe we were already doing it when in fact thinking was not happening at all: "preoccupation with philosophy more than anything else may give us the stubborn illusion that we are thinking just because we are incessantly 'philosophizing'" (WCT, 371). The obsession with science that has emerged in the past centuries has further exacerbated the problem, in Heidegger's view.

> Science itself does not think, and cannot think—which is its good fortune, here meaning the assurance of its own appointed course. Science does not think. . . . Nonetheless science always and in its own fashion has to do with thinking. That fashion, however, is generative and consequently fruitful only after the gulf has become visible that lies between thinking and the sciences, lies there unbridgeably. There is no bridge here—only the leap. (WCT, 373)

As Heidegger goes on to say, even *he* is not immune to the charge of a failure to think. This failure, in fact, is a failure of our era, not merely a failure of certain persons (or disciplines).

> A fog still surrounds the essence of modern science. That fog, however, is not produced by individual investigators and scholars in the sciences. It is not produced by man at all. It arises from the region of what is most thought-provoking—that we are still not thinking; none of us, including me who speaks to you, me first of all. (WCT, 379)

Heidegger's writing itself, he claims, is an attempt to learn thinking—an attempt to confront things as they are, not merely to procure true propositions about the world. This is one essential difference between thinking and science. Science is cumulative. It aims to assemble facts about the world in encyclopedic fashion—facts that will enable us to utilize the world around us in a way that will benefit us in the attempt to realize our ambitions and desires. Thinking does not function in this way. It adds nothing to knowledge by way of propositions that "correspond" to the world. Thinking does not seek explanatory laws that cover wide-ranging facts. Thinking is concerned, first and foremost, with the *immediate* and the particular. There is something of Aristotle here: the fundamentally real is not the logos that *describes* the particulars. What is real, rather, are *the things themselves.*

In our everyday grappling with things, our tendency, strangely enough, is to forget the very things we grapple with. This is a tendency that Heidegger had already diagnosed in *Being and Time*: Dasein tends to get lost in what's around it. Even those who work closely with the particular thing—even those who steer away from abstractions or laws that apply to particulars (like the scientific researcher, attempting to discover the underlying structure of things)—even these people fail to engage in *thinking*, fail to grapple with the things *qua* things. Instead, they come to see what they work with as an abstraction: as resources for revenue, jobs waiting to be completed, and so on. Heidegger's description of this workaday experience of things in the case of a cabinetmaker is as clear as can be: "[the cabinetmaker's] relatedness to wood is what maintains the whole craft. Without that relatedness, the craft will never be anything but empty busywork, any occupation with it will be determined exclusively by business concerns. Every handicraft, all human dealings, are constantly in that danger. The writing of poetry is no more exempt from it than is thinking" (WCT, 379).

Our greatest danger at present is that *we don't recognize our failure.* We don't recognize that our failure to think has resulted in an inability to dwell among beings in the world. This failure to see failure, moreover, culminates in a kind of ontological homelessness in which we become fundamentally alienated from our own Being. Thus, Heidegger says, "most thought-provoking for our thought-provoking time is that we are still not thinking" (WCT, 381). And because we are still not thinking, we are separated from our most basic Being in a fundamental way: "thinking itself is man's simplest, and for that reason hardest, handiwork, if from time to time it would be accomplished properly" (WCT, 381).

There is a way of being with objects that allows them to be what they are—that doesn't experience these objects as subordinate to our projects alone. This is a way of being with objects that is blocked by technological enframing. This kind of being Heidegger calls "dwelling." "Dwelling . . . is *the basic character* of Being, in keeping with which mortals exist" (BDT,

362). Moreover, "Man's relation to locales, and through locales to spaces, inheres in his dwelling. The relationship between man and space is none other than dwelling, thought essentially" (BDT, 359). Part of what is involved in our dwelling is, in fact, continuously *learning to dwell*, continuously reminding ourselves of what dwelling requires and demands of us—which is, ultimately, attentiveness to Being. "The proper dwelling plight lies in this, that mortals ever search anew for the essence of dwelling, that they *must ever learn to dwell.* What if man's homelessness consisted in this, that man still does not even think of the *proper* plight of dwelling as *the* plight?" (BDT, 363).

A return to dwelling requires that we see our current enframing—that we recognize how we have become blinded to Being. Heidegger's later work is, among other things, an attempt to get us to see just that.

CONCLUSION

Despite the different emphasis of Heidegger's later work, we can see that Heidegger has not turned away from the question that motivated *Being and Time*: the meaning of Being. Although Heidegger became more distrustful of the idea that Dasein provided the key to understanding Being, he never relinquished the question itself. His later work can be understood as the attempt to excavate Being without falling prey to the inherent perils of the philosophical tradition, on the one hand, and his own emphasis on Dasein, on the other. As Heidegger notes in his "Letter on Humanism," "It is time to break the habit of overestimating philosophy and of thereby asking too much of it. What is needed in the present world crisis is less philosophy, but more attentiveness to thinking; less literature, but more cultivation of the letter" (LH, 265).

Although *Being and Time* was indeed revolutionary, Heidegger came to think of it as still far too hostage to the philosophical tradition to which it responded. Heidegger's later work attempts to move beyond this tradition—beyond philosophy traditionally understood—and into a direct experience of Being. "The thinking that is to come is no longer philosophy, because it thinks more originally than metaphysics—a name identical to philosophy" (LH, 265).

The attempt to uncover Being, Heidegger thinks, is the way out of our current enframing. To uncover Being requires recognizing that not everything can be captured in the expository language of philosophical reflection—the conceit we find in *Being and Time*. It is this recognition that explains Heidegger's decidedly more poetic style in his later work—*not* some deliberate attempt to be obscure (a claim one hears surprisingly often from casual readers of Heidegger's later work). The style of writing and thinking is indeed more difficult than a standard philosophical treatise—it is a writing that dwells and cultivates rather than names and explains. But it is only through such approaches to Being, Heidegger thinks, that we'll ever make any progress. As Heidegger puts the point, in unsurprisingly poetic language:

> But if man is to find his way once again into the nearness of Being, he must first learn to exist in the nameless. In the same way he must recognize the seductions of the public realm as well as the impotence of the private. Before he speaks man must first let himself be claimed again by Being, taking the risk that under this claim he will seldom have much to say. Only thus will the pricelessness of its essence be once more bestowed upon the word, and upon man a home for dwelling in the truth of Being. (LH, 223).

NOTE

1. See Cornford, *From Religion to Philosophy*.

NINE

The Shadow of Heidegger

Heidegger casts a long shadow. Reflecting on his mentor's influence, Hans-Georg Gadamer remarked in 1979 that "no one can deny that the challenge presented by Heidegger's daring thought to the European philosophy of the last fifty years is simply unparalleled" (Gadamer, "Heidegger and Marburg Theology," 139). The only thing that has changed since this remark is the amount of time that has passed. Heidegger's influence seems only to have grown. In these brief concluding remarks, I want to highlight *some* of those areas where Heidegger's influence has been most forcefully felt.

Existentialism

Heidegger is often assimilated into the existentialist movement, though Heidegger himself explicitly denied being an existentialist. However one reads Heidegger's rejection of existentialism (in the "Letter on Humanism"), it is clear that there are a great many existential *themes* in Heidegger's work. It is the presence of such themes, no doubt, that led to the significant influence Heidegger's work had on existentialist writers like Sartre and Camus. Sartre, for example, took up many of the themes in *Being and Time*, offering his own particular (and sometimes peculiar) spin on them. In certain respects, Sartre was much more interested in developing the idea of authenticity than he was in Heidegger's claims about the inevitability of the inauthentic. In fact, Sartre largely ignores, if not rejects, the inevitability of inauthenticity, positing instead the idea of the "radical freedom" of human subjectivity to create itself out of whole cloth.

Poststructuralism

There are many versions of poststructuralism (one of which, of course, is deconstruction). Rather than trying to lay out the various versions, I will limit my attention to the work of Michel Foucault. Foucault's work can be read as building on the idea of the shared understanding one finds in inauthentic Dasein, but applied at the level of disciplines. Foucault's work, among other things, aims to explore how knowledge claims within particular disciplines (like psychology, criminology, and biology) construct subjects within power relations. In other words, what we call "knowledge" creates an understanding of the world (and ourselves) that exerts a power over human subjectivity. "Knowledge," seen from the point of view of a system for the production and transmission of statements, comes to dominate the way we see both ourselves and one another. We are labeled "criminals," "homosexuals," "mentally deranged," and so on in virtue of regimes of "truth" that, in turn, structure and control our lives. The idea of "regimes of truth," in one respect, is inauthentic, collective understanding writ large. Whereas Sartre develops the idea of authenticity, Foucault reveals to us, in painstaking historical detail, how inauthenticity emerges (and exerts power) even in our most "advanced" scientific enterprises.

Hermeneutics

As we've seen, Gadamer studied with Heidegger directly. Gadamer's own work sets out, in brilliant detail, what is involved in the deployment of hermeneutics one finds in Heidegger's work. Gadamer's *Truth and Method*, a classic in its own right, develops and expands some of the pregnant claims Heidegger makes in *Being and Time* about the structure of interpretation. In particular, Gadamer develops the idea of the hermeneutic circle as culminating in a "fusion of horizons" that alters the interpreter and the interpreted. In addition, Gadamer's notion of a "principle of charity" that makes comprehending a text *our responsibility* opens up fruitful pathways through the history of philosophy. This is a lesson, Gadamer often admits, that he learned from watching Heidegger confront the texts of the ancients.

Deconstruction

In certain ways, deconstruction can be understood as the antipode of hermeneutics. Whereas hermeneutics presumes the unity and coherence of the text (or text-analogue) to be interpreted, deconstruction assumes the *disunity* and *incoherence* of that which is interpreted. The aim of deconstructive interpretation, among other things, is to reveal that some of the core ideas of a text in fact rely on notions that *conflict with* a text.

Derrida, a leading proponent of this way of encountering texts, was explicit about his indebtedness to Heidegger.

Comparative Philosophy

Philosophers in the West have often overlooked the contributions of so-called Eastern philosophy—even when such disregard results in reinventing the proverbial wheel. Heidegger recognized an affinity between his own work and the work of philosophers working in the Buddhist and Taoist traditions. In particular, philosophers from Japan's Kyoto School saw in Heidegger's work a way of articulating some of the truths of traditional Buddhism. Among the most notable philosophers in the Kyoto school to interact with Heidegger (both in print and in person) was Nishitani Keiji.

Phenomenology and Ethics

There is simply no way to grasp the phenomenological tradition without grappling with Heidegger. Virtually everything written on phenomenology after Heidegger has to respond to him in some way. Some of the most significant developments in the tradition are to be found in Levinas, on the one hand, and Merleau-Ponty, on the other.

Levinas's work can be understood as a riposte to the absence of a developed ethics in Heidegger's work. Levinas offers an alternative to Heidegger's account of Being-in-the-world in which our guilt before the Other is our most fundamental experience (*not* our confrontation with our own mortality). This phenomenological account of our responsibility to others sends phenomenology in new directions and suggests that some crucial amendments might be needed for thinking through our Being-in-the-world. It makes ethics first philosophy, and obligation the primary state of our Being.

Phenomenology and Philosophy of Mind

Merleau-Ponty's unique approach to phenomenology can be understood as emphasizing the way that one's Being-in-the-world is essentially a *bodily* being-in-the-world. Our embodiment, in other words, is crucial to the way that our experience is structured, as well as the way we understand the possibilities that constitute us (our embodiment provides, among other things, a sense of the possibilities of movement available to us; our sense of "up" and "down," for example, are as crucial to our experience of an environment as are space and time). These insights have led to a growing recognition of the importance of embodiment in thinking about the mind, even in analytic philosophy (in the work of Andy Clark, Shaun Gallagher, and Sean D. Kelly, for example).

These are only some of the areas where Heidegger's influence has been felt. As should be obvious, the depth and breadth of this influence cannot be captured in a few paragraphs. My aim, in these final remarks, is simply to indicate the diversity of responses to Heidegger—and hence the fecundity of his philosophical work. Adequately mapping all of the influences Heidegger has exerted requires the diligence of an intellectual historian—and far more space than is available in an introductory text. Nevertheless, I have felt it worthwhile to at least point to those places where Heidegger casts a long shadow.

A Quick Terminology Guide for Getting Started

The definitions offered here are a reference point for those beginning to read *Being and Time*. The index can be used to find discussions of the many terms not defined here.

COMMON TERMS IN *BEING AND TIME*

Dasein: The term *Dasein* is the word Heidegger uses to talk about *us* in ontological terms. The verb *dasein*, in everyday German, means "to exist." As a noun, *Dasein* can be translated into its two constituent parts, *da* (there) and *sein* (being; to be), as "Being-there." The essence of Dasein is in its existence; essence is not given prior to our actual existence in the world. It is this feature of Dasein—that its essence lies in existence—that partially constitutes its unique mode of being.

existentiell and **existential:** An "existentiell" usually concerns an individual Dasein. An existentiell understanding is an individual's understanding of his or her own life and Being. Such an understanding will involve the roles one plays in society—for example, as student, teacher, patient, father, and so on. An "existential" concerns the structural features of existence. This is an understanding of ontology that must be worked out. Heidegger is after the existential constitution of Dasein. He wants to provide the ontology of Dasein by laying bare its structural constituents.

factical/facticity/fact and **factual/factuality/fact:** This burdensome family of terms is meant to distinguish two different German terms that are often both translated as "fact": the Latinate *Faktum* and the Germanic *Tatsache*. The "factical" concerns facts on an ontological level. Facticity, however, usually refers to Dasein's existential predicament (we exist in a world created by others, among possibilities that we did not create but from which we must choose). This is, of course, a fact about Dasein's ontology. *Factual*, by contrast, is the term used to discuss *ontical* facts (as opposed to ontological ones). Very roughly, something is ontological if it is about Being or the Being of a particular thing; something is ontical if it concerns something that presupposes an ontology.

ontological and **ontic:** The ontological is an investigation into Being. An ontology aims to uncover the structures involved in ways of Being— structures that lie beneath and within everyday perceptions. The ontic is a mode of investigating entities where an ontology is presupposed. To take a simple example: The claim "That chair is red" is ontic. It concerns the particular properties of an object in the world. An ontological claim, on the other hand, would say something about the Being of the chair— about what is involved in a chair's *very existence*. All of modern science involves ontic claims. To specify the gravitational force exerted on an object is to make an ontic claim. It does not touch on the question of what it means to be an *object*.

COMMON GREEK TERMS IN *BEING AND TIME*

Heidegger often gives translations of Greek terms he employs in the text, but not always. This list is meant as a reference source for terms Heidegger uses frequently (particularly in the introduction to *Being and Time*) or for which he provides no translation. Here is a list of Greek letters for those unfamiliar with the Greek alphabet: α, β, γ, δ, ε, ζ, η, θ, ι, κ, λ, μ, ν, ξ, ο, π, ρ, σ/ς, τ, υ, φ, χ, ψ, ω.

ἀγαθον **(agathon):** good
αἴσθησις **(aesthesis):** sensory perception
ἀληθές; ἀλήθεια; ἀληθεύειν **(aletheia):** truth; uncovering
ἀνθρωπως **(anthropos):** human
ἀπο **(apo):** from, away from
ἀποφαίνεσθαι **(apophanisthai):** show forth, display
ἀπόφανσις **(apophansis):** declaration, statement
ἀρχή **(arche):** beginning, origin, first cause

γένος **(genos):** race, kind, genus

δηλούν **(deloun):** to make visible, manifest
διανοείν **(dianoein):** to think, discriminate
δόχα **(doxa):** common belief, popular opinion

ἔίδος **(eidos):** that which is seen; form, shape
ἑρμηνεύειν; ἑρμηνεία **(hermeneia):** interpretation, explanation
εὐχή **(euche):** prayer, request

ζῷον λόγον ἔχον **(zoon logon echon):** animal with logos (speech, reason)

ἴδια **(idia):** separate, distinct; belonging to one uniquely

καθόλου **(katholou):** on the whole, in general

λανθάνω **(lanthano):** to be unnoticed, unseen
λέγειν **(legein):** to tell; to speak
λόγος **(logos):** word, speech, discourse; reason
λύπη **(lupe):** pain

μέθεξις **(methexis):** participation
μύθος **(mythos):** story, narrative; anything delivered by word of mouth, speech

νοείν; νόημα; νόησις **(noein, noema, noesis):** to see, observe, notice, consider

ούσία **(ousia):** being

πάθημα; πάθος **(pathema; pathos):** what one undergoes; passion, emotion
παρουσία **(parousia):** presence, being present
πράγμα **(pragma):** that which has been done, deed, act
πρᾶξις **(praxis):** action, deed; activity

συν- **(syn-):** with
συνφεσις **(synthesis):** putting together, combination

ὑποκείμενον **(hypokeimenon):** underlying thing, substratum

φαίνεσθαι **(phainesthai):** let something be seen
φαίνω; φαίνεσθαι; φαινόμενον **(phaino; phainesthai; phainomenon):** bring to light, make appear; what shows itself
φαντασία **(phantasia):** appearance
φωνή **(phone):** vocalization, utterance
φώς **(phos):** light

χρόνος **(chronos):** time

ψεύδεσθαι **(pseudesthai):** false
ψυχή **(psuche):** life, breath; mind, soul

COMMON LATIN TERMS IN *BEING AND TIME*

Heidegger often gives translations of Latin terms he employs in the text, but not always. This list is meant as a reference source for terms Heidegger uses frequently or for which he provides no translation.

anima: life, breath, soul
animal rationale: rational animal

bonum: good

cogitare: cogitations: to think, to imagine, to cogitate
cogito sum: I think [therefore] I am (from Descartes)

commercium: trade, commerce; communication
cura: care, cure, heal

ego: I, me (first person pronoun)
ego cogito: I think (from Descartes)
ens: an existing or real thing; an entity
ens creatum: created being/entity
ens infinitum: infinite being/entity
essentia: essence
existentia: existence
extensio: extension, in the sense of existing in space

habitare: to dwell, reside

intellectus: perception, discernment

lumen naturale: light of nature (from Descartes)

malum: evil, mischief
modus: a measure, extent, quantity; in the manner of

ratio: reason
res: thing, substance
res cogitans: thinking thing (Descartes contrasts this with *res extensa*)
res extensa: extended thing (a thing existing in space)

sensatio: sensation, the sensible
solus ipse: I alone
subjectum: underlying thing, substance
substantia: that of which something consists; essence, substance
sum: to be, Being

transcendens; transcendentia: what goes beyond, transcends

veritas: truth, reality

Selected Bibliography

One could fill volumes with a list of texts by, about, and responding to Heidegger. I have had to omit a great many books that deserve to be in this bibliography. What follows is thus only a selection of texts for further reading. I have organized the bibliography into the following divisions:

SELECTED WORKS BY HEIDEGGER

Basic Concepts. Translated by Gary Aylesworth. Bloomington: Indiana University Press, 1993.

Basic Concepts of Aristotelian Philosophy. Translated by Robert D. Metcalf and Mark B. Tanzer. Bloomington: Indiana University Press, 2009.

Basic Problems of Phenomenology. Translated by Albert Hofstadter. Bloomington and Indianapolis: Indiana University Press, 1982.

Basic Writings. Edited by David Farrell Krell. New York: HarperCollins, 1993.

Being and Time. Translated by John Macquarrie and Edward Robinson. New York: Harper & Row, 1962.

Being and Time. Translated by Joan Stambaugh. Albany: State University of New York Press, 1996.

"Building Dwelling Thinking." In *Basic Writings*, edited by David Farrell Krell, 343–65. New York: HarperCollins, 1993.

Contributions to Philosophy (from Enowning). Translated by Parvis Emad and Kenneth Maly. Bloomington: Indiana University Press, 1999.

The Fundamental Concepts of Metaphysics. Translated by William McNeill and Nicholas Walker. Bloomington: Indiana University Press, 1995.

History of the Concept of Time. Translated by Theodore Kisiel. Bloomington: Indiana University Press, 1985.

Introduction to Metaphysics. Translated by Gregory Fried and Richard Polt. New Haven, CT: Yale University Press, 2000.

Kant and the Problem of Metaphysics. Translated by Richard Taft. Bloomington: Indiana University Press, 1990.

"Letter on Humanism." In *Basic Writings*, edited by David Farrell Krell, 213–66. New York: HarperCollins, 1993.

"Letter to the Rector of Freiburg University. November 4, 1945." In *The Heidegger Controversy: A Critical Reader*, edited by Richard Wolin, 61–66. Cambridge, MA: MIT Press, 1993.

Letters to His Wife, 1915–1970. Malden, MA: Polity Press, 2008.

Logic: The Question of Truth. Translated by Thomas Sheehan. Bloomington: Indiana University Press, 2010.

"Modern Science, Metaphysics, and Mathematics." In *Basic Writings*, edited by David Farrell Krell, 267–306. New York: HarperCollins, 1993.

Off the Beaten Track. Edited by Julian Young and Kenneth Haynes. Cambridge: Cambridge University Press, 2002.

"The Origin of the Work of Art." In *Basic Writings*, edited by David Farrell Krell, 139–212. New York: HarperCollins, 1993.

Parmenides. Translated by Andre Schuwer and Richard Rojcewicz. Bloomington: Indiana University Press, 1992.

Pathmarks. Edited by William McNeill. Cambridge: Cambridge University Press, 1998.

Phenomenological Interpretations of Aristotle. Translated by Richard Rojcewicz. Bloomington: Indiana University Press, 2001.

Phenomenology of Religious Life. Translated by Matthias Fritsch and Jennifer Anna Gosetti-Ferencei. Bloomington: Indiana University Press, 2004.

Plato's Sophist. Translated by Richard Rojcewicz and Andre Schuwer. Bloomington: Indiana University Press, 1997.

"Political Texts, 1933–34." In *The Heidegger Controversy: A Critical Reader*, edited by Richard Wolin, 40–60. Cambridge, MA: MIT Press, 1993.

"The Question Concerning Technology." In *Basic Writings*, edited by David Farrell Krell, 307–42. New York: HarperCollins, 1993.

"What Calls for Thinking." In *Basic Writings*, edited by David Farrell Krell, 365–92. New York: HarperCollins, 1993.

SECONDARY WORKS ON *BEING AND TIME* (AND EARLIER)

Carman, Taylor. *Heidegger's Analytic: Interpretation, Discourse, and Authenticity in Being and Time*. Cambridge: Cambridge University Press, 2003.

Critchley, Simon, and Reiner Schuermann. *On Heidegger's Being and Time*. Edited by Steven Levine. New York: Routledge, 2008.

Dreyfus, Hubert. *Being-in-the-World: A Commentary on Heidegger's Being and Time, Division I*. Cambridge, MA: MIT Press, 1991.

King, Magda. *A Guide to Heidegger's Being and Time*. Albany: State University of New York Press, 2001.

Kisiel, Theodore. *The Genesis of Heidegger's Being and Time*. Berkeley: University of California Press, 1993.

———, and John van Buren, eds. *Reading Heidegger from the Start: Essays in His Earliest Thought*. Albany: State University of New York Press, 1994.

Mulhall, Stephen. *Heidegger and Being and Time*. New York: Routledge, 1996.

Polt, Richard, ed. *Heidegger's Being and Time: Critical Essays*. Lanham, MD: Rowman & Littlefield, 2005.

Van Buren, John. *The Young Heidegger*. Bloomington: Indiana University Press, 1994.

SECONDARY WORKS ON THE LATER HEIDEGGER

Mugeraur, Robert. *Heidegger and Homecoming: The Leitmotif in the Later Writings*. Toronto: University of Toronto Press, 2008.

Pattison, George. *The Later Heidegger*. New York: Routledge, 2000.

Risser, James, ed. *Heidegger toward the Turn: Essays on the Work of the 1930s*. Albany: State University of New York Press, 1999.

Wood, David. *Thinking after Heidegger*. Cambridge, MA: Polity Press, 2002.

COLLECTIONS OF ESSAYS ON HEIDEGGER

Dreyfus, Hubert L., and Mark Wrathal, eds. *A Companion to Heidegger*. Malden, MA: Blackwell, 2005.

Guignon, Charles, ed. *The Cambridge Companion to Heidegger*. Cambridge: Cambridge University Press, 1993.

Macann, Christopher, ed. *Critical Heidegger*. London: Routledge, 1996.

Malpas, Jeff, and Mark Wrathall, eds. *Heidegger, Authenticity, and Modernity: Essays in Honor of Hubert L. Dreyfus*. Vol. 1. Cambridge, MA: MIT Press, 2000.

———, eds. *Heidegger, Coping, and Cognitive Science: Essays in Honor of Hubert L. Dreyfus*. Vol. 2. Cambridge, MA: MIT Press, 2000.

ADDITIONAL NOTEWORTHY STUDIES OF HEIDEGGER

Blattner, William D. *Heidegger's Temporal Idealism*. Cambridge: Cambridge University Press, 1999.

Fynsk, Christopher. *Heidegger: Thought and Historicity*. Ithaca, NY: Cornell University Press, 1986.

Gordon, Peter E. *Continental Divide: Heidegger, Cassirer, and Davos*. Cambridge, MA: Harvard University Press, 2010.

Guignon, Charles B. *Heidegger and the Problem of Knowledge*. Indianapolis: Hackett, 1983.

Haar, Michel. *Heidegger and the Essence of Man*. Translated by William McNeil. Albany: State University of New York Press, 1993.

Haas, Andrew. *The Irony of Heidegger*. New York: Continuum, 2007.

LaFont, Cristina. *Heidegger, Language, and World-Disclosure*. Translated by Graham Harman. Cambridge: Cambridge University Press, 2000.

Malpas, Jeff. *Heidegger's Topology: Being, Place, World*. Cambridge, MA: MIT Press, 2006.

Mugerauer, Robert. *Heidegger's Language and Thinking*. Atlantic Highlands, NJ: Humanities Press, 1988.

Safranski, Rudiger. *Martin Heidegger: Between Good and Evil*. Translated by Ewald Osers. Cambridge, MA: Harvard University Press, 1998.

Schalow, Frank. *The Incarnality of Being: The Earth, Animals, and the Body in Heidegger's Thought*. Albany: State University of New York Press, 2006.

Schürmann, Reiner. *Heidegger: On Being and Acting: From Principles to Anarchy*. Bloomington: Indiana University Press, 1990.

Shahan, Robert W., and J. N. Mohanty. *Thinking about Being: Aspects of Heidegger's Thought*. Norman: University of Oklahoma Press, 1984.

Wrathal, Mark. *Heidegger and Unconcealment: Truth, Language, and History*. Cambridge: Cambridge University Press, 2010.

Zimmerman, Michael E. *Eclipse of the Self: The Development of Heidegger's Concept of Authenticity*. Athens: Ohio University Press, 1981.

WORKS INFLUENCED BY HEIDEGGER

Adorno, Theodor W. *The Jargon of Authenticity*. Translated by Knut Tarnowski and Frederick Will. Evanston, IL: Northwestern University Press, 1973.

Arendt, Hannah. *The Human Condition*. Chicago: University of Chicago Press, 1958.

Derrida, Jacques. *Of Spirit: Heidegger and the Question*. Translated by Geoffrey Bennington and Rachel Bowlby. Chicago: University of Chicago Press, 1989.

Foucault, Michel. *The Foucault Reader*. Edited by Paul Rabinow. New York: Pantheon, 1984.

———. *The Order of Things: An Archaeology of the Human Sciences*. New York: Random House, 1994.

Gadamer, Hans-Georg. "The Greeks." In *Heidegger's Ways*, by Hans-Georg Gadamer, 139–52. Albany: State University of New York Press, 1994.

———. "Heidegger and Marburg Theology." In *Philosophical Hermeneutics*, by Hans-Georg Gadamer. Translated by David E. Linge, 198–212. Berkeley: University of California Press, 1976.

———. *Heidegger's Ways*. Translated by Dennis J. Schmidt. Albany: State University of New York Press, 1994.

———. "Martin Heidegger—85 Years." In *Heidegger's Ways*, by Hans-Georg Gadamer, 111–20. Albany: State University of New York Press, 1994.

———. *Truth and Method*. Translated by Joel Weinsheimer and Donald G. Marshall. New York: Continuum, 2004.

Jonas, Hans. *Mortality and Morality: A Search for the Good after Auschwitz*. Edited by Lawrence Vogel. Evanston, IL: Northwestern University Press, 1996.

Levinas, Emmanuel. *Otherwise Than Being: Or, Beyond Essence*. Translated by Alphonso Lingis. Pittsburgh: Duquesne University Press, 1998.

———. *Time and the Other*. Translated by Richard A. Cohen. Pittsburgh: Duquesne University Press, 1987.

———. *Totality and Infinity: An Essay on Exteriority*. Translated by Alphonso Lingis. Pittsburgh: Duquesne University Press, 1969.

Lowith, Karl. *Martin Heidegger and European Nihilism*. Edited by Richard Wolin. Translated by Gary Steiner. New York: Columbia University Press, 1995.

Marcuse, Herbert. *One-Dimensional Man: Studies in the Ideology of Advanced Industrial Society*. Boston: Beacon Press, 1964.

Merleau-Ponty, Maurice. *Phenomenology of Perception*. Translated by Colin Smith. New York: Routledge, 1958.

HEIDEGGER AND ANCIENT PHILOSOPHY

Bowler, Michael. *Heidegger and Aristotle: Philosophy as Praxis*. New York: Continuum, 2008.

Brogan, Walter. *Heidegger and Aristotle: The Twofoldness of Being*. Albany: State University of New York Press, 2005.

Hyland, Drew A., and John Panteleimon Manoussakis. *Heidegger and the Greeks: Interpretive Essays*. Bloomington: Indiana University Press, 2006.

Jacobs, David C., ed. *The Presocratics after Heidegger*. Albany: State University of New York Press, 1999.

McNeill, William. *The Glance of the Eye: Heidegger, Aristotle, and the Ends of Theory*. Albany: State University of New York Press, 1999.

Rockmore, Tom, and Catalin Partenie. *Heidegger and Plato: Toward Dialogue*. Evanston, IL: Northwestern University Press, 2005.

HEIDEGGER AND ART

Thomson, Iain D. *Heidegger, Art, and Postmodernity*. Cambridge: Cambridge University Press, 2007.
Young, Julian. *Heidegger's Philosophy of Art*. Cambridge: Cambridge University Press, 2004.

HEIDEGGER AND ETHICS

Hatab, Lawrence J. *Ethics and Finitude: Heideggerian Contributions to Moral Philosophy*. Lanham, MD: Rowman & Littlefield, 2000.
Hodge, Joanna. *Heidegger and Ethics*. New York: Routledge, 1995.
McNeill, William. *The Time of Life: Heidegger and Ethos*. Albany: State University of New York Press, 2006.
Olafson, Frederick A. *Heidegger and the Ground of Ethics: A Study of Mitsein*. Cambridge: Cambridge University Press, 1998.
Raffoul, Francois, and David Pettigrew, eds. *Heidegger and Practical Philosophy*. Albany: State University of New York Press, 2002.
Vogel, Lawrence. *The Fragile "We": Ethical Implications of Heidegger's Being and Time*. Evanston, IL: Northwestern University Press, 1994.

HEIDEGGER AND POLITICS

Farías, Víctor. *Heidegger and Nazism*. Philadelphia: Temple University Press, 1989.
Faye, Emmanuel. *Heidegger: The Introduction of Nazism into Philosophy*. Translated by Michael B. Smith. New Haven, CT: Yale University Press, 2009.
Milchman, Alan, and Alan Rosenberg, eds. *Martin Heidegger and the Holocaust*. Atlantic Highlands, NJ: Humanities Press, 1996.
Rockmore, Tom, and Joseph Margolis, eds. *The Heidegger Case: On Philosophy and Politics*. Philadelphia: Temple University Press, 1992.
Sluga, Hans. *Heidegger's Crisis: Philosophy and Politics in Nazi Germany*. Cambridge, MA: Harvard University Press, 1993.
Wolin, Richard, ed. *The Heidegger Controversy: A Critical Reader*. Cambridge, MA: MIT Press, 1993.
Young, Julian. *Heidegger, Philosophy, Nazism*. Cambridge: Cambridge University Press, 1997.

HEIDEGGER AND RELIGION

Crowe, Benjamin D. *Heidegger's Phenomenology of Religion*. Bloomington: Indiana University Press, 2008.
———. *Heidegger's Religious Origins*. Bloomington: Indiana University Press, 2006.

HEIDEGGER AND TECHNOLOGY

Thomson, Iain D. *Heidegger on Ontotheology: Technology and the Politics of Education*. Cambridge: Cambridge University Press, 2005.
Zimmerman, Michael E. *Heidegger's Confrontation with Modernity: Technology, Politics, Art*. Bloomington: Indiana University Press, 1990.

HEIDEGGER AND TRUTH

Dahlstrom, Daniel. *Heidegger's Concept of Truth*. Cambridge: Cambridge University Press, 2009.
Frings, Manfred S., ed. *Heidegger and the Quest for Truth*. Chicago: Quadrangle Books, 1968.

ADDITIONAL WORKS CITED

Arendt, Hannah, and Martin Heidegger. *Letters, 1925–1975*. New York: Harcourt, 2004.
Austin, J. L. *Sense and Sensibilia*. Edited by G. J. Warnock. Oxford: Oxford University Press, 1962.
Ayer, A. J. *Language, Truth, and Logic*. New York: Dover, 1964.
Clark, Andy. *Being There: Putting Brain, Body, and World Together Again*. Cambridge, MA: MIT Press, 1998.
Cornford, F. M. *From Religion to Philosophy: A Study in the Origins of Western Speculation*. Princeton, NJ: Princeton University Press, 1991.
Der Spiegel. "'Only a God Can Save Us': Der Spiegel's Interview with Martin Heidegger." In *The Heidegger Controversy: A Critical Reader*, edited by Richard Wolin, 91–116. Cambridge, MA: MIT Press, 1993.
Frege, Gottlob. *The Frege Reader*. Edited by Michael Beaney. Hoboken, NJ: Wiley-Blackwell, 1997.
Gross, Daniel M., and Ansgar Kemmann, eds. *Heidegger and Rhetoric*. Albany: State University of New York Press, 2005.
Habermas, Jürgen. "Martin Heidegger: On the Publication of Lectures from the Year 1935." *Graduate Faculty Philosophy Journal* 6 (1977): 156.
Harrison, Robert Pogue. *Dominion of the Dead*. Chicago: University of Chicago Press, 2005.
Horkheimer, Max. *Eclipse of Reason*. London: Continuum, 2004.
Husserl, Edmund. *Logical Investigations*. 2 vols. New York: Routledge, 2004.
Jaspers, Karl. "Letter to the Denazification Committee." In *The Heidegger Controversy: A Critical Reader*, edited by Richard Wolin, 144–51. Cambridge, MA: MIT Press, 1993.
Kant, Immanuel. *Critique of Pure Reason*. Translated by Paul Guyer and Allen Wood. Cambridge: Cambridge University Press, 1998.
Kripke, Saul. *Naming and Necessity*. Cambridge, MA: Harvard University Press, 1980.
Kuhn, Thomas. *The Structure of Scientific Revolutions*. Chicago: University of Chicago Press, 1996.
Marcuse, Herbert, and Martin Heidegger. "An Exchange of Letters: Herbert Marcuse and Martin Heidegger." In *The Heidegger Controversy: A Critical Reader*, edited by Richard Wolin, 152–64. Cambridge, MA: MIT Press, 1993.
Mumford, Lewis. *Technics and Civilization*. New York: Harcourt, 1934.
Nietzsche, Friedrich. *Untimely Meditations*. Translated by R. J. Hollingdale. Edited by Daniel Breazeale. Cambridge: Cambridge University Press, 1997.
Rorty, Richard. *Philosophical Papers, Volume 2: Essays on Heidegger and Others*. Cambridge: Cambridge University Press, 1991.
Russell, Bertrand. *Wisdom of the West*. New York: Crescent Books, 1989.
Ryle, Gilbert. "Heidegger's *Sein und Zeit*." In *Critical Essays*. New York: Routledge, 2009.
Sartre, Jean-Paul. *Being and Nothingness: A Phenomenological Essay on Ontology*. Translated by Hazel E. Barnes. New York: Washington Square Press, 1992.
———. *Existentialism Is a Humanism*. Translated by Carol Macomber. New Haven, CT: Yale University Press, 2007.
Scheler, Max. *Formalism in Ethics and Non-Formal Ethics of Value*. Translated by Manfred Frings and Roger L. Funk. Evanston, IL: Northwestern University Press, 1973.

———. *The Nature of Sympathy*. Translated by Peter Heath. New Brunswick, NJ: Transaction, 2008.

Sheehan, Thomas. "Reading a Life: Heidegger and Hard Times." In *A Cambridge Companion to Heidegger*, edited by Charles Guignon, 70–96. Cambridge: Cambridge University Press, 1993.

Taylor, Charles. "The Concept of a Person." In *Philosophical Papers*. Vol. 1, *Human Agency and Language*, 97–114. Cambridge: Cambridge University Press, 1985.

———. *Sources of the Self: The Making of the Modern Identity*. Cambridge, MA: Harvard University Press, 1992.

Wittgenstein, Ludwig. *On Certainty*. Edited by G. E. M. Anscombe and G. H. von Wright. New York: Harper Torchbooks, 1972.

———. *Philosophical Investigations*. Translated by G. E. M. Anscombe. New York: Basil Blackwell, 1958.

Index

About the Author

J. Jeremy Wisnewski is associate professor of philosophy at Hartwick College. He has written widely on issues in moral philosophy, applied ethics, and phenomenology. His books include *Wittgenstein and Ethical Inquiry* (Continuum, 2007), *The Politics of Agency* (Ashgate, 2008), *The Ethics of Torture* (coauthored with R. D. Emerick, Continuum 2009) and *Understanding Torture* (EUP, 2010). He is coeditor, with Mark Sanders, of *Ethics and Phenomenology* (Lexington, 2012), and editor of the *Review Journal of Political Philosophy*. He has also edited six books in Blackwell's Philosophy and Pop Culture series.